Riverby Edition

THE WRITINGS OF
JOHN BURROUGHS

WITH PORTRAITS AND MANY ILLUSTRATIONS

VOLUME IX

Riverby

THE WRITINGS

OF

JOHN BURROUGHS

IX

RIVERBY

BOSTON AND NEW YORK

HOUGHTON MIFFLIN COMPANY

The Riverside Press, Cambridge

PREFATORY NOTE

I HAVE often said to myself, "Why should not one name his books as he names his children, arbitrarily, and let the name come to mean much or little, as the case may be?" In the case of the present volume — probably my last collection of Out-of-door Papers — I have taken this course, and have given to the book the name of my place here on the Hudson, "Riverby," — by the river, — where the sketches were written, and where for so many years I have been an interested spectator of the life of nature, as, with the changing seasons, it has ebbed and flowed past my door.

J. B.

CONTENTS

LIST OF ILLUSTRATIONS

RIVERBY

RIVERBY

I

AMONG THE WILD FLOWERS

I

NEARLY every season I make the acquaintance of one or more new flowers. It takes
years to exhaust the botanical treasures of any one
considerable neighborhood, unless one makes a dead
set at it, like an herbalist. One likes to have his
floral acquaintances come to him easily and naturally, like his other friends. Some pleasant occasion
should bring you together. You meet in a walk,
or touch elbows on a picnic under a tree, or get
acquainted on a fishing or camping-out expedition.
What comes to you in the way of birds or flowers,
while wooing only the large spirit of open-air nature, seems like special good fortune. At any rate,
one does not want to bolt his botany, but rather to
prolong the course. One likes to have something
in reserve, something to be on the lookout for on
his walks. I have never yet found the orchid called
calypso, a large, variegated purple and yellow

flower, Gray says, which grows in cold, wet woods and bogs, — very beautiful and very rare. Calypso, you know, was the nymph who fell in love with Ulysses and detained him seven years upon her island, and died of a broken heart after he left her. I have a keen desire to see her in her floral guise, reigning over some silent bog, or rising above the moss of some dark glen in the woods, and would gladly be the Ulysses to be detained at least a few hours by her.

I will describe her by the aid of Gray, so that if any of my readers come across her, they may know what a rarity they have found. She may be looked for in cold, mossy, boggy places in our northern woods. You will see a low flower, somewhat like a lady's-slipper, that is, with an inflated sac-shaped lip ; the petals and sepals much alike, rising and spreading; the color mingled purple and yellow; the stem, or scape, from three to five inches high, with but one leaf, — that one thin and slightly heart-shaped, with a stem which starts from a solid bulb. That is the nymph of our boggy solitudes, waiting to break her heart for any adventurous hero who may penetrate her domain.

Several of our harmless little wild flowers have been absurdly named out of the old mythologies: thus, Indian cucumber root, one of Thoreau's favorite flowers, is named after the sorceress Medea, and is called "medeola," because it was at one time

4

thought to possess rare medicinal properties; and medicine and sorcery have always been more or less confounded in the opinion of mankind. It is a pretty and decorative sort of plant, with, when perfect, two stages or platforms of leaves, one above the other. You see a whorl of five or six leaves, a foot or more from the ground, which seems to bear a standard with another whorl of three leaves at the top of it. The small, colorless, recurved flowers shoot out from above this top whorl. The whole expression of the plant is singularly slender and graceful. Sometimes, probably the first year, it only attains to the first circle of leaves. This is the platform from which it will rear its flower column the next year. Its white, tuberous root is crisp and tender, and leaves in the mouth distinctly the taste of cucumber. Whether or not the Indians used it as a relish as we do the cucumber, I do not know.

Still another pretty flower that perpetuates the name of a Grecian nymph, a flower that was a new find to me a few summers ago, is the arethusa. Arethusa was one of the nymphs who attended Diana, and was by that goddess turned into a fountain, that she might escape the god of the river, Alpheus, who became desperately in love with her on seeing her at her bath. Our Arethusa is one of the prettiest of the orchids, and has been pursued through many a marsh and quaking bog by her lovers. She is a bright pink-purple flower an inch or more long, with the odor of sweet violets. The sepals and petals rise up and arch over the column, which we may call the heart of the flower, as if shielding it. In Plymouth County, Massachusetts, where the arethusa seems common, I have heard it called Indian pink.

But I was going to recount my new finds. One sprang up in the footsteps of that destroying angel, Dynamite. A new railroad cut across my tramping-ground, with its hordes of Italian laborers and its mountains of giant-powder, was enough to banish all the gentler deities forever from the place. But it did not.

Scarcely had the earthquake passed when, walking at the base of a rocky cliff that had been partly blown away in the search for stone for two huge abutments that stood near by, I beheld the débris at the base of the cliff draped and festooned by one of our most beautiful foliage plants, and one I had long been on the lookout for, namely, the climbing fumitory. It was growing everywhere in the greatest profusion, affording, by its tenderness, delicacy, and grace, the most striking contrast to the destruction the black giant had wrought. The power that had smote the rock seemed to have called it into being. Probably the seeds had lain dormant in cracks and crevices for years, and when the catastrophe came, and they found themselves in new soil

6

amid the wreck of the old order of things, they sprang into new life, and grew as if the world had been created anew for them, as in a sense it had. Certainly, they grew most luxuriantly, and never was the ruin wrought by powder veiled by more delicate, lace-like foliage.[1] The panicles of drooping, pale flesh-colored flowers heightened the effect of the whole. This plant is a regular climber; it has no extra appendages for that purpose, and does not wind, but climbs by means of its young leafstalks, which lay hold like tiny hands or hooks. The end of every branch is armed with a multitude of these baby hands. The flowers are pendent, and swing like ear jewels. They are slightly heart-shaped, and when examined closely, look like little pockets made of crumpled silk, nearly white on the inside or under side, and pale purple on the side toward the light, and shirred up at the bottom. And pockets they are in quite a literal sense, for, though they fade, they do not fall, but become pockets full of seeds. The fumitory is a perpetual bloomer from July till killed by the autumn frosts.

The closely allied species of this plant, the dicentra (Dutchman's breeches and squirrel corn), are much more common, and are among our prettiest spring flowers. I have an eye out for the white-

[1] Strange to say, the plant did not appear in that locality the next season, and has never appeared since. Perhaps it will take another dynamite earthquake to wake it up.

hearts (related to the bleeding-hearts of the gardens, and absurdly called "Dutchman's breeches") the last week in April. It is a rock-loving plant, and springs up on the shelves of the ledges, or in the débris at their base, as if by magic. As soon as blood-root has begun to star the waste, stony places, and the first swallow has been heard in the sky, we are on the lookout for dicentra. The more northern species, called "squirrel corn" from the small golden tubers at its root, blooms in May, and has the fragrance of hyacinths. It does not affect the rocks, like all the other flowers of this family.

My second new acquaintance the same season was the showy lady's-slipper. Most of the floral ladies leave their slippers in swampy places in the woods; only the stemless one (*Cypripedium acaule*) leaves hers on dry ground before she reaches the swamp, commonly under evergreen trees, where the carpet of pine needles will not hurt her feet. But one may penetrate many wet, mucky places in the woods before he finds the prettiest of them all, the showy lady's-slipper, — the prettiest slipper, but the stoutest and coarsest plant ; the flower large and very showy, white, tinged with purple in front; the stem two feet high, very leafy, and coarser than bearweed. Report had come to me, through my botanizing neighbor, that in a certain quaking sphagnum bog in the woods the showy lady's-slipper could be

8

found. The locality proved to be the marrowy grave of an extinct lake or black tarn. On the borders of it the white azalea was in bloom, fast fading. In the midst of it were spruces and black ash and giant ferns, and, low in the spongy, mossy bottom, the pitcher plant. The lady's-slipper grew in little groups and companies all about. Never have I beheld a prettier sight, — so gay, so festive, so holiday-looking. Were they so many gay bonnets rising above the foliage? or were they flocks of white doves with purple-stained breasts just lifting up their wings to take flight? or were they little fleets of fairy boats, with sail set, tossing on a mimic sea of wild, weedy growths? Such images throng the mind on recalling the scene, and only faintly hint its beauty and animation. The long, erect, white sepals do much to give the alert, tossing look which the flower wears. The dim light, too, of its secluded haunts, and its snowy purity and freshness, contribute to the impression it makes. The purple tinge is like a stain of wine which has slightly overflowed the brim of the inflated lip or sac and run part way down its snowy sides.

This lady's-slipper is one of the rarest and choicest of our wild flowers, and its haunts and its beauty are known only to the few. Those who have the secret guard it closely, lest their favorite be exterminated. A well-known botanist in one of the large New England cities told me that it was found in

9

but one place in that neighborhood, and that the secret, so far as he knew, was known to but three persons, and was carefully kept by them.

A friend of mine, an enthusiast on orchids, came one June day a long way by rail to see this flower. I conducted him to the edge of the swamp, lifted up the branches as I would a curtain, and said, " There they are."

" Where ? " said he, peering far into the dim recesses.

" Within six feet of you," I replied.

He narrowed his vision, and such an expression of surprise and delight as came over his face! A group of a dozen or more of the plants, some of them twin-flowered, were there almost within reach, the first he had ever seen, and his appreciation of the scene, visible in every look and gesture, was greatly satisfying. In the fall he came and moved a few of the plants to a tamarack swamp in his own vicinity, where they throve and bloomed finely for a few years, and then for some unknown reason failed.

Nearly every June, my friend still comes to feast his eyes upon this queen of the cypripediums.

While returning from my first search for the lady's-slipper, my hat fairly brushed the nest of the red-eyed vireo, which was so cunningly concealed, such an open secret, in the dim, leafless underwoods, that I could but pause and regard it. It was suspended from the end of a small, curving sapling;

10

was flecked here and there by some whitish substance, so as to blend it with the gray mottled boles
of the trees; and, in the dimly lighted ground-floor
of the woods, was sure to escape any but the most
prolonged scrutiny. A couple of large leaves formed
a canopy above it. It was not so much hidden as
it was rendered invisible by texture and position
with reference to light and shade.

A few summers ago I struck a new and beautiful plant in the shape of a weed that had only recently appeared in that part of the country. I was
walking through an August meadow when I saw, on
a little knoll, a bit of most vivid orange, verging on
a crimson. I knew of no flower of such a complexion frequenting such a place as that. On investigation, it proved to be a stranger. It had a rough,
hairy, leafless stem about a foot high, surmounted
by a corymbose cluster of flowers or flower-heads of
dark vivid orange-color. The leaves were deeply
notched and toothed, very bristly, and were pressed
flat to the ground. The whole plant was a verita-
ble Esau for hairs, and it seemed to lay hold upon
the ground as if it was not going to let go easily.
And what a fiery plume it had! The next day, in
another field a mile away, I chanced upon more
of the flowers. On making inquiry, I found that a
small patch or colony of the plants had appeared
that season, or had first been noticed then, in a
meadow well known to me from boyhood. They had

11

been cut down with the grass in early July, and the first week in August had shot up and bloomed again. I found the spot aflame with them. Their leaves covered every inch of the surface where they stood, and not a spear of grass grew there. They were taking slow but complete possession; they were devouring the meadow by inches. The plant seemed to be a species of hieracium, or hawkweed, or some closely allied species of the composite family, but I could not find it mentioned in our botanies.

A few days later, on the edge of an adjoining county ten miles distant, I found, probably, its headquarters. It had appeared there a few years before, and was thought to have escaped from some farmer's door-yard. Patches of it were appearing here and there in the fields, and the farmers were thoroughly alive to the danger, and were fighting it like fire. Its seeds are winged like those of the dandelion, and it sows itself far and near. It would be a beautiful acquisition to our midsummer fields, supplying a tint as brilliant as that given by the scarlet poppies to English grain-fields. But it would be an expensive one, as it usurps the land completely.[1]

Parts of New England have already a midsummer flower nearly as brilliant, and probably far less ag-

[1] This observation was made ten years ago. I have since learned that the plant is *Hieracium aurantiacum* from Europe, a kind of hawkweed. It is fast becoming a common weed in New York and New England. (1894.)

gressive and noxious, in meadow-beauty, or rhexia, the sole northern genus of a family of tropical plants. I found it very abundant in August in the country bordering on Buzzard's Bay. It was a new flower to me, and I was puzzled to make it out. It seemed like some sort of scarlet evening primrose. The parts were in fours, the petals slightly heart-shaped and convoluted in the bud, the leaves bristly, the calyx-tube prolonged ; but the stem was square, the leaves opposite, and the tube urn-shaped. The flowers were an inch across, and bright purple. It grew in large patches in dry, sandy fields, making the desert gay with color ; and also on the edges of marshy places. It eclipses any flower of the open fields known to me farther inland. When we come to improve our wild garden, as recommended by Mr. Robinson in his book on wild gardening, we must not forget the rhexia.

Our seacoast flowers are probably more brilliant in color than the same flowers in the interior. I thought the wild rose on the Massachusetts coast deeper tinted and more fragrant than those I was used to. The steeple-bush, or hardhack, had more color, as had the rose gerardia and several other plants.

But when vivid color is wanted, what can surpass or equal our cardinal-flower ? There is a glow about this flower as if color emanated from it as from a live coal. The eye is baffled, and does not seem to

reach the surface of the petal; it does not see the
texture or material part as it does in other flowers,
but rests in a steady, still radiance. It is not so
much something colored as it is color itself. And
then the moist, cool, shady places it affects, usually where it has no floral rivals, and where the
large, dark shadows need just such a dab of fire!
Often, too, we see it double, its reflected image in
some dark pool heightening its effect. I never have
found it with its only rival in color, the monarda
or bee-balm, a species of mint. Farther north, the
cardinal-flower seems to fail, and the monarda takes
its place, growing in similar localities. One may
see it about a mountain spring, or along a meadow
brook, or glowing in the shade around the head of
a wild mountain lake. It stands up two feet high
or more, and the flowers show like a broad scarlet
cap.

The only thing I have seen in this country that
calls to mind the green grain-fields of Britain
splashed with scarlet poppies may be witnessed in
August in the marshes of the lower Hudson, when
the broad sedgy and flaggy spaces are sprinkled with
the great marsh-mallow. It is a most pleasing spectacle, — level stretches of dark green flag or waving
marsh-grass kindled on every square yard by these
bright pink blossoms, like great burning coals fanned
in the breeze. The mallow is not so deeply colored
as the poppy, but it is much larger, and has the tint

of youth and happiness. It is an immigrant from
Europe, but it is making itself thoroughly at home
in our great river meadows.

The same day your eye is attracted by the mal-
lows, as your train skirts or cuts through the broad
marshes, it will revel with delight in the masses of
fresh bright color afforded by the purple loosestrife,
which grows in similar localities, and shows here
and there like purple bonfires. It is a tall plant,
grows in dense masses, and affords a most striking
border to the broad spaces dotted with the mallow.
It, too, came to us from over seas, and first appeared along the Wallkill, many years ago. It used
to be thought by the farmers in that vicinity that
its seed was first brought in wool imported to this
country from Australia, and washed in the Wallkill
at Walden, where there was a woolen factory. This
is not probable, as it is a European species, and
I should sooner think it had escaped from cultivation. If one were to act upon the suggestions of
Robinson's "Wild Garden," already alluded to, he
would gather the seeds of these plants and sow
them in the marshes and along the sluggish inland
streams, till the banks of all our rivers were gay
with these brilliant exotics.

Among our native plants, the one that takes
broad marshes to itself and presents vast sheets of
color is the marsh milkweed, far less brilliant than
the loosestrife or the mallow, still a missionary in

15

the wilderness, lighting up many waste places with
its humbler tints of purple.

One sometimes seems to discover a familiar wild
flower anew by coming upon it in some peculiar and
striking situation. Our columbine is at all times
and in all places one of the most exquisitely beautiful of flowers ; yet one spring day, when I saw it
growing out of a small seam on the face of a great
lichen-covered wall of rock, where no soil or mould
was visible, — a jet of foliage and color shooting
out of a black line on the face of a perpendicular
mountain wall and rising up like a tiny fountain,
its drops turning to flame-colored jewels that hung
and danced in the air against the gray rocky surface, — its beauty became something magical and
audacious. On little narrow shelves in the rocky
wall the corydalis was blooming, and among the
loose boulders at its base the blood-root shone conspicuous, suggesting snow rather than anything
more sanguine.

Certain flowers one makes special expeditions for
every season. They are limited in their ranges,
and must generally be sought for in particular
haunts. How many excursions to the woods does
the delicious trailing arbutus give rise to! How
can one let the spring go by without gathering it
himself when it hides in the moss! There are arbutus days in one's calendar, days when the trailing
flower fairly calls him to the woods. With me,

16

they come the latter part of April. The grass is
greening here and there on the moist slopes and by
the spring runs ; the first furrow has been struck
by the farmer; the liver-leaf is in the height of its
beauty, and the bright constellations of the blood-
root shine out here and there; one has had his first
taste and his second taste of the spring and of the
woods, and his tongue is sharpened rather than
cloyed. Now he will take the most delicious and
satisfying draught of all, the very essence and soul
of the early season, of the tender brooding days,
with all their prophecies and awakenings, in the
handful of trailing arbutus which he gathers in his
walk. At the mere thought of it, one sees the sunlight flooding the woods, smells the warm earthy
odors which the heat liberates from beneath the dry
leaves, hears the mellow bass of the first bumblebee,

"Rover of the underwoods,"

or the finer chord of the adventurous honey-bee
seeking store for his empty comb. The arriving
swallows twitter above the woods ; the first chewink rustles the dry leaves; the northward-bound
thrushes, the hermit and the gray-cheeked, flit here
and there before you. The robin, the sparrow, and
the bluebird are building their first nests, and the
first shad are making their way slowly up the Hudson. Indeed, the season is fairly under way when

17

the trailing arbutus comes. Now look out for troops
of boys and girls going to the woods to gather it!
and let them look out that in their greed they do
not exterminate it. Within reach of our large towns,
the choicer spring wild flowers are hunted mercilessly. Every fresh party from town raids them as
if bent upon their destruction. One day, about ten
miles from one of our Hudson River cities, there
got into the train six young women loaded down
with vast sheaves and bundles of trailing arbutus.
Each one of them had enough for forty. They had
apparently made a clean sweep of the woods. It
was a pretty sight, — the pink and white of the
girls and the pink and white of the flowers! and
the car, too, was suddenly filled with perfume, —
the breath of spring loaded the air ; but I thought
it a pity to ravish the woods in that way. The next
party was probably equally greedy, and, because
a handful was desirable, thought an armful pro-
portionately so ; till, by and by, the flower will be
driven from those woods.

Another flower that one makes special excursions
for is the pond-lily. The pond-lily is a star, and
easily takes the first place among lilies ; and the
expeditions to her haunts, and the gathering her
where she rocks upon the dark secluded waters of
some pool or lakelet, are the crown and summit
of the floral expeditions of summer. It is the expedition about which more things gather than almost

18

any other: you want your boat, you want your lunch,
you want your friend or friends with you. You
are going to put in the greater part of the day; you
are going to picnic in the woods, and indulge in a
"green thought in a green shade." When my friend
and I go for pond-lilies, we have to traverse a distance of three miles with our boat in a wagon. The
road is what is called a "back road," and leads
through woods most of the way. Black Pond,
where the lilies grow, lies about one hundred feet
higher than the Hudson, from which it is separated
by a range of rather bold wooded heights, one of
which might well be called Mount Hymettus, for
I have found a great deal of wild honey in the forest that covers it. The stream which flows out of
the pond takes a northward course for two or three
miles, till it finds an opening through the rocky
hills, when it makes rapidly for the Hudson. Its
career all the way from the lake is a series of alter-
nating pools and cascades. Now a long, deep, level
stretch, where the perch and the bass and the pickerel lurk, and where the willow-herb and the royal
osmunda fern line the shores; then a sudden leap
of eight, ten, or fifteen feet down rocks to another
level stretch, where the water again loiters and suns
itself; and so on through its adventurous course till
the hills are cleared and the river is in sight. Our
road leads us along this stream, across its rude
bridges, through dark hemlock and pine woods,

19

under gray, rocky walls, now past a black pool, then within sight or hearing of a foaming rapid or fall, till we strike the outlet of the long level that leads to the lake. In this we launch our boat and paddle slowly upward over its dark surface, now pushing our way through half-submerged treetops, then ducking under the trunk of an overturned tree which bridges the stream and makes a convenient way for the squirrels and wood-mice, or else forcing the boat over it when it is sunk a few inches below the surface. We are traversing what was once a continuation of the lake; the forest floor is as level as the water and but a few inches above it, even in summer; it sweeps back a half mile or more, densely covered with black ash, red maple, and other deciduous trees, to the foot of the rocky hills which shut us in. What glimpses we get, as we steal along, into the heart of the rank, dense, silent woods! I carry in my eye yet the vision I had, on one occasion, of a solitary meadow lily hanging like a fairy bell there at the end of a chance opening, where a ray of sunlight fell full upon it, and brought out its brilliant orange against the dark green background. It appeared to be the only bit of bright color in all the woods. Then the song of a single hermit thrush immediately after did even more for the ear than the lily did for the eye. Presently the swamp sparrow, one of the rarest of the sparrows, was seen and heard ; and that nest there

20

in a small bough a few feet over the water proves
to be hers, — in appearance a ground-bird's nest
in a bough, with the same four speckled eggs. As
we come in sight of the lilies, where they cover the
water at the outlet of the lake, a brisk gust of
wind, as if it had been waiting to surprise us,
sweeps down and causes every leaf to leap from
the water and show its pink under side. Was it
a fluttering of hundreds of wings, or the clapping
of a multitude of hands? But there rocked the lilies
with their golden hearts open to the sun, and their
tender white petals as fresh as crystals of snow.
What a queenly flower, indeed, the type of unsul-
lied purity and sweetness! Its root, like a black,
corrugated, ugly reptile, clinging to the slime, but
its flower in purity and whiteness like a star. There
is something very pretty in the closed bud making
its way up through the water to meet the sun; and
there is something touching in the flower closing
itself up again after its brief career, and slowly
burying itself beneath the dark wave. One almost
fancies a sad, regretful look in it as the stem draws
it downward to mature its seed on the sunless bottom. The pond-lily is a flower of the morning; it
closes a little after noon; but after you have plucked
it and carried it home, it still feels the call of the
morning sun, and will open to him, if you give it
a good chance. Coil their stems up in the grass
on the lawn, where the sun's rays can reach them,

and sprinkle them copiously. By the time you are ready for your morning walk, there they sit upon the moist grass, almost as charmingly as upon the wave.

Our more choice wild flowers, the rarer and finer spirits among them, please us by their individual beauty and charm ; others, more coarse and common, delight us by mass and profusion; we regard not the one, but the many, as did Wordsworth his golden daffodils: —

> "Ten thousand saw I at a glance
> Tossing their heads in sprightly dance."

Of such is the marsh marigold, giving a golden lining to many a dark, marshy place in the leafless April woods, or marking a little water-course through a greening meadow with a broad line of new gold. One glances up from his walk, and his eye falls upon something like fixed and heaped-up sunshine there beneath the alders, or yonder in the freshening field.

In a measure, the same is true of our wild sunflowers, lighting up many a neglected bushy fence-corner or weedy roadside with their bright, beaming faces. The evening primrose is a coarse, rankly growing plant; but, in late summer, how many an untrimmed bank is painted over by it with the most fresh and delicate canary yellow!

We have one flower which grows in vast multi-

tudes, yet which is exquisitely delicate and beautiful
in and of itself: I mean the houstonia, or bluets.
In May, in certain parts of the country, I see vast
sheets of it; in old, low meadow bottoms that have
never known the plow, it covers the ground like
a dull bluish or purplish snow which has blown
unevenly about. In the mass it is not especially
pleasing ; it has a faded, indefinite sort of look.
Its color is not strong and positive enough to be
effective in the mass, yet each single flower is a gem
of itself. The color of the common violet is much
more firm and pronounced; and how many a grassy
bank is made gay with it in the mid-May days!
We have a great variety of violets, and they are
very capricious as to perfume. The only species
which are uniformly fragrant are the tall Canada
violet, so common in our northern woods, — white,
with a tinge of purple to the under side of its petals,
— and the small white violet of the marshy places;
yet one summer I came upon a host of the spurred
violet in a sunny place in the woods, which filled
the air with a delicate perfume. A handful of them
yielded a perceptible fragrance, but a single flower
none that I could detect. The Canada violet very
frequently blooms in the fall, and is more fragrant
at such times than in its earlier blooming. I must
not forget to mention that delicate and lovely
flower of May, the fringed polygala. You gather
it when you go for the fragrant, showy orchis, —

that is, if you are lucky enough to find it. It is rather a shy flower, and is not found in every wood. One day we went up and down through the woods looking for it, — woods of mingled oak, chestnut, pine, and hemlock, — and were about giving it up when suddenly we came upon a gay company of them beside an old wood-road. It was as if a flock of small rose-purple butterflies had alighted there on the ground before us. The whole plant has a singularly fresh and tender aspect. Its foliage is of a slightly purple tinge, and of very delicate texture. Not the least interesting feature about the plant is the concealed fertile flower which it bears on a subterranean shoot, keeping, as it were, one flower for beauty and one for use.

II

In our walks we note the most showy and beautiful flowers, but not always the most interesting. Who, for instance, pauses to consider that early species of everlasting, commonly called mouse-ear, that grows nearly everywhere by the roadside or about poor fields? It begins to be noticeable in May, its whitish downy appearance, its groups of slender stalks crowned with a corymb of paper-like buds, contrasting it with the fresh green of surrounding grass or weeds. It is a member of a very large family, the Compositæ, and does not attract one by its beauty; but it is interesting because of

24

The Study in Midsummer

its many curious traits and habits. For instance, it is diœcious, that is, the two sexes are represented by separate plants; and, what is more curious, these plants are usually found separated from each other in well-defined groups, like the men and women in an old-fashioned country church, — always in groups; here a group of females, there, a few yards away, a group of males. The females may be known by their more slender and graceful appearance, and, as the season advances, by their outstripping the males in growth. Indeed, they become real amazons in comparison with their brothers. The staminate or male plants grow but a few inches high; the heads are round, and have a more dusky or freckled appearance than do the pistillate ; and as soon as they have shed their pollen their work is done, they are of no further use, and by the middle of May, or before, their heads droop, their stalks wither, and their general collapse sets in. Then the other sex, or pistillate plants, seem to have taken a new lease of life ; they wax strong, they shoot up with the growing grass and keep their heads above it; they are alert and active; they bend in the breeze; their long, tapering flower-heads take on a tinge of color, and life seems full of purpose and enjoyment with them. I have discovered, too, that they are real sun-worshipers; that they turn their faces to the east in the morning, and follow the sun in his course across the sky till they all bend to the west at his going down. On the other hand, their brothers have stood stiff and stupid, and unresponsive to any influence of sky and air, so far as I could see, till they drooped and died.

Another curious thing is that the females seem vastly more numerous, — I should say almost ten times as abundant. You have to hunt for the males; the others you see far off. One season I used every day to pass several groups or circles of females in the grass by the roadside. I noted how they grew and turned their faces sunward. I observed how alert and vigorous they were, and what a purplish tinge came over their mammæ-shaped flower-heads as June approached. I looked for the males; to the east, south, west, none could be found for hundreds of yards. On the north, about two hundred feet away, I found a small colony of meek and lowly males. I wondered by what agency fertilization would take place, — by insects, or by the wind? I suspected it would not take place. No insects seemed to visit the flowers, and the wind surely could not be relied upon to hit the mark so far off, and from such an unlikely corner, too. But by some means the vitalizing dust seemed to have been conveyed. Early in June, the plants began to shed their down, or seed-bearing pappus, still carrying their heads at the top of the grass, so that the breezes could have free access to them, and sow the seeds far and wide.

AMONG THE WILD FLOWERS

As the seeds are sown broadcast by the wind, I was at first puzzled to know how the two sexes were kept separate, and always in little communities, till I perceived, what I might have read in the botany, that the plant is perennial and spreads by offsets and runners, like the strawberry. This would of course keep the two kinds in groups by themselves.

Another plant which has interesting ways and is beautiful besides is the adder's-tongue, or yellow erythronium, the earliest of the lilies, and one of the most pleasing. The April sunshine is fairly reflected in its revolute flowers. The lilies have bulbs that sit on or near the top of the ground. The onion is a fair type of the lily in this respect. But here is a lily with the bulb deep in the ground. How it gets there is well worth investigating. The botany says the bulb is deep in the ground, but offers no explanation. Now it is only the bulbs of the older or flowering plants that are deep in the ground. The bulbs of the young plants are near the top of the ground. The young plants have but one leaf, the older or flowering ones have two. If you happen to be in the woods at the right time in early April, you may see these leaves compactly rolled together, piercing the matted coating of sere leaves that covers the ground like some sharp-pointed instrument. They do not burst their covering or lift it up, but pierce through it like an awl.

27

But how does the old bulb get so deep into the ground? In digging some of them up one spring in an old meadow bottom, I had to cleave the tough fibrous sod to a depth of eight inches. The smaller ones were barely two inches below the surface. Of course they all started from the seed at the surface of the soil. The young botanist, or nature-lover, will find here a field for original research. If, in late May or early June, after the leaves of the plant have disappeared, he finds the ground where they stood showing curious, looping, twisting growths or roots, of a greenish white color, let him examine them. They are as smooth and as large as an angle-worm, and very brittle. Both ends will be found in the ground, one attached to the old bulb, the other boring or drilling downward and enlarged till it suggests the new bulb. I do not know that this mother root in all cases comes to the surface. Why it should come at all is a mystery, unless it be in some way to get more power for the downward thrust. My own observations upon the subject are not complete, but I think in the foregoing I have given the clew as to how the bulb each year sinks deeper and deeper into the ground.

It is a pity that this graceful and abundant flower has no good and appropriate common name. It is the earliest of the true lilies, and it has all the grace and charm that belong to this order of flowers.

28

AMONG THE WILD FLOWERS

Erythronium, its botanical name, is not good, as it is derived from a Greek word that means red, while one species of our flower is yellow and the other is white. How it came to be called "adder's-tongue" I do not know; probably from the spotted character of the leaf, which might suggest a snake, though it in no wise resembles a snake's tongue. A fawn is spotted, too, and "fawn-lily" would be better than "adder's-tongue." Still better is the name "trout-lily," which has recently been proposed for this plant. It blooms along the trout streams, and its leaf is as mottled as a trout's back. The name "dog's-tooth" may have been suggested by the shape and color of the bud, but how the "violet" came to be added is a puzzle, as it has not one feature of the violet. It is only another illustration of the haphazard way in which our wild flowers, as well as our birds, have been named.

In my spring rambles I have sometimes come upon a solitary specimen of this yellow lily growing beside a mossy stone where the sunshine fell full upon it, and have thought it one of the most beautiful of our wild flowers. Its two leaves stand up like a fawn's ears, and this feature, with its recurved petals, gives it an alert, wide-awake look. The white species I never have seen. I am told they are very abundant on the mountains in California.

Another of our common wild flowers, which I always look at with an interrogation-point in my

mind, is the wild ginger. Why should this plant
always hide its flower? Its two fuzzy, heart-shaped
green leaves stand up very conspicuously amid the
rocks or mossy stones; but its one curious, brown,
bell-shaped flower is always hidden beneath the
moss or dry leaves, as if too modest to face the
light of the open woods. As a rule, the one thing
which a plant is anxious to show and to make
much of, and to flaunt before all the world, is
its flower. But the wild ginger reverses the rule,
and blooms in secret. Instead of turning upward
toward the light and air, it turns downward toward
the darkness and the silence. It has no corolla,
but what the botanists call a lurid or brown-purple
calyx, which is conspicuous like a corolla. Its root
leaves in the mouth a taste precisely like that of
ginger.

This plant and the closed gentian are apparent
exceptions, in their manner of blooming, to the
general habit of the rest of our flowers. The closed
gentian does not hide its flower, but the corolla
never opens ; it always remains a closed bud. I
used to think that this gentian could never experience the benefits of insect visits, which Darwin
showed us were of such importance in the vegetable
world. I once plucked one of the flowers into which
a bumblebee had forced his way, but he had never
come out; the flower was his tomb.

I am assured, however, by recent observers, that

the bumblebee does successfully enter the closed corolla, and thus distribute its pollen.[1]

There is yet another curious exception which I will mention, namely, the witch-hazel. All our trees and plants bloom in the spring, except this one species ; this blooms in the fall. Just as its leaves are fading and falling, its flowers appear, giving out an odor along the bushy lanes and margins of the woods that is to the nose like cool water to the hand. Why it should bloom in the fall instead of in the spring is a mystery. And it is probably because of this very curious trait that its branches are used as divining-rods, by certain credulous persons, to point out where springs of water and precious metals are hidden.

Most young people find botany a dull study. So it is, as taught from the text-books in the schools; but study it yourself in the fields and woods, and you will find it a source of perennial delight. Find your flower, and then name it by the aid of the botany. There is so much in a name. To find out

[1] " A bumblebee came along and lit upon a cluster of asters. Leaving these, it next visited a head of gentians, and with some difficulty thrust its tongue through the valves of the nearest blossom ; then it pushed in its head and body until only the hind legs and the tip of the abdomen were sticking out. In this position it made the circuit of the blossom, and then emerged, resting a moment to brush the pollen from its head and thorax into the pollen-baskets, before flying again to a neighboring aster. The whole process required about twenty seconds." *Ten New England Blossoms and their Insect Visitors*, CLARENCE MOORES WEED, pp. 93, 94.

what a thing is called is a great help. It is the beginning of knowledge; it is the first step. When we see a new person who interests us, we wish to know his or her name. A bird, a flower, a place, — the first thing we wish to know about it is its name. Its name helps us to classify it; it gives us a handle to grasp it by; it sheds a ray of light where all before was darkness. As soon as we know the name of a thing, we seem to have established some sort of relation with it.

The other day, while the train was delayed by an accident, I wandered a few yards away from it along the river margin seeking wild flowers. Should I find any whose name I did not know? While thus loitering, a young English girl also left the train and came in my direction, plucking the flowers right and left as she came. But they were all unknown to her; she did not know the name of one of them, and she wished to send them home to her father, too. With what satisfaction she heard the names! The words seemed to be full of meaning to her, though she had never heard them before in her life. It was what she wanted: it was an introduction to the flowers, and her interest in them increased at once.

"That orange-colored flower which you just plucked from the edge of the water, — that is our jewel-weed," I said.

"It looks like a jewel," she replied.

"You have nothing like it in England, or did not have till lately; but I hear it is now appearing along certain English streams, having been brought from this country."

"And what is this?" she inquired, holding up a blue flower with a very bristly leaf and stalk.

"That is viper's bugloss, or blue-weed, a plant from your side of the water, one that is making itself thoroughly at home along the Hudson, and in the valleys of some of its tributaries among the Catskills. It is a rough, hardy weed, but its flower, with its long, conspicuous purple stamens and blue corolla, as you see, is very pretty."

"Here is another emigrant from across the Atlantic," I said, holding up a cluster of small white flowers, each mounted upon a little inflated brown bag or balloon, — the bladder campion. "It also runs riot in some of our fields, as I am sure you will not see it at home." She went on filling her hands with flowers, and I gave her the names of each, — sweet clover or melilotus, a foreign plant; vervain (foreign); purple loosestrife (foreign); toad-flax (foreign); chelone, or turtle-head, a native; and the purple mimulus, or monkey-flower, also a native. It was a likely place for the cardinal-flower, but I could not find any. I wanted this hearty English girl to see one of our native wild flowers so intense in color that it would fairly make her eyes water to gaze upon it.

Just then the whistle of the engine summoned us all aboard, and in a moment we were off.

When one is stranded anywhere in the country in the season of flowers or birds, if he feels any interest in these things, he always has something ready at hand to fall back upon. And if he feels no interest in them, he will do well to cultivate an interest. The tedium of an eighty-mile drive which I lately took (in September), cutting through parts of three counties, was greatly relieved by noting the various flowers by the roadside. First my attention was attracted by wild thyme making purple patches here and there in the meadows and pastures. I got out of the wagon and gathered some of it. I found honey-bees working upon it, and remembered that it was a famous plant for honey in parts of the Old World. It had probably escaped from some garden; I had never seen it growing wild in this way before. Along the Schoharie Kill, I saw acres of blue-weed, or viper's bugloss, the hairy stems of the plants, when looked at toward the sun, having a frosted appearance.

What is this tall plant by the roadside, thickly hung with pendent clusters of long purplish buds or tassels? The stalk is four feet high, the lower leaves are large and lobed, and the whole effect of the plant is striking. The clusters of purple pendents have a very decorative effect. This is a species of nabalus, of the great composite family, and is sometimes called lion's-foot. The flower is cream-colored, but quite inconspicuous. The noticeable thing about it is the drooping or pendulous clusters of what appear to be buds, but which are the involucres, bundles of purple scales, like little staves, out of which the flower emerges.

In another place I caught sight of something intensely blue in a wet, weedy place, and, on getting some of it, found it to be the closed gentian, a flower to which I have already referred as never opening, but always remaining a bud. Four or five of these blue buds, each like the end of your little finger and as long as the first joint, crown the top of the stalk, set in a rosette of green leaves. It is one of our rarer flowers, and a very interesting one, well worth getting out of the wagon to gather. As I drove through a swampy part of Ulster County, my attention was attracted by a climbing plant over-running the low bushes by the sluggish streams, and covering them thickly with clusters of dull white flowers. I did not remember ever to have seen it before, and, on taking it home and examining it, found it to be climbing boneset. The flowers are so much like those of boneset that you would suspect their relationship at once.

Without the name, any flower is still more or less a stranger to you. The name betrays its family, its relationship to other flowers, and gives the mind something tangible to grasp. It is very difficult for persons who have had no special training to learn the names of the flowers from the botany. The botany is a sealed book to them. The descriptions of the flowers are in a language which they do not understand at all. And the key is no help to them. It is as much a puzzle as the botany itself. They need a key to unlock the key.

One of these days some one will give us a hand-book of our wild flowers, by the aid of which we shall all be able to name those we gather in our walks without the trouble of analyzing them. In this book we shall have a list of all our flowers arranged according to color, as white flowers, blue flowers, yellow flowers, pink flowers, with place of growth and time of blooming; also lists or sub-lists of fragrant flowers, climbing flowers, marsh flowers, meadow flowers, wood flowers, so that, with flower in hand, by running over these lists we shall be pretty sure to find its name. Having got its name, we can turn to Gray or Wood and find a more technical description of it if we choose.

II

THE HEART OF THE SOUTHERN
CATSKILLS

ON looking at the southern and more distant
Catskills from the Hudson River on the east,
or on looking at them from the west from some
point of vantage in Delaware County, you see, amid
the group of mountains, one that looks like the back
and shoulders of a gigantic horse. The horse has
got his head down grazing; the shoulders are high,
and the descent from them down his neck very
steep; if he were to lift up his head, one sees that
it would be carried far above all other peaks, and
that the noble beast might gaze straight to his peers
in the Adirondacks or the White Mountains. But
the lowered head never comes up; some spell or
enchantment keeps it down there amid the mighty
herd; and the high round shoulders and the smooth
strong back of the steed are alone visible. The
peak to which I refer is Slide Mountain, the highest of the Catskills by some two hundred feet, and
probably the most inaccessible; certainly the hard-
est to get a view of, it is hedged about so completely
by other peaks, — the greatest mountain of them

all, and apparently the least willing to be seen; only at a distance of thirty or forty miles is it seen to stand up above all other peaks. It takes its name from a landslide which occurred many years ago down its steep northern side, or down the neck of the grazing steed. The mane of spruce and balsam fir was stripped away for many hundred feet, leaving a long gray streak visible from afar.

Slide Mountain is the centre and the chief of the southern Catskills. Streams flow from its base, and from the base of its subordinates, to all points of the compass, — the Rondout and the Neversink to the south; the Beaverkill to the west; the Esopus to the north; and several lesser streams to the east. With its summit as the centre, a radius of ten miles would include within the circle described but very little cultivated land; only a few poor, wild farms in some of the numerous valleys. The soil is poor, a mixture of gravel and clay, and is subject to slides. It lies in the valleys in ridges and small hillocks, as if dumped there from a huge cart. The tops of the southern Catskills are all capped with a kind of conglomerate, or "pudden stone," — a rock of cemented quartz pebbles which underlies the coal measures. This rock disintegrates under the action of the elements, and the sand and gravel which result are carried into the valleys and make up the most of the soil. From the northern Catskills, so far as I know them, this rock has been swept clean.

38

Low down in the valleys the old red sandstone crops out, and, as you go west into Delaware County, in many places it alone remains and makes up most of the soil, all the superincumbent rock having been carried away.

Slide Mountain had been a summons and a challenge to me for many years. I had fished every stream that it nourished, and had camped in the wilderness on all sides of it, and whenever I had caught a glimpse of its summit I had promised myself to set foot there before another season should pass. But the seasons came and went, and my feet got no nimbler, and Slide Mountain no lower, until finally, one July, seconded by an energetic friend, we thought to bring Slide to terms by approaching him through the mountains on the east. With a farmer's son for guide we struck in by way of Weaver Hollow, and, after a long and desperate climb, contented ourselves with the Wittenberg, instead of Slide. The view from the Wittenberg is in many respects more striking, as you are perched immediately above a broader and more distant sweep of country, and are only about two hundred feet lower. You are here on the eastern brink of the southern Catskills, and the earth falls away at your feet and curves down through an immense stretch of forest till it joins the plain of Shokan, and thence sweeps away to the Hudson and beyond. Slide is southwest of you, six or seven miles distant, but is visible only when you climb into a treetop. I climbed and saluted him, and promised to call next time.

We passed the night on the Wittenberg, sleeping on the moss, between two decayed logs, with balsam boughs thrust into the ground and meeting and forming a canopy over us. In coming off the mountain in the morning we ran upon a huge porcupine, and I learned for the first time that the tail of a porcupine goes with a spring like a trap. It seems to be a set-lock; and you no sooner touch with the weight of a hair one of the quills than the tail leaps up in a most surprising manner, and the laugh is not on your side. The beast cantered along the path in my front, and I threw myself upon him, shielded by my roll of blankets. He submitted quietly to the indignity, and lay very still under my blankets, with his broad tail pressed close to the ground. This I proceeded to investigate, but had not fairly made a beginning when it went off like a trap, and my hand and wrist were full of quills. This caused me to let up on the creature, when it lumbered away till it tumbled down a precipice. The quills were quickly removed from my hand, when we gave chase. When we came up to him, he had wedged himself in between the rocks so that he presented only a back bristling with quills, with the tail lying in ambush below. He had chosen his position well, and seemed to defy us. After amusing ourselves by repeatedly springing his tail and receiving the quills in a rotten stick, we made a slip-noose out of a spruce root, and, after much manœuvring, got it over his head and led him forth. In what a peevish, injured tone the creature did complain of our unfair tactics! He protested and protested, and whimpered and scolded like some infirm old man tormented by boys. His game after we led him forth was to keep himself as much as possible in the shape of a ball, but with two sticks and the cord we finally threw him over on his back and exposed his quill-less and vulnerable under side, when he fairly surrendered and seemed to say, " Now you may do with me as you like." His great chisel-like teeth, which are quite as formidable as those of the woodchuck, he does not appear to use at all in his defense, but relies entirely upon his quills, and when those fail him, he is done for.

After amusing ourselves with him awhile longer, we released him and went on our way. The trail to which we had committed ourselves led us down into Woodland Valley, a retreat which so took my eye by its fine trout brook, its superb mountain scenery, and its sweet seclusion, that I marked it for my own, and promised myself a return to it at no distant day. This promise I kept, and pitched my tent there twice during that season. Both occasions were a sort of laying siege to Slide, but we only skirmished with him at a distance; the actual assault was not undertaken. But the following year, reinforced by two other brave climbers, we determined upon the assault, and upon making it from this the most difficult side. The regular way is by Big Ingin Valley, where the climb is comparatively easy, and where it is often made by women. But from Woodland Valley only men may essay the ascent. Larkins is the upper inhabitant, and from our camping-ground near his clearing we set out early one June morning.

One would think nothing could be easier to find than a big mountain, especially when one is encamped upon a stream which he knows springs out of its very loins. But for some reason or other we had got an idea that Slide Mountain was a very slippery customer and must be approached cautiously. We had tried from several points in the valley to get a view of it, but were not quite sure we had seen its very head. When on the Wittenberg, a neighboring peak, the year before, I had caught a brief glimpse of it only by climbing a dead tree and craning up for a moment from its topmost branch. It would seem as if the mountain had taken every precaution to shut itself off from a near view. It was a shy mountain, and we were about to stalk it through six or seven miles of primitive woods, and we seemed to have some unreasonable fear that it might elude us. We had been told of parties who had essayed the ascent from this side, and had returned baffled and bewildered. In a tangle of prim-

itive woods, the very bigness of the mountain baffles
one. It is all mountain; whichever way you turn
— and one turns sometimes in such cases before he
knows it — the foot finds a steep and rugged ascent.

The eye is of little service ; one must be sure of
his bearings and push boldly on and up. One is
not unlike a flea upon a great shaggy beast, looking
for the animal's head; or even like a much smaller
and much less nimble creature, — he may waste his
time and steps, and think he has reached the head
when he is only upon the rump. Hence I ques-
tioned our host, who had several times made the
ascent, closely. Larkins laid his old felt hat upon
the table, and, placing one hand upon one side of it
and the other upon the other, said: "There Slide
lies, between the two forks of the stream, just as my
hat lies between my two hands. David will go with
you to the forks, and then you will push right on up."
But Larkins was not right, though he had traversed
all those mountains many times over. The peak we
were about to set out for did not lie between the
forks, but exactly at the head of one of them; the
beginnings of the stream are in the very path of the
slide, as we afterward found. We broke camp early
in the morning, and with our blankets strapped to
our backs and rations in our pockets for two days,
set out along an ancient and in places an obliterated
bark road that followed and crossed and recrossed
the stream. The morning was bright and warm, but

the wind was fitful and petulant, and I predicted rain. What a forest solitude our obstructed and dilapidated wood-road led us through! five miles of primitive woods before we came to the forks, three miles before we came to the "burnt shanty," a name merely, — no shanty there now for twenty-five years past. The ravages of the barkpeelers were still visible, now in a space thickly strewn with the soft and decayed trunks of hemlock-trees, and overgrown with wild cherry, then in huge mossy logs scattered through the beech and maple woods. Some of these logs were so soft and mossy that one could sit or recline upon them as upon a sofa.

But the prettiest thing was the stream soliloquizing in such musical tones there amid the moss-covered rocks and boulders. How clean it looked, what purity! Civilization corrupts the streams as it corrupts the Indian; only in such remote woods can you now see a brook in all its original freshness and beauty. Only the sea and the mountain forest brook are pure; all between is contaminated more or less by the work of man. An ideal trout brook was this, now hurrying, now loitering, now deepening around a great boulder, now gliding evenly over a pavement of green-gray stone and pebbles; no sediment or stain of any kind, but white and sparkling as snow-water, and nearly as cool. Indeed, the water of all this Catskill region is the best in the world. For the first few days, one feels as if he could almost live on

the water alone; he cannot drink enough of it. In
this particular it is indeed the good Bible land, " a
land of brooks of water, of fountains and depths that
spring out of valleys and hills."

Near the forks we caught, or thought we caught,
through an opening, a glimpse of Slide. Was it
Slide? was it the head, or the rump, or the shoulder
of the shaggy monster we were in quest of? At the
forks there was a bewildering maze of underbrush
and great trees, and the way did not seem at all certain; nor was David, who was then at the end of his
reckoning, able to reassure us. But in assaulting a
mountain, as in assaulting a fort, boldness is the
watchword. We pressed forward, following a line
of blazed trees for nearly a mile, then, turning to the
left, began the ascent of the mountain. It was steep,
hard climbing. We saw numerous marks of both
bears and deer; but no birds, save at long intervals
the winter wren flitting here and there, and darting
under logs and rubbish like a mouse. Occasionally
its gushing, lyrical song would break the silence.
After we had climbed an hour or two, the clouds
began to gather, and presently the rain began to
come down. This was discouraging; but we put our
backs up against trees and rocks, and waited for the
shower to pass.

"They were wet with the showers of the mountain, and embraced the rocks for want of shelter,"
as they did in Job's time. But the shower was

light and brief, and we were soon under way again.
Three hours from the forks brought us out on the
broad level back of the mountain upon which Slide,
considered as an isolated peak, is reared. After a
time we entered a dense growth of spruce which
covered a slight depression in the table of the mountain. The moss was deep, the ground spongy, the
light dim, the air hushed. The transition from the
open, leafy woods to this dim, silent, weird grove
was very marked. It was like the passage from the
street into the temple. Here we paused awhile and
ate our lunch, and refreshed ourselves with water
gathered from a little well sunk in the moss.

The quiet and repose of this spruce grove proved
to be the calm that goes before the storm. As we
passed out of it, we came plump upon the almost
perpendicular battlements of Slide. The mountain
rose like a huge, rock-bound fortress from this plain-
like expanse. It was ledge upon ledge, precipice
upon precipice, up which and over which we made
our way slowly and with great labor, now pulling
ourselves up by our hands, then cautiously finding
niches for our feet and zigzagging right and left from
shelf to shelf. This northern side of the mountain
was thickly covered with moss and lichens, like the
north side of a tree. This made it soft to the foot,
and broke many a slip and fall. Everywhere a
stunted growth of yellow birch, mountain-ash, and
spruce and fir opposed our progress. The ascent at

such an angle with a roll of blankets on your back
is not unlike climbing a tree: every limb resists your
progress and pushes you back; so that when we at
last reached the summit, after twelve or fifteen hundred feet of this sort of work, the fight was about
all out of the best of us. It was then nearly two
o'clock, so that we had been about seven hours in
coming seven miles.

Here on the top of the mountain we overtook
spring, which had been gone from the valley nearly
a month. Red clover was opening in the valley
below, and wild strawberries just ripening; on the
summit the yellow birch was just hanging out its
catkins, and the claytonia, or spring-beauty, was in
bloom. The leaf-buds of the trees were just bursting, making a faint mist of green, which, as the eye
swept downward, gradually deepened until it became a dense, massive cloud in the valleys. At the
foot of the mountain the clintonia, or northern green
lily, and the low shadbush were showing their ber-
ries, but long before the top was reached they were
found in bloom. I had never before stood amid
blooming claytonia, a flower of April, and looked
down upon a field that held ripening strawberries.
Every thousand feet elevation seemed to make about
ten days' difference in the vegetation, so that the
season was a month or more later on the top of the
mountain than at its base. A very pretty flower
which we began to meet with well up on the moun-

tain-side was the painted trillium, the petals white,
veined with pink.

The low, stunted growth of spruce and fir which
clothes the top of Slide has been cut away over a
small space on the highest point, laying open the
view on nearly all sides. Here we sat down and
enjoyed our triumph. We saw the world as the
hawk or the balloonist sees it when he is three thousand feet in the air. How soft and flowing all the
outlines of the hills and mountains beneath us
looked! The forests dropped down and undulated
away over them, covering them like a carpet. To
the east we looked over the near-by Wittenberg
range to the Hudson and beyond; to the south,
Peak-o'-Moose, with its sharp crest, and Table
Mountain, with its long level top, were the two
conspicuous objects; in the west, Mt. Graham and
Double Top, about three thousand eight hundred
feet each, arrested the eye; while in our front to the
north we looked over the top of Panther Mountain
to the multitudinous peaks of the northern Catskills.
All was mountain and forest on every hand. Civilization seemed to have done little more than to have
scratched this rough, shaggy surface of the earth
here and there. In any such view, the wild, the
aboriginal, the geographical greatly predominate.
The works of man dwindle, and the original features of the huge globe come out. Every single
object or point is dwarfed; the valley of the Hud-

son is only a wrinkle in the earth's surface. You discover with a feeling of surprise that the great thing is the earth itself, which stretches away on every hand so far beyond your ken.

The Arabs believe that the mountains steady the earth and hold it together; but they have only to get on the top of a high one to see how insignificant mountains are, and how adequate the earth looks to get along without them. To the imaginative Oriental people, mountains seemed to mean much more than they do to us. They were sacred; they were the abodes of their divinities. They offered their sacrifices upon them. In the Bible, mountains are used as a symbol of that which is great and holy. Jerusalem is spoken of as a holy mountain. The Syrians were beaten by the Children of Israel because, said they, "their gods are gods of the hills; therefore were they stronger than we." It was on Mount Horeb that God appeared to Moses in the burning bush, and on Sinai that He delivered to him the law. Josephus says that the Hebrew shepherds never pasture their flocks on Sinai, believing it to be the abode of Jehovah. The solitude of mountain-tops is peculiarly impressive, and it is certainly easier to believe the Deity appeared in a burning bush there than in the valley below. When the clouds of heaven, too, come down and envelop the top of the mountain, — how such a circumstance must have impressed the old God-fearing Hebrews! Moses

49

knew well how to surround the law with the pomp
and circumstance that would inspire the deepest awe
and reverence.

But when the clouds came down and enveloped
us on Slide Mountain, the grandeur, the solemnity,
were gone in a twinkling; the portentous-looking
clouds proved to be nothing but base fog that wet
us and extinguished the world for us. How tame,
and prosy, and humdrum the scene instantly became! But when the fog lifted, and we looked from
under it as from under a just-raised lid, and the eye
plunged again like an escaped bird into those vast
gulfs of space that opened at our feet, the feeling of
grandeur and solemnity quickly came back.

The first want we felt on the top of Slide, after
we had got some rest, was a want of water. Several
of us cast about, right and left, but no sign of water
was found. But water must be had, so we all
started off deliberately to hunt it up. We had not
gone many hundred yards before we chanced upon
an ice-cave beneath some rocks, — vast masses of
ice, with crystal pools of water near. This was good
luck, indeed, and put a new and a brighter face on
the situation.

Slide Mountain enjoys a distinction which no
other mountain in the State, so far as is known, does
— it has a thrush peculiar to itself. This thrush was
discovered and described by Eugene P. Bicknell, of
New York, in 1880, and has been named Bicknell's

50

thrush. A better name would have been Slide Mountain thrush, as the bird so far has been found only on this mountain.[1] I did not see or hear it upon the Wittenberg, which is only a few miles distant, and only two hundred feet lower. In its appearance to the eye among the trees, one would not distinguish it from the gray-cheeked thrush of Baird, or the olive-backed thrush, but its song is totally different. The moment I heard it I said, "There is a new bird, a new thrush," for the quality of all thrush songs is the same. A moment more, and I knew it was Bicknell's thrush. The song is in a minor key, finer, more attenuated, and more under the breath than that of any other thrush. It seemed as if the bird was blowing in a delicate, slender, golden tube, so fine and yet so flute-like and resonant the song appeared. At times it was like a musical whisper of great sweetness and power. The birds were numerous about the summit, but we saw them nowhere else. No other thrush was seen, though a few times during our stay I caught a mere echo of the hermit's song far down the mountain-side. A bird I was not prepared to see or to hear was the black-poll warbler, a bird usually found much farther north, but here it was, amid the balsam firs, uttering its simple, lisping song.

[1] Bicknell's thrush turns out to be the more southern form of the gray-cheeked thrush, and is found on the higher mountains of New York and New England.

The rocks on the tops of these mountains are quite sure to attract one's attention, even if he have no eye for such things. They are masses of light reddish conglomerate, composed of round wave-worn quartz pebbles. Every pebble has been shaped and polished upon some ancient seacoast, probably the Devonian. The rock disintegrates where it is most exposed to the weather, and forms a loose sandy and pebbly soil. These rocks form the floor of the coal formation, but in the Catskill region only the floor remains; the superstructure has never existed, or has been swept away; hence one would look for a coal mine here over his head in the air, rather than under his feet.

This rock did not have to climb up here as we did; the mountain stooped and took it upon its back in the bottom of the old seas, and then got lifted up again. This happened so long ago that the memory of the oldest inhabitants of these parts yields no clew to the time.

A pleasant task we had in reflooring and reroofing the log-hut with balsam boughs against the night. Plenty of small balsams grew all about, and we soon had a huge pile of their branches in the old hut. What a transformation, this fresh green carpet and our fragrant bed, like the deep-furred robe of some huge animal, wrought in that dingy interior! Two or three things disturbed our sleep. A cup of strong beef-tea taken for supper disturbed mine; then the porcupines kept up such a grunting and chattering near our heads, just on the other side of the log, that sleep was difficult. In my wakeful mood I was a good deal annoyed by a little rabbit that kept whipping in at our dilapidated door and nibbling at our bread and hardtack. He persisted even after the gray of the morning appeared. Then about four o'clock it began gently to rain. I think I heard the first drop that fell. My companions were all in sound sleep. The rain increased, and gradually the sleepers awoke. It was like the tread of an advancing enemy which every ear had been expecting. The roof over us was of the poorest, and we had no confidence in it. It was made of the thin bark of spruce and balsam, and was full of hollows and depressions. Presently these hollows got full of water, when there was a simultaneous downpour of bigger and lesser rills upon the sleepers beneath. Said sleepers, as one man, sprang up, each taking his blanket with him; but by the time some of the party had got themselves stowed away under the adjacent rock, the rain ceased. It was little more than the dissolving of the nightcap of fog which so often hangs about these heights. With the first appearance of the dawn I had heard the new thrush in the scattered trees near the hut, — a strain as fine as if blown upon a fairy flute, a suppressed musical whisper from out the tops of the dark spruces. Probably never did there go up from the top of a great mountain a

53

smaller song to greet the day, albeit it was of the purest harmony. It seemed to have in a more marked degree the quality of interior reverberation than any other thrush song I had ever heard. Would the altitude or the situation account for its minor key? Loudness would avail little in such a place. Sounds are not far heard on a mountain-top; they are lost in the abyss of vacant air. But amid these low, dense, dark spruces, which make a sort of canopied privacy of every square rod of ground, what could be more in keeping than this delicate musical whisper? It was but the soft hum of the balsams, interpreted and embodied in a bird's voice.

It was the plan of two of our companions to go from Slide over into the head of the Rondout, and thence out to the railroad at the little village of Shokan, an unknown way to them, involving nearly an all-day pull the first day through a pathless wilderness. We ascended to the topmost floor of the tower, and from my knowledge of the topography of the country I pointed out to them their course, and where the valley of the Rondout must lie. The vast stretch of woods, when it came into view from under the foot of Slide, seemed from our point of view very uniform. It swept away to the southeast, rising gently toward the ridge that separates Lone Mountain from Peak-o'-Moose, and presented a comparatively easy problem. As a clew to the course, the line where the dark belt or saddle-cloth of spruce, which covered the top of the ridge they were to skirt, ended, and the deciduous woods began, a sharp, well-defined line was pointed out as the course to be followed. It led straight to the top of the broad level-backed ridge which connected two higher peaks, and immediately behind which lay the headwaters of the Rondout. Having studied the map thoroughly, and possessed themselves of the points, they rolled up their blankets about nine o'clock, and were off, my friend and I purposing to spend yet another day and night on Slide. As our friends plunged down into that fearful abyss, we shouted to them the old classic caution, "Be bold, be bold, *be not too bold*." It required courage to make such a leap into the unknown, as I knew those young men were making, and it required prudence. A faint heart or a bewildered head, and serious consequences might have resulted. The theory of a thing is so much easier than the practice! The theory is in the air, the practice is in the woods; the eye, the thought, travel easily where the foot halts and stumbles. However, our friends made the theory and the fact coincide ; they kept the dividing line between the spruce and the birches, and passed over the ridge into the valley safely; but they were torn and bruised and wet by the showers, and made the last few miles of their journey on will and pluck alone, their last pound of positive strength having been exhausted in making the descent through the chaos of rocks and

logs into the head of the valley. In such emergen-
cies one overdraws his account ; he travels on the
credit of the strength he expects to gain when he
gets his dinner and some sleep. Unless one has
made such a trip himself (and I have several times
in my life), he can form but a faint idea what it is
like, — what a trial it is to the body, and what a trial
it is to the mind. You are fighting a battle with
an enemy in ambush. How those miles and leagues
which your feet must compass lie hidden there in
that wilderness; how they seem to multiply themselves; how they are fortified with logs, and rocks,
and fallen trees; how they take refuge in deep gullies, and skulk behind unexpected eminences! Your
body not only feels the fatigue of the battle, your
mind feels the strain of the undertaking; you may
miss your mark; the mountains may outmanœuvre
you. All that day, whenever I looked upon that
treacherous wilderness, I thought with misgivings
of those two friends groping their way there, and
would have given much to know how it fared with
them. Their concern was probably less than my
own, because they were more ignorant of what was
before them. Then there was just a slight shadow
of a fear in my mind that I might have been in error
about some points of the geography I had pointed
out to them. But all was well, and the victory
was won according to the campaign which I had
planned. When we saluted our friends upon their

own doorstep a week afterward, the wounds were nearly healed and the rents all mended.

When one is on a mountain-top, he spends most of the time in looking at the show he has been at such pains to see. About every hour we would ascend the rude lookout to take a fresh observation. With a glass I could see my native hills forty miles away to the northwest. I was now upon the back of the horse, yea, upon the highest point of his shoulders, which had so many times attracted my attention as a boy. We could look along his balsam-covered back to his rump, from which the eye glanced away down into the forests of the Neversink, and on the other hand plump down into the gulf where his head was grazing or drinking. During the day there was a grand procession of thunder-clouds filing along over the northern Catskills, and letting down veils of rain and enveloping them. From such an elevation one has the same view of the clouds that he does from the prairie or the ocean. They do not seem to rest across and to be upborne by the hills, but they emerge out of the dim west, thin and vague, and grow and stand up as they get nearer and roll by him, on a level but invisible highway, huge chariots of wind and storm.

In the afternoon a thick cloud threatened us, but it proved to be the condensation of vapor that announces a cold wave. There was soon a marked fall in the temperature, and as night drew near it became pretty certain that we were going to have a cold time of it. The wind rose, the vapor above us thickened and came nearer, until it began to drive across the summit in slender wraiths, which curled over the brink and shut out the view. We became very diligent in getting in our night wood, and in gathering more boughs to calk up the openings in the hut. The wood we scraped together was a sorry lot, roots and stumps and branches of decayed spruce, such as we could collect without an axe, and some rags and tags of birch bark. The fire was built in one corner of the shanty, the smoke finding easy egress through large openings on the east side and in the roof over it. We doubled up the bed, making it thicker and more nest-like, and as darkness set in, stowed ourselves into it beneath our blankets. The searching wind found out every crevice about our heads and shoulders, and it was icy cold. Yet we fell asleep, and had slept about an hour when my companion sprang up in an unwonted state of excitement for so placid a man. His excitement was occasioned by the sudden discovery that what appeared to be a bar of ice was fast taking the place of his backbone. His teeth chattered, and he was convulsed with ague. I advised him to replenish the fire, and to wrap himself in his blanket and cut the liveliest capers he was capable of in so circumscribed a place. This he promptly did, and the thought of his wild and desperate dance there in the dim light, his tall form, his blanket flapping, his teeth chattering, the porcupines outside marking time with their squeals and grunts, still provokes a smile, though it was a serious enough matter at the time. After a while, the warmth came back to him, but he dared not trust himself again to the boughs; he fought the cold all night as one might fight a besieging foe. By carefully husbanding the fuel, the beleaguering enemy was kept at bay till morning came; but when morning did come, even the huge root he had used as a chair was consumed. Rolled in my blanket beneath a foot or more of balsam boughs, I had got some fairly good sleep, and was most of the time oblivious of the melancholy vigil of my friend. As we had but a few morsels of food left, and had been on rather short rations the day before, hunger was added to his other discomforts. At that time a letter was on the way to him from his wife, which contained this prophetic sentence : " I hope thee is not suffering with cold and hunger on some lone mountain-top."

Mr. Bicknell's thrush struck up again at the first signs of dawn, notwithstanding the cold. I could hear his penetrating and melodious whisper as I lay buried beneath the boughs. Presently I arose and invited my friend to turn in for a brief nap, while I gathered some wood and set the coffee brewing. With a brisk, roaring fire on, I left for the spring to fetch some water, and to make my toilet. The leaves of the mountain goldenrod, which everywhere covered the ground in the opening, were covered with frozen particles of vapor, and the scene, shut in by fog, was chill and dreary enough.

We were now not long in squaring an account with Slide, and making ready to leave. Round pellets of snow began to fall, and we came off the mountain on the 10th of June in a November storm and temperature. Our purpose was to return by the same valley we had come. A well-defined trail led off the summit to the north; to this we committed ourselves. In a few minutes we emerged at the head of the slide that had given the mountain its name. This was the path made by visitors to the scene; when it ended, the track of the avalanche began; no bigger than your hand, apparently, had it been at first, but it rapidly grew, until it became several rods in width. It dropped down from our feet straight as an arrow until it was lost in the fog, and looked perilously steep. The dark forms of the spruce were clinging to the edge of it, as if reaching out to their fellows to save them. We hesitated on the brink, but finally cautiously began the descent. The rock was quite naked and slippery, and only on the margin of the slide were there any boulders to stay the foot, or bushy growths to aid the hand. As we paused, after some minutes, to select our course, one of the finest surprises of the trip awaited us:

the fog in our front was swiftly whirled up by the breeze, like the drop-curtain at the theatre, only much more rapidly, and in a twinkling the vast gulf opened before us. It was so sudden as to be almost bewildering. The world opened like a book, and there were the pictures; the spaces were without a film, the forests and mountains looked surprisingly near; in the heart of the northern Catskills a wild valley was seen flooded with sunlight. Then the curtain ran down again, and nothing was left but the gray strip of rock to which we clung, plunging down into the obscurity. Down and down we made our way. Then the fog lifted again. It was Jack and his beanstalk renewed ; new wonders, new views, awaited us every few moments, till at last the whole valley below us stood in the clear sunshine. We passed down a precipice, and there was a rill of water, the beginning of the creek that wound through the valley below ; farther on, in a deep depression, lay the remains of an old snow-bank ; Winter had made his last stand here, and April flowers were springing up almost amid his very bones. We did not find a palace, and a hungry giant, and a princess, at the end of our beanstalk, but we found a humble roof and the hospitable heart of Mrs. Larkins, which answered our purpose better. And we were in the mood, too, to have undertaken an eating-bout with any giant Jack ever discovered.

RIVERBY

Of all the retreats I have found amid the Catskills, there is no other that possesses quite so many
charms for me as this valley, wherein stands Larkins's humble dwelling; it is so wild, so quiet, and
has such superb mountain views. In coming up the
valley, you have apparently reached the head of civilization a mile or more lower down; here the rude
little houses end, and you turn to the left into the
woods. Presently you emerge into a clearing again,
and before you rises the rugged and indented crest
of Panther Mountain, and near at hand, on a low
plateau, rises the humble roof of Larkins, — you get
a picture of the Panther and of the homestead at
one glance. Above the house hangs a high, bold cliff
covered with forest, with a broad fringe of blackened
and blasted tree-trunks, where the cackling of the
great pileated woodpecker may be heard; on the left
a dense forest sweeps up to the sharp spruce-covered
cone of the Wittenberg, nearly four thousand feet
high, while at the head of the valley rises Slide
over all. From a meadow just back of Larkins's
barn, a view may be had of all these mountains,
while the terraced side of Cross Mountain bounds
the view immediately to the east. Running from
the top of Panther toward Slide one sees a gigantic
wall of rock, crowned with a dark line of fir. The
forest abruptly ends, and in its stead rises the face
of this colossal rocky escarpment, like some barrier built by the mountain gods. Eagles might nest

here. It breaks the monotony of the world of woods very impressively.

I delight in sitting on a rock in one of these upper fields, and seeing the sun go down behind Panther. The rapid-flowing brook below me fills all the valley with a soft murmur. There is no breeze, but the great atmospheric tide flows slowly in toward the cooling forest; one can see it by the motes in the air illuminated by the setting sun: presently, as the air cools a little, the tide turns and flows slowly out. The long, winding valley up to the foot of Slide, five miles of primitive woods, how wild and cool it looks, its one voice the murmur of the creek! On the Wittenberg the sunshine lingers long ; now it stands up like an island in a sea of shadows, then slowly sinks beneath the wave. The evening call of a robin or a veery at his vespers makes a marked impression on the silence and the solitude.

The following day my friend and I pitched our tent in the woods beside the stream where I had pitched it twice before, and passed several delightful days, with trout in abundance and wild strawberries at intervals. Mrs. Larkins's cream-pot, butter-jar, and bread-box were within easy reach. Near the camp was an unusually large spring, of icy coldness, which served as our refrigerator. Trout or milk immersed in this spring in a tin pail would keep sweet four or five days. One night some creature, probably a lynx or a raccoon, came and lifted the stone from the pail that held the trout and took out a fine string of them, and ate them up on the spot, leaving only the string and one head. In August bears come down to an ancient and now brushy bark-peeling near by for blackberries. But the creature that most infests these backwoods is the porcupine. He is as stupid and indifferent as the skunk; his broad, blunt nose points a witless head. They are great gnawers, and will gnaw your house down if you do not look out. Of a summer evening they will walk coolly into your open door if not prevented. The most annoying animal to the camper-out in this region, and the one he needs to be most on the look-out for, is the cow. Backwoods cows and young cattle seem always to be famished for salt, and they will fairly lick the fisherman's clothes off his back, and his tent and equipage out of existence, if you give them a chance. On one occasion some wood-ranging heifers and steers that had been hovering around our camp for some days made a raid upon it when we were absent. The tent was shut and everything snugged up, but they ran their long tongues under the tent, and, tasting something savory, hooked out John Stuart Mill's "Essays on Religion," which one of us had brought along, thinking to read in the woods. They mouthed the volume around a good deal, but its logic was too tough for them, and they contented themselves with devouring the paper in which it was wrapped. If the cattle had not been surprised at just that point, it is probable the tent would have gone down before their eager curiosity and thirst for salt.

The raid which Larkins's dog made upon our camp was amusing rather than annoying. He was a very friendly and intelligent shepherd dog, probably a collie. Hardly had we sat down to our first lunch in camp before he called on us. But as he was disposed to be too friendly, and to claim too large a share of the lunch, we rather gave him the cold shoulder. He did not come again; but a few evenings afterward, as we sauntered over to the house on some trifling errand, the dog suddenly conceived a bright little project. He seemed to say to himself, on seeing us, "There come both of them now, just as I have been hoping they would; now, while they are away, I will run quickly over and know what they have got that a dog can eat." My companion saw the dog get up on our arrival, and go quickly in the direction of our camp, and he said something in the cur's manner suggested to him the object of his hurried departure. He called my attention to the fact, and we hastened back. On cautiously nearing camp, the dog was seen amid the pails in the shallow water of the creek investigating them. He had uncovered the butter, and was about to taste it, when we shouted, and he made quick steps for home, with a very "kill-sheep" look. When we again met him at the house next day, he could not look us in the face, but sneaked off, utterly crest-fallen. This was a clear case of reasoning on the part of the dog, and afterward a clear case of a sense of guilt from wrong-doing. The dog will probably be a man before any other animal.

III

BIRDS' EGGS

ADMIRE the bird's egg and leave it in its nest" is a wiser forbearance than "Love the wood-rose and leave it on its stalk." We will try to leave these eggs in the nest, and as far as possible show the bird and the nest with them.

The first egg of spring is undoubtedly a hen's egg. The domestic fowls, not being compelled to shift for themselves, and having artificial shelter, are not so mindful of the weather and the seasons as the wild birds. But the hen of the woods and the hen of the prairie, namely, the ruffed and the pinnated grouse, do not usually nest till the season is so far advanced that danger from frost is past.

The first wild egg, in New York and New England, is probably that of an owl, the great horned owl, it is said, laying as early as March. They probably shelter their eggs from the frost and the snow before incubation begins. The little screech owl waits till April, and seeks the deep, snug cavity of an old tree; the heart of a decayed apple-tree suits him well. Begin your search by the middle of April, and before the month is past you will find the

RIVERBY

four white, round eggs resting upon a little dry
grass or a few dry leaves in the bottom of a long cavity. Owls' eggs are inclined to be spherical. You
would expect to see a big, round-headed, round-eyed
creature come out of such an egg.

The passenger pigeon nests before danger from
frost is passed; but as it lays but two eggs, probably
in two successive days, the risks from this source
are not great, though occasionally a heavy April
snow-storm breaks them up.

Which is the earliest song-bird's egg? One cannot be quite so certain here, as he can as to which
the first wild flower is, for instance; but I would
take my chances on finding that of the phœbe-bird
first, and finding it before the close of April, unless
the season is very backward. The present season
(1883) a pair built their nest under the eaves of my
house, and deposited their eggs, the last days of the
month. Some English sparrows that had been hanging around, and doubtless watching the phœbes,
threw the eggs out and took possession of the nest.
How shrewd and quick to take the hint these little
feathered John Bulls are! With a handful of rat-
tling pebble-stones I told this couple very plainly
that they were not welcome visitors to my premises.
They fled precipitately. The next morning they
appeared again, but were much shyer. Another dis-
charge of pebbles, and they were off as if bound
for the protection of the British flag, and did not

return. I notice wherever I go that these birds have got a suspicion in their heads that public opinion has changed with regard to them, and that they are no longer wanted.

The eggs of the phœbe-bird are snow-white, and when, in threading the gorge of some mountain trout brook, or prowling about some high, overhanging ledge, one's eye falls upon this mossy structure planted with such matchless art upon a little shelf of the rocks, with its complement of five or six pearl-like eggs, he is ready to declare it the most pleasing nest in all the range of our bird architecture. It was such a happy thought for the bird to build there, just out of the reach of all four-footed beasts of prey, sheltered from the storms and winds, and, by the use of moss and lichens, blending its nest so perfectly with its surroundings that only the most alert eye can detect it. An egg upon a rock, and thriving there, — the frailest linked to the strongest, as if the geology of the granite mountain had been bent into the service of the bird. I doubt if crows, or jays, or owls ever rob these nests. Phœbe has outwitted them. They never heard of the bird that builded its house upon a rock. "Strong is thy dwelling-place, and thou puttest thy nest in a rock."

The song sparrow sometimes nests in April, but not commonly in our latitude. Emerson says, in "May-Day:" —

"The sparrow meek, prophetic-eyed,
    Her nest beside the snow-drift weaves,
    Secure the osier yet will hide
    Her callow brood in mantling leaves."

But the sparrow usually prefers to wait till the snow-drift is gone. I never have found the nest of one till long after the last drift had disappeared from the fields, though a late writer upon New England birds says the sparrow sometimes lays in April, when snow is yet upon the ground.

The sparrow is not a beautiful bird except in our affections and associations, and its eggs are not beautiful as eggs go, — four or five little freckled spheres, that, like the bird itself, blend well with the ground upon which they are placed.

The eggs of the " chippie," or social sparrow, are probably the most beautiful of sparrow eggs, being of a bright bluish green with a ring of dark purple spots around the larger end.

Generally there is but little relation between the color of the bird and the color of its egg. For the most part, the eggs of birds that occupy open, exposed nests are of some tint that harmonizes well with the surroundings. With the addition of specks of various hues, they are rendered still less conspicuous. The eggs of the scarlet tanager are greenish blue, with faint brown or purplish markings. The blackbird lays a greenish blue egg also, with various markings. Indeed, the favorite ground tint of the birds that build open nests is a greenish blue; sometimes the blue predominates, sometimes the green; while the eggs of birds that build concealed nests, or lay in dark cavities, are generally white, as is the case with the eggs of all our woodpeckers, for instance. The eggs of the bluebird are bluish white.

Among the flycatchers, the nest of the phœbe is most concealed, at least from above, and her eggs are white, while those of nearly all the other species are more or less tinted and marked. The eggs of the hummingbird are white, but the diminutiveness of their receptacle is a sufficient concealment. Another white egg is that of the kingfisher, deposited upon fish-bones at the end of a hole in the bank eight or nine feet long. The bank swallow also lays white eggs, as does the chimney swallow, the white-bellied swallow, and the purple martin. The eggs of the barn swallow and the cliff swallow are more or less speckled. In England the kingfisher (smaller and much more brilliantly colored than ours), the woodpecker, the bank swallow, the swift, the wryneck (related to the woodpecker), and the dipper also lay white eggs.

A marked exception to the above rule is furnished by the eggs of the Baltimore oriole, perhaps the most fantastically marked of all our birds' eggs. One would hardly expect a plainly marked egg in such a high-swung, elaborately woven, deeply pouched, aristocratic nest. The threads and strings and horse-hairs with which the structure is sewed and bound and stayed are copied in the curious lines and markings of the treasures it holds. After the oriole is through with its nest, it is sometimes taken possession of by the house wren in which to rear its second brood. The long, graceful cavity, with its fine carpet of hair, is filled with coarse twigs, as if one were to build a log hut in a palace, and the rusty-colored eggs of the little busybody deposited there. The wren would perhaps stick to its bundle of small fagots in the box or pump tree, and rear its second brood in the cradle of the first, were it not that by seeking new lodgings time can be saved. The male bird builds and furnishes the second nest, and the mother bird has begun to lay in it before the first is empty.

The chatter of a second brood of nearly fledged wrens is heard now (August 20) in an oriole's nest suspended from the branch of an apple-tree near where I write. Earlier in the season the parent birds made long and determined attempts to establish themselves in a cavity that had been occupied by a pair of bluebirds. The original proprietor of the place was the downy woodpecker. He had excavated it the autumn before, and had passed the winter there, often to my certain knowledge lying abed till nine o'clock in the morning. In the spring he went elsewhere, probably with a female, to begin

72

the season in new quarters. The bluebirds early took possession, and in June their first brood had flown. The wrens had been hanging around, evidently with an eye on the place (such little comedies may be witnessed anywhere), and now very naturally thought it was their turn. A day or two after the young bluebirds had flown, I noticed some fine, dry grass clinging to the entrance to the cavity; a circumstance which I understood a few moments later, when the wren rushed by me into the cover of a small Norway spruce, hotly pursued by the male bluebird. It was a brown streak and a blue streak pretty close together. The wrens had gone to house-cleaning, and the bluebird had returned to find his bed and bedding being pitched out of doors, and had thereupon given the wrens to understand in the most emphatic manner that he had no intention of vacating the premises so early in the season. Day after day, for more than two weeks, the male bluebird had to clear his premises of these intruders. It occupied much of his time and not a little of mine, as I sat with a book in a summer-house near by, laughing at his pretty fury and spiteful onset. On two occasions the wren rushed under the chair in which I sat, and a streak of blue lightning almost flashed in my very face. One day, just as I had passed the tree in which the cavity was placed, I heard the wren scream desperately; turning, I saw the little vagabond fall into the grass with the wrathful blue-

bird fairly upon him; the latter had returned just
in time to catch him, and was evidently bent on
punishing him well. But in the squabble in the grass
the wren escaped and took refuge in the friendly
evergreen. The bluebird paused for a moment with
outstretched wings looking for the fugitive, then
flew away. A score of times during the month of
June did I see the wren taxing every energy to get
away from the bluebird. He would dart into the
stone wall, under the floor of the summer-house, into
the weeds, — anywhere to hide his diminished head.
The bluebird, with his bright coat, looked like an
officer in uniform in pursuit of some wicked, rusty
little street gamin. Generally the favorite house of
refuge of the wrens was the little spruce, into which
their pursuer made no attempt to follow them. The
female would sit concealed amid the branches, chattering in a scolding, fretful way, while the male with
his eye upon his tormentor would perch on the topmost shoot and sing. Why he sang at such times,
whether in triumph and derision, or to keep his
courage up and reassure his mate, I could not make
out. When his song was suddenly cut short, and
I glanced to see him dart down into the spruce, my
eye usually caught a twinkle of blue wings hovering
near. The wrens finally gave up the fight, and their
enemies reared their second brood in peace.

That the wren should use such coarse, refractory
materials, especially since it builds in holes where

twigs are so awkward to carry and adjust, is curious
enough. All its congeners, the marsh wrens, the
Carolina wren, the winter wren, build of soft flexible
materials. The nest of the winter wren, and of the
English "Jenny Wren," is mainly of moss, and is a
marvel of softness and warmth.

One day a swarm of honey-bees went into my
chimney, and I mounted the stack to see into which
flue they had gone. As I craned my neck above the
sooty vent, with the bees humming about my ears,
the first thing my eye rested upon in the black interior was two long white pearls upon a little shelf
of twigs, the nest of the chimney swallow, or swift, —
honey, soot, and birds' eggs closely associated. The
bees, though in an unused flue, soon found the gas
of anthracite that hovered about the top of the
chimney too much for them, and they left. But the
swallows are not repelled by smoke. They seem to
have entirely abandoned their former nesting-places
in hollow trees and stumps, and to frequent only
chimneys. A tireless bird, never perching, all day
upon the wing, and probably capable of flying one
thousand miles in twenty-four hours, they do not
even stop to gather materials for their nests, but snap
off the small dry twigs from the treetops as they fly
by. Confine one of these swallows to a room and
it does not perch, but after flying till it becomes
bewildered and exhausted, it clings to the side of
the wall till it dies. I once found one in my room

on returning, after several days' absence, in which life seemed nearly extinct; its feet grasped my finger as I removed it from the wall, but its eyes closed, and it seemed about on the point of joining its companion, which lay dead upon the floor. Tossing it into the air, however, seemed to awaken its wonderful powers of flight, and away it went straight toward the clouds. On the wing the chimney swallow looks like an athlete stripped for the race. There is the least appearance of quill and plumage of any of our birds, and, with all its speed and marvelous evolutions, the effect of its flight is stiff and wiry. There appears to be but one joint in the wing, and that next the body. This peculiar inflexible motion of the wings, as if they were little sickles of sheet iron, seems to be owing to the length and development of the primary quills and the smallness of the secondary. The wing appears to hinge only at the wrist. The barn swallow lines its rude masonry with feathers, but the swift begins life on bare twigs, glued together by a glue of home manufacture as adhesive as Spaulding's.

I have wondered if Emerson referred to any particular bird in these lines from "The Problem:" —

"Know'st thou what wove yon wood-bird's nest
Of leaves, and feathers from her breast?"

Probably not, but simply availed himself of the general belief that certain birds or fowls line their nests with their own feathers. This is notably true of the eider duck, and in a measure of our domestic fowls, but so far as I know is not true of any of our small birds. The barn swallow and the house wren feather their nests at the expense of the hens and the geese. The winter wren picks up the feathers of the ruffed grouse. The chickadee, Emerson's favorite bird, uses a few feathers in its upholstering, but not its own. In England, I noticed that the little willow warbler makes a free use of feathers from the poultry-yard. Many of our birds use hair in their nests, and the kingbird and the cedar-bird like wool. I have found a single feather of the bird's own in the nest of the phœbe. Such a circumstance would perhaps justify the poet.

About the first of June there is a nest in the woods upon the ground with four creamy white eggs in it, spotted with brown or lilac, chiefly about the larger ends, that always gives the walker who is so lucky as to find it a thrill of pleasure. It is like a ground sparrow's nest with a roof or canopy to it. The little brown or olive backed bird starts away from your feet and runs swiftly and almost silently over the dry leaves, and then turns her speckled breast to see if you are following. She walks very prettily, by far the prettiest pedestrian in the woods. But if she thinks you have discovered her secret, she feigns lameness and disability of both leg and wing, to decoy you into the pursuit of her. This is

the golden-crowned thrush, or accentor, a strictly
wood-bird, about the size of a song sparrow, with
the dullest of gold upon his crown, but the brightest
of songs in his heart. The last nest of this bird I
found was while in quest of the pink cypripedium.
We suddenly spied a couple of the flowers a few
steps from the path along which we were walking,
and had stooped to admire them, when out sprang
the bird from beside them, doubtless thinking she
was the subject of observation instead of the flowers
that swung their purple bells but a foot or two above
her. But we never should have seen her had she
kept her place. She had found a rent in the matted
carpet of dry leaves and pine needles that covered
the ground, and into this had insinuated her nest,
the leaves and needles forming a canopy above it,
sloping to the south and west, the source of the more
frequent summer rains.

At about the same time one finds the nest above
described, if he were to explore the woods very
thoroughly, he might chance upon two curious eggs
lying upon the leaves as if dropped there by chance.
They are elliptical, both ends of a size, about an inch
and a quarter long, of a creamy white spotted with
lavender. These are the eggs of the whip-poor-
will, a bird that has absolutely no architectural instincts or gifts. Perhaps its wide, awkward mouth
and short beak are ill-adapted to carrying nest
materials. It is awkward upon the ground and

78

awkward upon the tree, being unable to perch upon
a limb, except lengthwise of it.

The song and game birds lay pointed eggs, but the
night birds lay round or elliptical eggs.

The egg-collector sometimes stimulates a bird to
lay an unusual number of eggs. A youth, whose
truthfulness I do not doubt, told me he once induced
a high-hole to lay twenty-nine eggs by robbing her
of an egg each day. The eggs became smaller and
smaller, till the twenty-ninth one was only the size
of a chippie's egg. At this point the bird gave up
the contest.

There is a last egg of summer as well as a first
egg of spring, but one cannot name either with much
confidence. Both the robin and the chippie sometimes rear a third brood in August; but the birds
that delay their nesting till midsummer are the goldfinch and the cedar-bird, the former waiting for the
thistle to ripen its seeds, and the latter probably
for the appearance of certain insects which it takes
on the wing. Often the cedar-bird does not build
till August, and will line its nest with wool if it
can get it, even in this sultry month. The eggs are
marked and colored, as if a white egg were to be
spotted with brown, then colored a pale blue, then
again sharply dotted or blotched with blackish or
purplish spots.

But the most common August nest with me —
early August — is that of the goldfinch, — a deep,

snug, compact nest, with no loose ends hanging, placed in the fork of a small limb of an apple-tree, a peach-tree, or an ornamental shade-tree. The eggs are a faint bluish white.

While the female is sitting, the male feeds her regularly. She calls to him on his approach, or when she hears his voice passing by, in the most affectionate, feminine, childlike tones, the only case I know where the sitting bird makes any sound while in the act of incubation. When a rival male invades the tree, or approaches too near, the male whose nest it holds pursues and reasons or expostulates with him in the same bright, amicable, confiding tones. Indeed, most birds make use of their sweetest notes in war. The song of love is the song of battle, too. The male yellowbirds flit about from point to point, apparently assuring each other of the highest sentiments of esteem and consideration, at the same time that one intimates to the other that he is carrying his joke a little too far. It has the effect of saying with mild and good-humored surprise, "Why, my dear sir, this is my territory; you surely do not mean to trespass; permit me to salute you, and to escort you over the line." Yet the intruder does not always take the hint. Occasionally the couple have a brief sparring match in the air, and mount up and up, beak to beak, to a considerable height, but rarely do they actually come to blows.

The yellowbird becomes active and conspicuous after the other birds have nearly all withdrawn from the stage and become silent, their broods reared and flown. August is his month, his festive season. It is his turn now. The thistles are ripening their seeds, and his nest is undisturbed by jay-bird or crow. He is the first bird I hear in the morning, circling and swinging through the air in that peculiar undulating flight, and calling out on the downward curve of each stroke, "Here we go, here we go!" Every hour in the day he indulges in his circling, billowy flight. It is a part of his musical performance. His course at such times is a deeply undulating line, like the long gentle roll of the summer sea, the distance from crest to crest or from valley to valley being probably thirty feet; this distance is made with but one brief beating of the wings on the downward curve. As he quickly opens them, they give him a strong upward impulse, and he describes the long arc with them closely folded. Thus, falling and recovering, rising and sinking like dolphins in the sea, he courses through the summer air. In marked contrast to this feat is his manner of flying when he indulges in a brief outburst of song in the air. Now he flies level, with broad expanded wings nearly as round and as concave as two shells, which beat the air slowly. The song is the chief matter now, and the wings are used only to keep him afloat while delivering it. In the other case, the flight is the main concern, and the voice merely punctuates it.

I know no autumn egg but a hen's egg, though a certain old farmer tells me he finds a quail's nest full of eggs nearly every September; but fall progeny of any kind has a belated start in life, and the chances are against it.

IV

BIRD COURTSHIP

THERE is something about the matchmaking of birds that is not easily penetrated. The jealousies and rivalries of the males and of the females are easily understood, — they are quite human; but those sudden rushes of several males, some of them already mated, after one female, with squeals and screams and a great clatter of wings, — what does it mean? There is nothing human about that, unless it be illustrative of a trait that has at times cropped out in the earlier races, and which is still seen among the Eskimos, where the male carries off the female by force. But in these sudden sallies among the birds, the female, so far as I have observed, is never carried off. One may see half a dozen English sparrows engaged in what at first glance appears to be a general mêlée in the gutter or on the sidewalk; but if you look more closely, you will see a single female in the midst of the mass, beating off the males, who, with plumage puffed out and screaming and chattering, are all making a set at her. She strikes right and left, and seems to be equally displeased with them all. But her anger may be all put on, and she may be giving the wink all the time to her favorite.

The Eskimo maiden is said by Doctor Nansen to resist stoutly being carried off even by the man she is desperately in love with.

In the latter half of April, we pass through what I call the "robin racket," — trains of three or four birds rushing pell-mell over the lawn and fetching up in a tree or bush, or occasionally upon the ground, all piping and screaming at the top of their voices, but whether in mirth or anger it is hard to tell. The nucleus of the train is a female. One cannot see that the males in pursuit of her are rivals; it seems rather as if they had united to hustle her out of the place. But somehow the matches are no doubt made and sealed during these mad rushes. Maybe the female shouts out to her suitors, "Who touches me first wins," and away she scurries like an arrow. The males shout out, "Agreed!" and away they go in pursuit, each trying to outdo the other. The game is a brief one. Before one can get the clew to it, the party has dispersed.

Earlier in the season the pretty sparring of the males is the chief feature. You may see two robins apparently taking a walk or a run together over the sward or along the road; only first one bird runs, and then the other. They keep a few feet apart, stand very erect, and the course of each describes the segment of an arc about the other, thus: —

How courtly and deferential their manners toward each other are! often they pipe a shrill, fine strain, audible only a few yards away. Then, in a twinkling, one makes a spring and they are beak to beak, and claw to claw, as they rise up a few feet into the air. But usually no blow is delivered; not a feather is ruffled; each, I suppose, finds the guard of the other perfect. Then they settle down upon the ground again, and go through with the same running challenge as before. How their breasts glow in the strong April sunlight; how perk and military the bearing of each! Often they will run about each other in this way for many rods. After a week or so the males seem to have fought all their duels, when the rush and racket I have already described begin.

The bluebird wins his mate by the ardor of his attentions and the sincerity of his compliments, and by finding a house ready built which cannot be surpassed. The male bluebird is usually here several days before the female, and he sounds forth his note as loudly and eloquently as he can till she appears. On her appearance he flies at once to the box or tree cavity upon which he has had his eye, and, as he looks into it, calls and warbles in his most persuasive tones. The female at such times is always shy and backward, and the contrast in the manners of the two birds is as striking as the contrast in their colors. The male is brilliant and ardent; the female is dim and retiring, not to say indifferent. She may take a

hasty peep into the hole in the box or tree and then
fly away, uttering a lonesome, homesick note. Only
by a wooing of many days is she to be fully won.

The past April I was witness one Sunday morning
to the jealousies that may rage in these little brown
breasts. A pair of bluebirds had apparently mated
and decided to occupy a woodpecker's lodge in the
limb of an old apple-tree near my study. But that
morning another male appeared on the scene, and
was bent on cutting the first male out, and carrying off his bride. I happened to be near by when
the two birds came into collision. They fell to the
grass, and kept their grip upon each other for half
a minute. Then they separated, and the first up flew
to the hole and called fondly to the female. This
was too much for the other male, and they clinched
again and fell to the ground as before. There they
lay upon the grass, blue and brown intermingled.
But not a feather was tweaked out, or even disturbed,
that I could see. They simply held each other down.
Then they separated again, and again rushed upon
each other. The battle raged for about fifteen minutes, when one of the males — which one, of course,
I could not tell — withdrew and flew to a box under
the eaves of the study, and exerted all the eloquence
he possessed to induce the female to come to him
there. How he warbled and called, and lifted his
wings and flew to the entrance to the box and called
again! The female was evidently strongly attracted;

she would respond and fly about halfway to an apple-tree, and look toward him. The other male, in the mean time, did his best to persuade her to cast her lot with him. He followed her to the tree toward his rival, and then flew back to the nest and spread his plumage and called and warbled, oh, so confidently, so fondly, so reassuringly! When the female would return and peep into the hole in the tree, what fine, joyous notes he would utter! then he would look in and twinkle his wings, and say something his rival could not hear. This vocal and pantomimic contest went on for a long time. The female was evidently greatly shaken in her allegiance to the male in the old apple-tree. In less than an hour another female responded to the male who had sought the eaves of the study, and flew with him to the box. Whether this was their first meeting or not I do not know, but it was clear enough that the heart of the male was fixed upon the bride of his rival. He would devote himself a moment to the new-comer, and then turn toward the old apple-tree and call and lift his wings; then, apparently admonished by the bird near him, he would turn again to her and induce her to look into the box, and would warble fondly; then up on a higher branch again, with his attention directed toward his first love, between whom and himself salutations seemed constantly passing. This little play went on for some time, when the two females came into collision, and fell to the ground tweaking each other spitefully. Then the four birds drifted away from me down into the vineyard, where the males closed with each other again and fell to the plowed ground and lay there a surprisingly long time, nearly two minutes, as we calculated. Their wings were outspread, and their forms were indistinguishable. They tugged at each other most doggedly; one or the other brown breast was generally turned up, partly overlaid by a blue coat. They were determined to make a finish of it this time, but which got the better of the fight I could not tell. But it was the last battle; they finally separated, neither, apparently, any the worse for the encounter. The females fought two more rounds, the males looking on and warbling approvingly when they separated, and the two pairs drifted away in different directions. The next day they were about the box and tree again, and seemed to have definitely settled matters. Who won and who lost I do not know, but two pairs of bluebirds have since been very busy and very happy about the two nesting-places. One of the males I recognize as a bird that appeared early in March; I recognize him from one peculiar note in the midst of his warble, a note that suggests a whistle.

The matchmaking of the high-holes, which often comes under my observation, is in marked contrast to that of the robins and the bluebirds. There does not appear to be any anger or any blows. The male or two males will alight on a limb in front of the female, and go through with a series of bowings and scrapings that are truly comical. He spreads his tail, he puffs out his breast, he throws back his head, and then bends his body to the right and to the left, uttering all the while a curious musical hic-cough. The female confronts him unmoved, but whether her attitude is critical or defensive, I can-not tell. Presently she flies away, followed by her suitor or suitors, and the little comedy is enacted on another stump or tree. Among all the woodpeckers the drum plays an important part in the match-making. The male takes up his stand on a dry, resonant limb, or on the ridgeboard of a building, and beats the loudest call he is capable of. The downy woodpecker usually has a particular branch to which he resorts for advertising his matrimonial wants. A favorite drum of the high-holes about me is a hollow wooden tube, a section of a pump, which stands as a bird-box upon my summer-house. It is a good instrument; its tone is sharp and clear. A high-hole alights upon it, and sends forth a rattle that can be heard a long way off. Then he lifts up his head and utters that long April call, *Wick, wick, wick, wick.* Then he drums again. If the female does not find him, it is not because he does not make noise enough. But his sounds are all welcome to the ear. They are simple and primitive, and voice well a certain sentiment of the April days. As I

89

write these lines I hear through the half-open door his call come up from a distant field. Then I hear the steady hammering of one that has been for three days trying to penetrate the weather boarding of the big icehouse by the river, and to reach the saw-dust filling for a nesting-place.

Among our familiar birds the matchmaking of none other is quite so pretty as that of the goldfinch. The goldfinches stay with us in loose flocks and clad in a dull-olive suit throughout the winter. In May the males begin to put on their bright summer plumage. This is the result of a kind of super-ficial moulting. Their feathers are not shed, but their dusky covering or overalls are cast off. When the process is only partly completed, the bird has a smutty, unpresentable appearance. But we seldom see them at such times. They seem to retire from society. When the change is complete, and the males have got their bright uniforms of yellow and black, the courting begins. All the goldfinches of a neigh-borhood collect together and hold a sort of musical festival. To the number of many dozens they may be seen in some large tree, all singing and calling in the most joyous and vivacious manner. The males sing, and the females chirp and call. Whether there is actual competition on a trial of musical abil-ities of the males before the females or not, I do not know. The best of feeling seems to pervade the company; there is no sign of quarreling or fight-

BIRD COURTSHIP

ing; "all goes merry as a marriage bell," and the matches seem actually to be made during these musical picnics. Before May is passed the birds are seen in couples, and in June housekeeping usually begins. This I call the ideal of love-making among birds, and is in striking contrast to the squabbles and jealousies of most of our songsters.

I have known the goldfinches to keep up this musical and love-making festival through three consecutive days of a cold northeast rainstorm. Bedraggled, but ardent and happy, the birds were not to be dispersed by wind or weather.

All the woodpeckers, so far as I have observed, drum up their mates; the male advertises his wants by hammering upon a dry, resonant limb, when in due time the female approaches and is duly courted and won. The drumming of the ruffed grouse is for the same purpose; the female hears, concludes to take a walk that way, approaches timidly, is seen and admired, and the match is made. That the male accepts the first female that offers herself is probable. Among all the birds the choice, the selection, seems to belong to the female. The males court promiscuously; the females choose discreetly. The grouse, unlike the woodpecker, always carries his drum with him, which is his own proud breast; yet, if undisturbed, he selects some particular log or rock in the woods from which to sound forth his willingness to wed. What determines the choice of the female it would be hard to say. Among song-birds, it is probably the best songster, or the one whose voice suits her taste best. Among birds of bright plumage, it is probably the gayest dress; among the drummers, she is doubtless drawn by some quality of the sound. Our ears and eyes are too coarse to note any differences in these things, but doubtless the birds themselves note differences.

Birds show many more human traits than do quad-rupeds. That they actually fall in love admits of no doubt; that there is a period of courtship, during which the male uses all the arts he is capable of to win his mate, is equally certain; that there are jeal-ousies and rivalries, and that the peace of families is often rudely disturbed by outside males or females is a common observation. The females, when they come to blows, fight much more spitefully and reck-lessly than do the males. One species of bird has been known to care for the young of another species which had been made orphans. The male turkey will sometimes cover the eggs of his mate and hatch and rear the brood alone. Altogether, birds often present some marked resemblances in their actions to men, when love is the motive.

Mrs. Martin, in her "Home Life on an Ostrich Farm," relates this curious incident: —

"One undutiful hen — having apparently im-bibed advanced notions — absolutely refused to sit at all, and the poor husband, determined not to be disappointed of his little family, did all the work himself, sitting bravely and patiently day and night, though nearly dead with exhaustion, till the chicks were hatched out. The next time this pair of birds had a nest, the cock's mind was firmly made up that he would stand no more nonsense. He fought the hen [kicked her], giving her so severe a thrashing that she was all but killed, and this Petruchio-like treatment had the desired effect, for the wife never again rebelled, but sat submissively."

In the case of another pair of ostriches of which Mrs. Martin tells, the female was accidentally killed, when the male mourned her loss for over two years, and would not look at another female. He wandered up and down, up and down, the length of his camp, utterly disconsolate. At last he mated again with a most magnificent hen, who ruled him tyrannically; he became the most hen-pecked, or rather hen-kicked, of husbands.

V

NOTES FROM THE PRAIRIE

THE best lesson I have had for a long time in the benefits of contentment, and of the value of one's own nook or corner of the world, however circumscribed it may be, as a point from which to observe nature and life, comes to me from a prairie correspondent, an invalid lady, confined to her room year in and year out, and yet who sees more and appreciates more than many of us who have the freedom of a whole continent. Having her permission, why should I not share these letters with my readers, especially since there are other house-bound or bed-bound invalids whom they may reach, and who may derive some cheer or suggestion from them? Words uttered in a popular magazine like "The Century" are like the vapors that go up from the ground and the streams: they are sure to be carried far and wide, and to fall again as rain or dew, and one little knows what thirsty plant or flower they may reach and nourish. I am thinking of another fine spirit, couch-bound in one of the northern New England States, who lives in a town that bears the same name as that in which my Western correspondent resides, and into whose chamber my slight and desultory papers have also brought something of the breath of the fields and woods, and who in return has given me many glimpses of nature through eyes purified by suffering.

Women are about the best lovers of Nature, after all; at least of Nature in her milder and more familiar forms. The feminine character, the feminine perceptions, intuitions, delicacy, sympathy, quickness, are more responsive to natural forms and influences than is the masculine mind.

My Western correspondent sees existence as from an altitude, and sees where the complements and compensations come in. She lives upon the prairie, and she says it is as the ocean to her, upon which she is adrift, and always expects to be, until she reaches the other shore. Her house is the ship which she never leaves. "What is visible from my window is the sea, changing only from winter to summer, as the sea changes from storm to sunshine. But there is one advantage, — messages can come to me continually from all the wide world."

One summer she wrote she had been hoping to be well enough to renew her acquaintance with the birds, the flowers, the woods, but instead was confined to her room more closely than ever.

"It is a disappointment to me, but I decided long ago that the wisest plan is to make the best of things ; to take what is given you, and make the most of it. To gather up the fragments, that nothing may be lost, applies to one's life as well as to other things. Though I cannot walk, I can think and read and write ; probably I get my share of pleasure from sources that well people are apt to neglect. I have learned that the way to be happy is to keep so busy that thoughts of self are forced out of sight; and to live for others, not for ourselves.

"Sometimes, when I think over the matter, I am half sorry for well people, because, you see, I have so much better company than they can have, for I have so much more time to go all over the world and meet all the best and wisest people in it. Some of them died long ago to the most of people, but to me they are just as much alive as they ever were; they give me their best and wisest thoughts, without the disagreeable accompaniments others must endure. Other people use their eyes and ears and pens for me ; all I have to do is to sit still and enjoy the results. Dear friends I have everywhere, though I am unknown to them ; what right have I to wish for more privileges than I have ? "

There is philosophy for you, — philosophy which looks fate out of countenance. It seems that if we only have the fortitude to take the ills of life cheerfully and say to fortune, "Thy worst is good enough for me," behold the worst is already repentant and fast changing to the best. Love softens the heart of the inevitable. The magic phrase which turns

the evil spirits into good angels is, "I am contented." Happiness is always at one's elbow, it
seems, in one disguise or another; all one has to do
is to stop seeking it afar, or stop *seeking* it at all,
and say to this unwelcome attendant, "Be thou my
friend," when, lo! the mask falls, and the angel is
disclosed. Certain rare spirits in this world have
accepted poverty with such love and pride that
riches at once become contemptible.

My correspondent has the gift of observation. In
renouncing self, she has opened the door for many
other things to enter. In cultivating the present
moment, she cultivates the present incident. The
power to see things comes of that mental attitude
which is directed to the now and the here: keen,
alert perceptions, those faculties that lead the mind
and take the incident as it flies. Most persons fail
to see things, because the print is too small for their
vision; they read only the large-lettered events like
the newspaper headings, and are apt to miss a part
of these, unless they see in some way their own
initials there.

The small type of the lives of bird and beast
about her is easily read by this cheerful invalid.
"To understand that the sky is everywhere blue,"
says Goethe, "we need not go around the world;"
and it would seem that this woman has got all the
good and pleasure there is in natural history from
the pets in her room, and the birds that build before

her window. I had been for a long time trying to determine whether or not the blue jay hoarded up nuts for winter use, but had not been able to settle the point. I applied to her, and, sitting by her window, she discovered that jays do indeed hoard food in a tentative, childish kind of way, but not with the cunning and provident foresight of the squirrels and the native mice. She saw a jay fly to the ground with what proved to be a peanut in its beak, and carefully cover it up with leaves and grass. "The next fall, looking out of my own window, I saw two jays hiding chestnuts with the same blind instinct. They brought them from a near tree, and covered them up in the grass, putting but one in a place. Subsequently, in another locality, I saw jays similarly employed. It appears to be simply the crow instinct to steal, or to carry away and hide any superfluous morsel of food." The jays were really planting chestnuts instead of hoarding them. There was no possibility of such supplies being available in winter, and in spring a young tree might spring from each nut. This fact doubtless furnishes a key to the problem why a forest of pine is usually succeeded by a forest of oak. The acorns are planted by the jays. Their instinct for hiding things prompts them to seek the more dark and secluded pine woods with their booty, and the thick layer of needles furnishes an admirable material with which to cover the nut. The germ sprouts and remains a low slender shoot for years, or until the pine woods are cut away, when it rapidly becomes a tree.

My correspondent thinks the birds possess some of the frailties of human beings; among other things, fickle-mindedness. "I believe they build nests just for the fun of it, to pass away the time, to have something to chatter about and dispute over. [I myself have seen a robin play at nest-building late in October, and have seen two young bluebirds ensconce themselves in an old thrush's nest in the fall and appear to amuse themselves like children, while the wind made the branch sway to and fro.] Now my wrens' nest is so situated that nothing can disturb them, and where I can see it at any time. They have often made a nest and left it. A year ago, during the latter part of May, they built a nest, and in a few days they kicked everything out of the box and did the work all over again, repeating the operation all July, then left the country without accomplishing anything further. This season they reared one brood, built another nest, and, I think, laid one or more eggs, idled around a few weeks, and then went away. [This last was probably a "cock-nest," built by the male as a roosting-place.] I have noticed, too, that blue jays build their apology for a nest, and abandon it for another place in the same tree." Her jays and wrens do not live together on the most amicable terms. "I had much amusement while the jay was on the nest, watching the actions

Blue Jay

of the wrens, whose nest was under the porch close by the oak. Perched on a limb over the jay, the male wren sat flirting his tail and scolding, evidently saying all the insulting things he could think of ; for, after enduring it for some time, the jay would fly off its nest in a rage, and, with the evident intention of impaling Mr. Wren with his bill, strike down vengefully and — find his bill fast in the bark, while his enemy was somewhere else, squeaking in derision. They kept that up day after day; but the wren is too lively to be caught by a large bird.

"I have never had the opportunity to discover whether there was any difference in the dispositions of birds of the same species; it would take a very close and extended observation to determine that; but I do know there is as much difference between animals as between human beings in that respect. Horses, cats, dogs, squirrels, all have their own individuality. I have had five gray squirrels for pets, and even their features were unlike. Fred and Sally were mates, who were kept shut up in their cages all the time. Fred was wonderfully brave, would strut and scold until there was something to be afraid of, then would crouch down behind Sally and let her defend him, the sneak! He abused her shamefully, but she never resented it. Being the larger, she could have whipped him and not half tried; but she probably labored under the impression, which is shared by some people, that it is a wife's duty to submit to whatever abuse the husband chooses to inflict. Their characters reminded me so strongly of some people I have seen that I used to take Fred out and whip him regularly, as a sort of vicarious punishment of those who deserved it. Chip was a gentle, pretty squirrel, fond of being petted, spent most of her time in my pocket or around my neck, but she died young; probably she was too good to live.

"Dick, lazy and a glutton, also died young, from over-eating. Chuck, the present pet, has Satan's own temper — very ugly — but so intelligent that she is the plague of our lives, though at the same time she is a constant source of amusement. It is impossible to remain long angry with her, however atrocious her crimes are. We are obliged to let her run loose through the house, for, when shut up, she squeals and chatters and rattles her cage so we can't endure it. From one piece of mischief to another as fast as she can go, she requires constant watching. She knows what is forbidden very well, for, if I chance to look at her after she has been up to mischief, she quickly drops down flat, spreads her tail over her back, looking all the time so very innocent that she betrays herself. If I go toward her, she springs on my back, where I cannot reach her to whip her. She never bites *me*, but if others tease her, she is very vicious. When I tease her, she relieves her feelings by biting any one else who

102

happens to be in the room; and it is no slight matter being bitten by a squirrel's sharp teeth. Know-
ing that the other members of the family are afraid
of her, she amuses herself by putting nuts in their
shoes, down their necks, or in their hair, then standing guard, so that if they remove the nuts she flies
at them.

"Chuck will remember an injury for months,
and take revenge whenever opportunity offers. She
claims all the nuts and candy that come into the
house, searching Mr. B——'s pockets *on Sundays,*
never on other days. I don't see how she distin-
guishes, unless from the fact that he comes home
early on that day. Once, when she caught one of
the girls eating some of her nuts, she flew at her, bit
her, and began carrying off the nuts to hide as fast
as she could. For months afterward she would slip
slyly up and bite the girl. She particularly despises
my brother, he teases her so, and gives her no chance
to bite; so she gets even with him by tearing up
everything of his she can find, — his books, his
gloves, etc.; and if she can get into the closet where
I keep the soiled clothing, she will select such arti-
cles as belong to him, and tear them up! And she
has a wonderful memory; never forgets where she
puts things; people whom she has not seen for several years she remembers.

"She had the misfortune to have about two inches
of her tail cut off, by being caught in the door, which

made it too short to be used for wiping her face ; it would slip out of her hands, making her stamp her feet and chatter her teeth with anger. By experimenting, she found by backing up in a corner it was prevented from slipping out of her reach. Have had her five years ; wonder how long their lives usually are. One of my neighbors got a young squirrel, so young that it required milk; so they got a small nursing-bottle for it. Until that squirrel was over a year old, whenever he got hungry he would get his bottle and sit and hold it up as if he thought that quite the proper way for a squirrel to obtain his nourishment. It was utterly comical to see him. We have no black squirrels ; a few red ones, and a great many gray ones of different kinds."

I was much interested in her pet squirrel, and made frequent inquiries about it. A year later she writes: "My squirrel still lives and rules the house. She has an enemy that causes her much trouble, — a rat that comes into the wood-shed. I had noticed that, whenever she went out there, she investigated the dark corners with care before she ventured to play, but did not understand it till I chanced to be sitting in the kitchen door once, as she was digging up a nut she had buried. Just as she got it up, a great rat sprung on her back; there ensued a trial of agility and strength to see which should have that nut. Neither seemed to be angry, for they did not attempt to bite, but raced around the shed, cuffing each other at every opportunity ; sometimes one had the nut, sometimes the other. I regret to say my squirrel, whenever she grew tired, took a base advantage of the rat by coming and sitting at my feet, gnawing the nut, and plainly showing by her motions her exultation over her foe. Finally the rat became so exasperated that he forgot prudence, and forced her to climb up on my shoulder.

"In an extract from a London paper I see it asserted that birds and snakes cannot taste. As to the snakes I cannot say, but I know birds can taste, from observing my canary when I give him something new to eat. He will edge up to it carefully, take a bit, back off to meditate; then, if he decides he likes it, he walks up boldly and eats his fill. But if there is anything disagreeable in what I offer him, acid, for instance, there is such a fuss! He scrapes his bill, raises and lowers the feathers on the top of his head, giving one the impression that he is making a wry face. He cannot be induced to touch it a second time.

"I have taught him to think I am afraid of him, and how he tyrannizes over me, chasing me from place to place, pecking and squeaking! He delights in pulling out my hair. When knitting or crocheting, he tries to prevent my pulling the yarn by standing on it; when that fails, he takes hold with his bill and pulls with all his little might."

Some persons have a special gift or quality that

enables them to sustain more intimate relations with wild creatures than others. Women, as a rule, are ridiculously afraid of cattle and horses turned loose in a field, but my correspondent, when a young girl, had many a lark with the prairie colts. "Is it not strange," she says, "that a horse will rarely hurt a child, or any person that is fond of them? To see a drove of a hundred or even a hundred and fifty unbroken colts branded and turned out to grow up was a common occurrence then [in her childhood]. I could go among them, catch them, climb on their backs, and they never offered to hurt me; they seemed to consider it *fun*. They would come up and touch me with their noses, and prance off around and around me; but just let a man come near them, and they were off like the wind."

All her reminiscences of her early life in Iowa, thirty years ago, are deeply interesting to me. Her parents, a Boston family, moved to that part of the State in advance of the railroads, making the journey from the Mississippi in a wagon. "My father had been fortunate enough to find a farm with a frame house upon it (the houses were mostly log ones) built by an Englishman whose homesickness had driven him back to England. It stood upon a slight elevation in the midst of a prairie, though not a very level one. To the east and to the west of us, about four miles away, were the woods along the banks of the streams. It was in the month of June when we came, and the prairie was tinted pink with wild roses. From early spring till late in the fall the ground used to be so covered with some kinds of flowers that it had almost as decided a color as the sky itself, and the air would be fragrant with their perfume. First it is white with ' dog-toes' [probably an orchid], then a cold blue from being covered with some kind of light-blue flower; next come the roses; in July and August it is pink with the ' prairie pink,' dotted with scarlet lilies; as autumn comes on, it is vivid with orange-colored flowers. I never knew their names ; they have woody stalks ; one kind that grows about a foot high has a feathery spray of little blossoms [goldenrod ?]. There are several kinds of tall ones; the blossom has yellow leaves and brown velvety centres [cone-flower, or rudbeckia, probably, now common in the East]. We youngsters used to gather the gum that exuded from the stalk. Every one was poor in those days, and no one was ashamed of it. Plenty to eat, such as it was. We introduced some innovations in that line that shocked the people here. We used *corn meal;* they said it was only fit for hogs. Worse than that, we ate 'greens,' — weeds, they called them. It does not seem possible, but it is a fact, that with all those fertile acres around them waiting for cultivation, and to be had almost for the asking, those people (they were mainly Hoosiers) lived on fried salt pork swimming in fat, and hot biscuit, all the

year round ; no variety, no vegetables, no butter
saved for winter use, no milk after cold weather began, for it was too much trouble to milk the cows —
such a shiftless set! And the hogs they raised, —
you should have seen them! 'Prairie sharks' and
'razor-backs' were the local names for them, and
either name fitted them; long noses, long legs, bodies
about five inches thick, and no amount of food
would make them fat. They were allowed to run
wild to save the trouble of caring for them, and
when the pork-barrel was empty, they *shot* one.

"Everybody drove oxen and used lumber-wagons
with a board across the box for a seat. How did
we ever endure it, riding over the roadless prairies!
Then, any one who owned a horse was considered
an aristocrat and despised accordingly. One yoke of
oxen that we had were not to be sneezed at as a fast
team. They were trained to trot, and would make
good time, too. [I love to hear oxen praised. An
old Michigan farmer, an early settler, told me of a
famous pair of oxen he once had; he spoke of them
with great affection. They would draw any log he
hitched them to. When they had felt of the log and
found they had their match, he said they would
nudge each other, give their tails a kink, lift up their
heads, and say *eh-h-h-h!* then something had to
come.]

"One phrase you used in your last letter — 'the
start from the stump' — shows how locality governs

the illustrations we use. The start was not from the *stump* here, quite the reverse. Nature made the land ready for man's hand, and there were no obstacles in the shape of stumps and stones to overcome. Probably in the East a pine-stump fence is not regarded as either particularly attractive or odd; but to me, when I first saw one in York State, it was both. I had never even heard of the stumps being utilized in that way. Seen for the first time, there is something grotesque in the appearance of those long arms forever reaching out after something they never find, like a petrified octopus. Those fences are an evidence of Eastern thrift, — making an enemy serve as a friend. I think they would frighten our horses and cattle, used as they are to the almost invisible wire fence. 'Worm' fences were the fashion at first. But they soon learned the necessity of economizing wood. The people were extravagant, too, in the outlay of power in tilling the soil, sixteen yoke of oxen being thought absolutely necessary to run a breaking-plow; and I have seen twenty yoke used, requiring three men to drive and attend the great clumsy plow. Every summer you might see them in any direction, looking like 'thousand-legged worms.' They found out after a while that two yoke answered quite as well. There is something very queer about the boulders that are supposed to have been brought down from northern regions during the glacial period; like Banquo's ghost, they refuse

109

to stay down. Other stones beside them gradually become buried, but the boulders are always on top of the ground. Is there something repellent about them, that the earth refuses to cover them? They seem to be of no use, for they cannot be worked as other stone; they have to be broken open with heat in some way, though I did see a building made of them once. The boulders had been broken and put in big squares and little squares, oblong pieces and triangles. The effect was curious, if not fine.

"In those days there were such quantities of game-birds, it was the sportsman's paradise, and during the summer a great many gunners from the cities came there. Prairie-chickens without number, as great a nuisance as the crows in the East, only we could eat them to pay for the grain they ate; also geese, turkeys, ducks, quail, and pigeons. Did you ever hear the prairie-chickens during the spring? I never felt sure spring had come to stay till, in the early morning, there came the boom of the chickens, *Poor old booff*. It is an indescribable sound, as if there were a thousand saying the same thing and keeping perfect time. No trouble then getting a child up early in the morning, for it is time for hunting prairie-chickens' nests. In the most unexpected places in the wild grass the nests would be found, with about sixteen eggs in them, looking somewhat like a guinea-hen's egg. Of course, an omelet made out of them tasted ever so much better than if made out of home-laid eggs; now I should not like the taste so well, probably, for there is a wild flavor to the egg, as there is to the flesh of the bird. Many a time I've stepped right into the nest, so well was it hidden. After a prairie fire is a good time to go egging, the nests being in plain sight and the eggs already roasted. I have tried again and again to raise the chickens by setting the eggs under the tame hens, but it cannot be done; they seem to inherit a shyness that makes them refuse to eat, and at the first opportunity they slip off in the grass and are gone. Every kind of food, even to live insects, they will refuse, and will starve to death rather than eat in captivity. There are but few chickens here now; they have taken Horace Greeley's advice and gone west. As to four-footed game, there were any number of the little prairie-wolves and some big gray ones. Could see the little wolves running across the prairie any time o' day, and at night their continual *yap, yap* was almost unendurable. They developed a taste for barn-yard fowl that made it necessary for hens to roost high. They are cowards in the daytime, but brave enough to come close to the house at night. If people had only had foxhounds, they would have afforded an opportunity for some sport. I have seen people try to run them down on horseback, but never knew them to succeed.

"One of my standard amusements was to go every little while to a den the wolves had, where the rocks cropped out of the ground, and poke in there with a stick, to see a wolf pop out scared almost to death. As to the big wolves, it was dangerous sport to meddle with them. I had an experience with them one winter that would have begotten a desire to keep a proper distance from them, had I not felt it before. An intensely cold night three of us were riding in an open wagon on one seat. The road ran for about a mile through the woods, and as we entered it four or five gray wolves sprang out at us; the horse needed no urging, you may be sure, but to me it seemed an âge before we got out into the moonlight on the prairie; then the wolves slunk back into the woods. Every leap they made it seemed as if they would jump into the wagon. I could hear them strike against the back of it, and hear their teeth *click* together as they barely missed my hand where I held on to the seat to keep from being thrown out. My most prominent desire about that time was to sit in the middle, and let some one else have the outside seat.

"Grandfather was very fond of trapping, and used to catch a great many wolves for their skins and the bounty; also minks and muskrats. I always had to help skin them, which I considered dreadful, especially skinning the muskrats; but as that was the only condition under which I was allowed to go along, of course I submitted, for I would n't miss the excitement of seeing whether we had succeeded in outwitting and catching the sly creatures for any consideration. The beautiful minks, with their slender satiny bodies, it seemed a pity to catch them. Muskrats I had no sympathy for, they looked so ratty, and had so unpleasant a smell. The gophers were one of the greatest plagues the farmers had. The ground would be dotted with their mounds, so round and regular, the black dirt pulverized so finely. I always wondered how they could make them of such a perfect shape, and wished I could see way down into their houses. They have more than one entrance to them, because I've tried to drown them out, and soon I would see what I took to be my gopher, that I thought I had covered so nicely, skipping off. They took so much corn out of the hills after it was planted that it was customary to mix corn soaked with strychnine with the seed corn. Do they have pocket gophers in the East? [No.] They are the cutest little animals, with their pockets on each side of their necks, lined with fur; when they get them stuffed full they look as broad as they are long, and so saucy. I have met them, and had them show fight because I would n't turn out of their path, — the little impudent things!

"One nuisance that goes along with civilization we escaped until the railroad was built, and that was *rats*. The railroads brought other nuisances, too, the weeds; they soon crowded out the native plants. I don't want to be understood as calling *all* weeds nuisances; the beautiful flowers some of them bear save their reputations, — the dandelion, for instance; I approve of the dandelion, whatever others may think. I shall never forget the first one I found in the West; it was like meeting an old friend. It grew alongside of an emigrant road, about five miles from my home; here I spied the golden treasure in the grass. Some of the many 'prairie schooners' that had passed that way had probably dropped the one seed. Mother dug it up and planted it in our flower-bed, and in two years the neighborhood was yellow with them, — all from that one root. The prairies are gone now, and the wild flowers, those that have not been civilized to death like the Indians, have taken refuge in the fence-corners."

I had asked her what she knew about cranes, and she replied as follows: —

"During the first few years after we came West, cranes, especially the sand-hill variety, were very plentiful. Any day in the summer you might see a triangle of them flying over, with their long legs dragging behind them; or, if you had sharp eyes, could see them stalking along the sloughs sometimes found on the prairie. In the books I see them described as being brown in color. Now I should not call them brown, for they are more of a yellow. They are just the color of a gosling, should it get its down somewhat soiled, and they look much like overgrown goslings set up on stilts. I have often

114

found their nests, and always in the shallow water in the slough, built out of sticks, — much as the children build cob-houses, — about a foot high, with two large flat eggs in them. I have often tried to catch them on their nests, so as to see how they disposed of their long legs, but never quite succeeded. They are very shy, and their nests are always so situated as to enable them to see in every direction. I had a great desire to possess a pet crane, but every attempt to raise one resulted in failure, all on account of those same slender legs.

"The egg I placed under a 'sitting hen' (one was as much as a hen could conveniently manage); it would hatch out all right, and I had no difficulty in feeding the young crane, for it would eat anything, and showed no shyness, — quite different from a young prairie-chicken; in fact, their tameness was the cause of their death, for, like Mary's little lamb, they insisted on going everywhere I went. When they followed me into the house, and stepped upon the smooth floor, one leg would go in one direction and the other in the opposite, breaking one or both of them. They seemed to be unable to walk upon any smooth surface. Such ridiculous-looking things they were! I have seen a few pure white ones, but only on the wing. They seem more shy than the yellow ones.

"Once I saw a curious sight; I saw seven or eight cranes dance a cotillon, or something very

115

much like it. I have since read of wild fowl performing in that way, but then I had never heard of it. They were in a meadow about half a mile from the house; I did not at all understand what they were doing, and proceeded to investigate. After walking as near as I could without frightening them, I crept through the tall grass until I was within a rod of the cranes, and then lay and watched them. It was the most comical sight to see them waltz around, sidle up to each other and back again, their long necks and legs making the most clumsy motions. With a little stretch of the imagination one might see a smirk on their faces, and suspect them of caricaturing human beings. There seemed to be a regular method in their movements, for the changes were repeated. How long they kept it up I do not know, for I tired of it, and went back to the house, but they had danced until the grass was trampled down hard and smooth. I always had a mania for trying experiments, so I coaxed my mother to cook one the men had shot, though I had never heard of any one's eating crane. It was not very good, tasted somewhat peculiar, and the thought that maybe it was poison struck me with horror. I was badly scared, for I reflected that I had no proof that it was *not* poison, and I had been told so many times that I was bound to come to grief, sooner or later, from trying to find out things."

I am always glad to have the views of a sensible

person, outside of the literary circles, upon my favorite authors, especially when the views are spontaneous. "Speaking of Thoreau," says my correspondent, "I am willing to allow most that is said in his praise, but *I do not like him*, all the same. Do you know I feel that he was not altogether human. There is something uncanny about him. I guess that, instead of having a human soul, his body was inhabited by some sylvan deity that flourished in Grecian times; he seemed out of place among human beings."

Of Carlyle, too, she has an independent opinion. "It is a mystery to me why men so universally admire Carlyle; women do not, or, if there is occasionally one who does, she does not *like* him. A woman's first thought about him would be, 'I pity his wife!' Do you remember what he said in answer to Mrs. Welsh's proposal to come and live with them and help support them? He said they could only live pleasantly together on the condition that she looked up to him, not he to her. Here is what he says: 'Now, think, Liebchen, whether your mother will consent to forget her riches and our poverty, and uncertain, more probably scanty, income, and consent in the spirit of Christian meekness to make me her guardian and director, and be a second wife to her daughter's husband?' Now, is n't that insufferable conceit for you? To expect that a woman old enough to be his mother would lay aside her self-respect and individuality to accept him, a comparatively young and inexperienced man, as her master? The cheekiness of it! Here you have the keynote of his character, — 'great I and little u.'

"I have tried faithfully to like him, for it seemed as if the fault must be in me because I did not; I have labored wearily through nearly all his works, stumbling over his superlatives (why, he is an adjective factory ; his pages look like the alphabet struck by a cyclone. You call it picturesqueness; I call it grotesqueness). But it was of no use; it makes me tired all over to think of it. All the time I said to myself, 'Oh, do stop your scolding ; you are not so much better than the rest of us.' One is willing to be led to a higher life, but who wants to be pushed and cuffed along? How can people place him and our own Emerson, the dear guide and friend of so many of us, on the same level? It may be that the world had need of him, just as it needs lightning and rain and cold and pain, but must we *like* these things?" [1]

[1] My correspondent was Mrs. Beardslee of Manchester, Iowa. She died in October, 1885.

VI

EYE–BEAMS

I

A WEASEL IN HIS DEN

MY most interesting note of the season of 1893 relates to a weasel. One day in early November, my boy and I were sitting on a rock at the edge of a tamarack swamp in the woods, hoping to get a glimpse of some grouse which we knew were in the habit of feeding in the swamp. We had not sat there very long before we heard a slight rustling in the leaves below us, which we at once fancied was made by the cautious tread of a grouse. (We had no gun.) Presently, through the thick brushy growth, we caught sight of a small animal running along, that we at first took for a red squirrel. A moment more, and it came into full view but a few yards from us, and we saw that it was a weasel. A second glance showed that it carried something in its mouth which, as it drew near, we saw was a mouse or a mole of some sort. The weasel ran nimbly along, now the length of a decayed log, then over stones and branches, pausing a moment every three or four yards, and passed within twenty feet of us, and disappeared behind some rocks on the bank at the edge of the swamp. "He is carrying food into his den," I said; "let us watch him." In four or five minutes he reappeared, coming back over the course along which he had just passed, running over and under the same stones and down the same decayed log, and was soon out of sight in the swamp. We had not moved, and evidently he had not noticed us. After about six minutes we heard the same rustle as at first, and in a moment saw the weasel coming back with another mouse in his mouth. He kept to his former route as if chained to it, making the same pauses and gestures, and repeating exactly his former movements. He disappeared on our left as before, and, after a few moments' delay, reëmerged and took his course down into the swamp again. We waited about the same length of time as before, when back he came with another mouse. He evidently had a big crop of mice down there amid the bogs and bushes, and he was gathering his harvest in very industriously. We became curious to see exactly where his den was, and so walked around where he had seemed to disappear each time, and waited. He was as punctual as usual, and was back with his game exactly on time. It happened that we had stopped within two paces of his hole, so that, as he approached it, he evidently discovered us. He paused, looked steadily at us, and then, without any sign of fear, entered his den. The entrance was not under the rocks as we had expected, but was in the bank a few feet beyond them. We remained motionless for some time, but he did not reappear. Our presence had made him suspicious and he was going to wait awhile. Then I removed some dry leaves and exposed his doorway, a small, round hole, hardly as large as the chipmunk makes, going straight down into the ground. We had a lively curiosity to get a peep into his larder. If he had been carrying in mice at this rate very long, his cellars must be packed with them. With a sharp stick I began digging into the red clayey soil, but soon encountered so many roots from near trees that I gave it up, deciding to return next day with a mattock. So I repaired the damages I had done as well as I could, replaced the leaves, and we moved off.

The next day, which was mild and still as usual, I came back armed, as I thought, to unearth the weasel and his treasures. I sat down where we had sat the day before and awaited developments. I was curious to know if the weasel was still carrying in his harvest. I had sat but a few minutes when I heard again the rustle in the dry leaves, and saw the weasel coming home with another mouse. I observed him till he had made three trips; about every six or seven minutes, I calculated, he brought in a mouse. Then I went and stood near his hole. This time he had a fat meadow-mouse. He laid it down

near the entrance, went in and turned around, and
reached out and drew the mouse in after him. That
store of mice I am bound to see, I thought, and then
fell to with the heavy mattock. I followed the hole
down about two feet, when it turned to the north.
I kept the clew by thrusting into the passage slender
twigs; these it was easy to follow. Two or three feet
more and the hole branched, one part going west,
the other northeast. I followed the west one a few
feet till it branched. Then I turned to the easterly
tunnel, and pursued it till it branched. I followed
one of these ways till it divided. I began to be em-
barrassed and hindered by the accumulations of
loose soil. Evidently this weasel had foreseen just
such an assault upon his castle as I was making, and
had planned it accordingly. He was not to be caught
napping. I found several enlargements in the various tunnels, breathing-spaces, or spaces to turn
around in, or to meet and chat with a companion,
but nothing that looked like a terminus, a permanent
living-room. I tried removing the soil a couple of
paces away with the mattock, but found it slow
work. I was getting warm and tired, and my task
was apparently only just begun. The farther I dug,
the more numerous and intricate became the passages. I concluded to stop, and come again the next
day, armed with a shovel in addition to the mattock.

Accordingly, I came back on the morrow, and fell
to work vigorously. I soon had quite a large exca-

vation; I found the bank a labyrinth of passages, with here and there a large chamber. One of the latter I struck only six inches under the surface, by making a fresh breach a few feet away.

While I was leaning upon my shovel-handle and recovering my breath, I heard some light-footed creature tripping over the leaves above me just out of view, which I fancied might be a squirrel. Presently I heard the bay of a hound and the yelp of a cur, and then knew that a rabbit had passed near me. The dogs came hurrying after, with a great rumpus, and then presently the hunters followed. The dogs remained barking not many rods south of me on the edge of the swamp, and I knew the rabbit had run to hole. For half an hour or more I heard the hunters at work there, digging their game out; then they came along and discovered me at my work. (An old trapper and woodsman and his son.) I told them what I was in quest of. "A mountain weasel," said the old man. "Seven or eight years ago I used to set deadfalls for rabbits just over there, and the game was always partly eaten up. It must have been this weasel that visited my traps." So my game was evidently an old resident of the place. This swamp, maybe, had been his hunting-ground for many years, and he had added another hall to his dwelling each year. After further digging, I struck at least one of his banqueting-halls, a cavity about the size of one's hat, arched over by a network of fine tree-roots. The occupant evidently lodged or rested here also. There was a warm, dry nest, made of leaves and the fur of mice and moles. I took out two or three hand-fuls. In finding this chamber I had followed one of the tunnels around till it brought me within a foot of the original entrance. A few inches to one side of this cavity there was what I took to be a back alley where the weasel threw his waste; there were large masses of wet, decaying fur here, and fur pellets such as are regurgitated by hawks and owls. In the nest there was the tail of a flying squirrel, showing that the weasel sometimes had a flying squirrel for supper or dinner.

I continued my digging with renewed energy; I should yet find the grand depot where all these pas-sages centred; but the farther I excavated, the more complex and baffling the problem became; the ground was honeycombed with passages. What enemy has this weasel, I said to myself, that he should provide so many ways of escape, that he should have a back door at every turn? To corner him would be impossible; to be lost in his fortress were like being lost in Mammoth Cave. How he could bewilder his pursuer by appearing now at this door, now at that; now mocking him from the attic, now defying him from the cellar! So far, I had dis-covered but one entrance; but some of the cham-bers were so near the surface that it looked as if the

planner had calculated upon an emergency when he
might want to reach daylight quickly in a new place.

Finally I paused, rested upon my shovel awhile,
eased my aching back upon the ground, and then
gave it up, feeling as I never had before the force of
the old saying, that you cannot catch a weasel asleep.
I had made an ugly hole in the bank, had handled
over two or three times a ton or more of earth, and
was apparently no nearer the weasel and his store
of mice than when I began.

Then I regretted that I had broken into his castle
at all; that I had not contented myself with coming
day after day and counting his mice as he carried
them in, and continued my observation upon him
each succeeding year. Now the rent in his fortress
could not be repaired, and he would doubtless move
away, as he most certainly did, for his doors, which
I had closed with soil, remained unopened after
winter had set in.

But little seems known about the intimate private
lives of any of our lesser wild creatures. It was news
to me that any of the weasels lived in dens in this
way, and that they stored up provision against a day
of need. This species was probably the little ermine,
eight or nine inches long, with tail about five inches.
It was still in its summer dress of dark chestnut-
brown above and whitish below.

It was a mystery where the creature had put the
earth which it must have removed in digging its

den; not a grain was to be seen anywhere, and yet a bushel or more must have been taken out. Externally, there was not the slightest sign of that curious habitation there under the ground. The entrance was hidden beneath dry leaves, and was surrounded by little passages and flourishes between the leaves and the ground. If any of my readers find a weasel's den, I hope they will be wiser than I was, and observe his goings and comings without disturbing his habitation.

II

KEEN PERCEPTIONS

Success in observing nature, as in so many other things, depends upon alertness of mind and quickness to take a hint. One's perceptive faculties must be like a trap lightly and delicately set; a touch must suffice to spring it. But how many people have I walked with, whose perceptions are rusty and unpracticed, — nothing less than a bear would spring their trap! All the finer play of nature, all the small deer, they miss. The little dramas and tragedies that are being enacted by the wild creatures in the fields and woods are more or less veiled and withdrawn; and the actors all stop when a spectator appears upon the scene. One must be able to interpret the signs, to penetrate the screens, to put this and that together.

126

Then nature speaks a different language from our own; the successful observer translates this language into human speech. He knows the meaning of every sound, movement, gesture, and gives the human equivalent. Careless or hasty observers, on the other hand, make the mistake of reading their own thoughts or mental and emotional processes into nature; plans and purposes are attributed to the wild creatures which are quite beyond them. Some people in town saw an English sparrow tangled up in a horsehair, and suspended from a tree, with other sparrows fluttering and chattering about it. They concluded at once that the sparrows had executed one of their number, doubtless for some crime. I have several times seen sparrows suspended in this way about their nesting and roosting places. Accidents happen to birds as well as to other folks. But they do not yet imitate us in the matter of capital punishment.

One day I saw a little bush sparrow fluttering along in the grass, disabled in some way, and a large number of its mates flitting and calling about it. I captured the bird, and, in doing so, its struggles in my hand broke the bond that held it, — some kind of web or silken insect thread that tied together the quills of one wing. When I let it fly away, all its mates followed it as if wondering at the miracle that had been wrought. They no doubt experienced some sort of emotion. Birds sympathize with each other in their distress, and will make common cause against an enemy. Crows will pursue and fight a tame crow. They seem to look upon him as an alien and an enemy. He is never so shapely and bright and polished as his wild brother. He is more or less demoralized, and has lost caste. Probably a pack of wolves would in the same way destroy a tame wolf, should such an one appear in their midst. The wild creatures are human, — with a difference, a wide difference. They have the keenest powers of perception, — what observers they are! how quickly they take a hint, — but they have little or no powers of reflection. The crows do not meet in parliaments and caucuses, as has been fancied, and try offenders, and discuss the tariff, or consider ways and means. They are gregarious and social, and probably in the fall have something like a reunion of the tribe. At least their vast assemblages upon the hills at this season have a decidedly festive appearance.

The crow has fine manners. He always has the walk and air of a lord of the soil. One morning I put out some fresh meat upon the snow near my study window. Presently a crow came and carried it off, and alighted with it upon the ground in the vineyard. While he was eating of it, another crow came, and, alighting a few yards away, slowly walked up to within a few feet of this fellow and stopped. I expected to see a struggle over the food, as would have been the case with domestic fowls or animals. Nothing of the kind. The feeding crow stopped eating, regarded the other for a moment, made a gesture or two, and flew away. Then the second crow went up to the food, and proceeded to take his share. Presently the first crow came back, when each seized a portion of the food and flew away with it. Their mutual respect and good-will seemed perfect. Whether it really was so in our human sense, or whether it was simply an illustration of the instinct of mutual support which seems to prevail among gregarious birds, I know not. Birds that are solitary in their habits, like hawks or woodpeckers, behave quite differently toward each other in the presence of their food.

The lives of the wild creatures revolve about two facts or emotions, appetite and fear. Their keenness in discovering food and in discovering danger are alike remarkable. But man can nearly always outwit them, because, while his perceptions are not as sharp, his power of reflection is so much greater. His cunning carries a great deal farther. The crow will quickly discover anything that looks like a trap or snare set to catch him, but it takes him a long time to see through the simplest contrivance. As I have above stated, I sometimes place meat on the snow in front of my study window to attract him. On one occasion, after a couple of crows had come to expect something there daily, I suspended a piece of meat by a string from a branch of the tree just over the spot where I usually placed the food. A crow soon discovered it, and came into the tree to see what it meant. His suspicions were aroused. There was some design in that suspended meat evidently. It was a trap to catch him. He surveyed it from every near branch. He peeked and pried, and was bent on penetrating the mystery. He flew to the ground, and walked about and surveyed it from all sides. Then he took a long walk down about the vineyard as if in hope of hitting upon some clew. Then he came to the tree again, and tried first one eye, then the other, upon it ; then to the ground beneath; then he went away and came back; then his fellow came, and they both squinted and investigated, and then disappeared. Chickadees and woodpeckers would alight upon the meat and peck it swinging in the wind, but the crows were fearful. Does this show reflection ? Perhaps it does, but I look upon it rather as that instinct of fear and cunning so characteristic of the crow. Two days passed thus: every morning the crows came and surveyed the suspended meat from all points in the tree, and then went away. The third day I placed a large bone on the snow beneath the suspended morsel. Presently one of the crows appeared in the tree, and bent his eye upon the tempting bone. "The mystery deepens," he seemed to say to himself. But after half an hour's investigation, and after

approaching several times within a few feet of the
food upon the ground, he seemed to conclude there
was no connection between it and the piece hanging
by the string. So he finally walked up to it and fell
to pecking it, flickering his wings all the time, as a
sign of his watchfulness. He also turned up his eye,
momentarily, to the piece in the air above, as if it
might be some disguised sword of Damocles ready
to fall upon him. Soon his mate came and alighted
on a low branch of the tree. The feeding crow regarded him a moment, and then flew up to his side,
as if to give him a turn at the meat. But he refused
to run the risk. He evidently looked upon the whole
thing as a delusion and a snare, and presently went
away, and his mate followed him. Then I placed
the bone in one of the main forks of the tree, but
the crows kept at a safe distance from it. Then
I put it back to the ground, but they grew more
and more suspicious; some evil intent in it all, they
thought. Finally a dog carried off the bone, and
the crows ceased to visit the tree.

III

A SPARROW'S MISTAKE

IF one has always built one's nest upon the ground,
and if one comes of a race of ground-builders, it is
a risky experiment to build in a tree. The conditions

131

are vastly different. One of my near neighbors, a little song sparrow, learned this lesson the past season. She grew ambitious; she departed from the traditions of her race, and placed her nest in a tree. Such a pretty spot she chose, too — the pendent cradle formed by the interlaced sprays of two parallel branches of a Norway spruce. These branches shoot out almost horizontally; indeed, the lower ones become quite so in spring, and the side shoots with which they are clothed droop down, forming the slopes of miniature ridges; where the slopes of two branches join, a little valley is formed, which often looks more stable than it really is. My sparrow selected one of these little valleys about six feet from the ground, and quite near the walls of the house. Here, she thought, I will build my nest, and pass the heat of June in a miniature Norway. This tree is the fir-clad mountain, and this little vale on its side I select for my own. She carried up a great quantity of coarse grass and straws for the foundation, just as she would have done upon the ground. On the top of this mass there gradually came into shape the delicate structure of her nest, compacting and refining till its delicate carpet of hairs and threads was reached. So sly as the little bird was about it, too, — every moment on her guard lest you discover her secret! Five eggs were laid, and incubation was far advanced, when the storms and winds came. The cradle indeed did

Nest of the Song Sparrow

rock. The boughs did not break, but they swayed and separated as you would part your two inter-locked hands. The ground of the little valley fairly gave way, the nest tilted over till its contents fell into the chasm. It was like an earthquake that destroys a hamlet.

No born tree-builder would have placed its nest in such a situation. Birds that build at the end of the branch, like the oriole, tie the nest fast; others, like the robin, build against the main trunk; still others build securely in the fork. The sparrow, in her ignorance, rested her house upon the spray of two branches, and when the tempest came, the branches parted company and the nest was en-gulfed.

Another sparrow friend of mine met with a curi-ous mishap the past season. It was the little social sparrow, or chippie. She built her nest on the arm of a grapevine in the vineyard, a favorite place with chippie. It had a fine canopy of leaves, and was firmly and securely placed. Just above it hung a bunch of young grapes, which in the warm July days grew very rapidly. The little bird had not fore-seen the calamity that threatened her. The grapes grew down into her nest and completely filled it, so that, when I put my hand in, there were the eggs sat upon by the grapes. The bird was crowded out, and had perforce abandoned her nest, ejected by a bunch of grapes. How long she held her

ground I do not know; probably till the fruit began
to press heavily upon her.

IV

A POOR FOUNDATION

IT is a curious habit the wood thrush has of starting its nest with a fragment of newspaper or other
paper. Except in remote woods, I think it nearly
always puts a piece of paper in the foundation of its
nest. Last spring I chanced to be sitting near a tree
in which a wood thrush had concluded to build. She
came with a piece of paper nearly as large as my
hand, placed it upon the branch, stood upon it a
moment, and then flew down to the ground. A little
puff of wind caused the paper to leave the branch
a moment afterward. The thrush watched it eddy
slowly down to the ground, when she seized it and
carried it back. She placed it in position as before,
stood upon it again for a moment, and then flew
away. Again the paper left the branch, and sailed
away slowly to the ground. The bird seized it again,
jerking it about rather spitefully, I thought ; she
turned it around two or three times, then labored
back to the branch with it, upon which she shifted
it about as if to hit upon some position in which it
would lie more securely. This time she sat down
upon it for a moment, and then went away, doubt-

less with the thought in her head that she would
bring something to hold it down. The perverse
paper followed her in a few seconds. She seized it
again, and hustled it about more than before. As
she rose with it toward the nest, it in some way impeded her flight, and she was compelled to return to
the ground with it. But she kept her temper remark-
ably well. She turned the paper over and took it
up in her beak several times before she was satisfied with her hold, and then carried it back to the
branch, where, however, it would not stay. I saw
her make six trials of it, when I was called away. I
think she finally abandoned the restless fragment,
probably a scrap that held some "breezy" piece of
writing, for later in the season I examined the nest
and found no paper in it.

V

A FRIGHTENED MINK

IN walking through the woods one day in early
winter, we read upon the newly fallen snow the
record of a mink's fright the night before. The mink
had been traveling through the woods post-haste,
not along the water-courses where one sees them by
day, but over ridges and across valleys. We followed his track some distance to see what adventures he had met with. We tracked him through a

bushy swamp, saw where he had left it to explore a
pile of rocks, then where he had taken to the swamp
again, then to the more open woods. Presently the
track turned sharply about, and doubled upon itself
in long hurried strides. What had caused the mink
to change its mind so suddenly? We explored a few
paces ahead, and came upon a fox track. The mink
had seen the fox stalking stealthily through the
woods, and the sight had probably brought his heart
into his mouth. I think he climbed a tree, and
waited till the fox passed. His track disappeared
amid a clump of hemlocks, and then reappeared
again a little beyond them. It described a big loop
around, and then crossed the fox track only a few
yards from the point where its course was interrupted. Then it followed a little water-course, went
under a rude bridge in a wood-road, then mingled
with squirrel tracks in a denser part of the thicket.
If the mink met a muskrat or a rabbit in his travels,
or came upon a grouse, or quail, or a farmer's hen-
roost, he had the supper he was in quest of.

VI

A LEGLESS CLIMBER

THE eye always sees what it wants to see, and the
ear hears what it wants to hear. If I am intent upon
birds'-nests in my walk, I find birds'-nests every-

where. Some people see four-leaved clovers wherever they look in the grass. A friend of mine picks up Indian relics all about the fields; he has Indian relics in his eye. I have seen him turn out of the path at right angles, as a dog will when he scents something, and walk straight away several rods, and pick up an Indian pounding-stone. He saw it out of the corner of his eye. I find that without conscious effort I see and hear birds with like ease. Eye and ear are always on the alert.

One day in early June I was walking with some friends along a secluded wood-road. Above the hum of the conversation I caught the distressed cry of a pair of blue jays. My companions heard it also, but did not heed it.

But to my ear the cry was peculiar. It was uttered in a tone of anguish and alarm. I said, "Let us see what is the trouble with these jays." I presently saw a nest twenty-five or thirty feet from the ground in a small hemlock which I at once concluded belonged to the jays. The birds were but a few yards away, hopping about amid the neighboring branches uttering now and then their despairing note. Looking more intently at the nest, I became aware in the dim light of the tree of something looped about it, or else there was a dark, very crooked limb that partly held it. Suspecting the true nature of the case, I threw a stone up through the branches, and then another and another, when the dark loops and folds

137

upon one side of the nest began to disappear, and the head and neck of a black snake to slowly slide out on a horizontal branch on the other; in a moment the snake had cleared the nest, and stretched himself along the branch.

Another rock-fragment jarred his perch, when he slid cautiously along toward the branch of a large pine-tree which came out and mingled its spray with that of the hemlock. It was soon apparent that the snake was going to take refuge in the pine. As he made the passage from one tree to the other, we sought to dislodge him by a shower of sticks and stones, but without success; he was soon upon a large branch of the pine, and, stretched out on top of the limb, thought himself quite hidden. And so he was; but we knew his hiding-place, and the stones and clubs we hurled soon made him uneasy. Presently a club struck the branch with such force that he was fairly dislodged, but saved himself by quickly wrapping his tail about the limb. In this position he hung for some moments, but the intervening branches shielded him pretty well from our missiles, and he soon recovered himself and gained a still higher branch that reached out over the road and nearly made a bridge to the trees on the other side.

Seeing the monster was likely to escape us, unless we assailed him at closer quarters, I determined to climb the tree. A smaller tree growing near helped me up to the first branches, where the ascent was not very difficult. I finally reached the branch upon which the snake was carefully poised, and began shaking it. But he did not come down; he wrapped his tail about it, and defied me. My own position was precarious, and I was obliged to move with great circumspection.

After much manœuvring I succeeded in arming myself with a dry branch eight or ten feet long, where I had the serpent at a disadvantage. He kept his hold well. I clubbed him about from branch to branch, while my friends, with cautions and directions, looked on from beneath. Neither man nor snake will indulge in very lively antics in a treetop thirty or forty feet from the ground. But at last I dislodged him, and, swinging and looping like a piece of rubber hose, he went to the ground, where my friends pounced upon him savagely and quickly made an end of him.

I worked my way carefully down the tree, and was about to drop upon the ground from the lower branches, when I saw another black snake coiled up at the foot of the tree, as if lying in wait for me. Had he started to his mate's rescue, and, seeing the battle over, was he now waiting to avenge himself upon the victor? But the odds were against him; my friends soon had him stretched beside his comrade.

The first snake killed had swallowed two young jays just beginning to feather out.

How the serpent discovered the nest would be very interesting to know. What led him to search in this particular tree amid all these hundreds of trees that surrounded it ? It is probable that the snake watches like a cat, or, having seen the parent birds about this tree, explored it. Nests upon the ground and in low boughs are frequently rifled by black snakes, but I never before have known one to climb to such a height in a forest tree.

It would also be interesting to know if the other snake was in the secret of this nest, and was waiting near to share in its contents. One rarely has the patience to let these little dramas or tragedies be played to the end ; one cannot look quietly on, and see a snake devour anything. Not even when it is snake eat snake. Only a few days later my little boy called me to the garden to see a black snake in the act of swallowing a garter snake. The little snake was holding back with all his might and main, hooking his tail about the blackberry bushes, and pulling desperately; still his black enemy was slowly engulfing him, and had accomplished about eight or ten inches of him, when he suddenly grew alarmed at some motion of ours, and ejected the little snake from him with unexpected ease and quickness, and tried to escape. The little snake's head was bleeding, but he did not seem otherwise to have suffered from the adventure.

Still a few days later, the man who was mowing

the lawn called to me to come and witness a similar tragedy, but on a smaller scale, — a garter snake swallowing a little green snake. Half the length of the green snake had disappeared from sight, and it was quite dead. The process had been a slow one, as the garter snake was only two or three inches longer than his victim. There seems to be a sort of poetic justice in snake swallowing snake, shark eating shark, and one can look on with more composure than when a bird or frog is the victim. It is said that in the deep sea there is a fish that will swallow another fish eight or ten times its own size. It seizes its victim by the tail and slowly sucks it in, stretching and expanding itself at the same time, and probably digesting the big fish by inches, till, after many days, it is completely engulfed. Would it be hard to find something analogous to this in life, especially in American politics?

VII

A YOUNG MARSH HAWK

MOST country boys, I fancy, know the marsh hawk. It is he you see flying low over the fields, beating about bushes and marshes and dipping over the fences, with his attention directed to the ground beneath him. He is a cat on wings. He keeps so low that the birds and mice do not see him till he is fairly upon them. The hen-hawk swoops down upon the meadow-mouse from his position high in air, or from the top of a dead tree; but the marsh hawk stalks him and comes suddenly upon him from over the fence, or from behind a low bush or tuft of grass. He is nearly as large as the hen-hawk, but has a much longer tail. When I was a boy, I used to call him the long-tailed hawk. The male is a bluish slate color; the female a reddish brown, like the hen-hawk, with a white rump.

Unlike the other hawks, they nest on the ground in low, thick marshy places. For several seasons a pair have nested in a bushy marsh a few miles back of me, near the house of a farmer friend of mine, who has a keen eye for the wild life about him. Two years ago he found the nest, but when I got over to see it the next week, it had been robbed, probably by some boys in the neighborhood. The past season, in April or May, by watching the mother bird, he found the nest again. It was in a marshy place, several acres in extent, in the bottom of a valley, and thickly grown with hardhack, prickly ash, smilax, and other low thorny bushes. My friend brought me to the brink of a low hill, and pointed out to me in the marsh below us, as nearly as he could, just where the nest was located. Then we crossed the pasture, entered upon the marsh, and made our way cautiously toward it. The wild thorny growths, waist high, had to be carefully dealt with. As we neared the spot, I used my eyes the best I could, but I did not see the hawk till she sprang into the air not ten yards away from us. She went screaming upward, and was soon sailing in a circle far above us. There, on a coarse matting of twigs and weeds, lay five snow-white eggs, a little more than half as large as hens' eggs. My companion said the male hawk would probably soon appear and join the female, but he did not. She kept drifting away to the east, and was soon gone from our sight.

We soon withdrew and secreted ourselves behind the stone wall, in hopes of seeing the mother hawk return. She appeared in the distance, but seemed to know she was being watched, and kept away. About ten days later we made another visit to the nest. An adventurous young Chicago lady also wanted to see a hawk's nest, and so accompanied us. This time three of the eggs were hatched, and as the mother hawk sprang up, either by accident or intentionally, she threw two of the young hawks some feet from the nest. She rose up and screamed angrily. Then, turning toward us, she came like an arrow straight at the young lady, a bright plume in whose hat probably drew her fire. The damsel gathered up her skirts about her and beat a hasty retreat. Hawks were not so pretty as she thought they were. A large hawk launched at one's face from high in the air is calculated to make one a little nervous. It is such a fearful incline down which the bird comes, and she is aiming exactly toward your eye. When within about thirty feet of you, she turns upward with a rushing sound, and, mounting higher, falls toward you again. She is only firing blank cartridges, as it were ; but it usually has the desired effect, and beats the enemy off.

After we had inspected the young hawks, a neighbor of my friend offered to conduct us to a quail's nest. Anything in the shape of a nest is always welcome, it is such a mystery, such a centre of interest and affection, and, if upon the ground, is usually something so dainty and exquisite amid the natural wreckage and confusion. A ground-nest seems so exposed, too, that it always gives a little thrill of pleasurable surprise to see the group of frail eggs resting there behind so slight a barrier. I will walk a long distance any day just to see a song sparrow's nest amid the stubble or under a tuft of grass. It is a jewel in a rosette of jewels, with a frill of weeds or turf. A quail's nest I had never seen, and to be shown one within the hunting-ground of this murderous hawk would be a double pleasure. Such a quiet, secluded, grass-grown highway as we moved along was itself a rare treat. Sequestered was the word that the little valley suggested, and peace the feeling the road evoked. The farmer, whose fields lay about us, half grown with weeds and bushes, evidently did not make stir or noise enough to disturb anything. Beside this rustic highway, bounded by old mossy stone walls, and within a stone's throw of the farmer's barn, the quail had made her nest. It was just under the edge of a prostrate thorn-bush.

"The nest is right there," said the farmer, pausing within ten feet of it, and pointing to the spot with his stick.

In a moment or two we could make out the mottled brown plumage of the sitting bird. Then we approached her cautiously till we bent above her.

She never moved a feather.

Then I put my cane down in the brush behind her. We wanted to see the eggs, yet did not want rudely to disturb the sitting hen.

A YOUNG MARSH HAWK

She would not move.

Then I put down my hand within a few inches of her; still she kept her place. Should we have to lift her off bodily?

Then the young lady put down her hand, probably the prettiest and the whitest hand the quail had ever seen. At least it started her, and off she sprang, uncovering such a crowded nest of eggs as I had never before beheld. Twenty-one of them! a ring or disk of white like a china tea-saucer. You could not help saying How pretty! How cunning! like baby hens' eggs, as if the bird were playing at sitting as children play at housekeeping.

If I had known how crowded her nest was, I should not have dared disturb her, for fear she would break some of them. But not an egg suffered harm by her sudden flight; and no harm came to the nest afterward. Every egg hatched, I was told, and the little chicks, hardly bigger than bumblebees, were led away by the mother into the fields.

In about a week I paid another visit to the hawk's nest. The eggs were all hatched, and the mother bird was hovering near. I shall never forget the curious expression of those young hawks sitting there on the ground. The expression was not one of youth, but of extreme age. Such an ancient, infirm look as they had, — the sharp, dark, and shrunken look about the face and eyes, and their feeble, tottering motions! They sat upon their elbows and the hind part of their bodies, and their pale, withered legs and feet extended before them in the most helpless fashion. Their angular bodies were covered with a pale yellowish down, like that of a chicken; their heads had a plucked, seedy appearance; and their long, strong, naked wings hung down by their sides till they touched the ground: power and ferocity in the first rude draught, shorn of everything but its sinister ugliness. Another curious thing was the gradation of the young in size; they tapered down regularly from the first to the fifth, as if there had been, as probably there was, an interval of a day or two between the hatchings.

The two older ones showed some signs of fear on our approach, and one of them threw himself upon his back, and put up his impotent legs, and glared at us with open beak. The two smaller ones regarded us not at all. Neither of the parent birds appeared during our stay.

When I visited the nest again, eight or ten days later, the birds were much grown, but of as marked a difference in size as before, and with the same look of extreme old age, — old age in men of the aquiline type, nose and chin coming together, and eyes large and sunken. They now glared upon us with a wild, savage look, and opened their beaks threateningly.

The next week, when my friend visited the nest, the larger of the hawks fought him savagely. But one of the brood, probably the last to hatch, had made but little growth. It appeared to be on the point of starvation. The mother hawk (for the male seemed to have disappeared) had perhaps found her family too large for her, and was deliberately allowing one of the number to perish; or did the larger and stronger young devour all the food before the weaker member could obtain any? Probably this was the case.

Arthur brought the feeble nestling away, and the same day my little boy got it and brought it home, wrapped in a woolen rag. It was clearly a starved bantling. It cried feebly, but would not lift up its head.

We first poured some warm milk down its throat, which soon revived it, so that it would swallow small bits of flesh. In a day or two we had it eating ravenously, and its growth became noticeable. Its voice had the sharp whistling character of that of its parents, and was stilled only when the bird was asleep. We made a pen for it, about a yard square, in one end of the study, covering the floor with several thicknesses of newspapers; and here, upon a bit of brown woolen blanket for a nest, the hawk waxed strong day by day. An uglier-looking pet, tested by all the rules we usually apply to such things, would have been hard to find. There he would sit upon his elbows, his helpless feet out in front of him, his great featherless wings touching

the floor, and shrilly cry for more food. For a time
we gave him water daily from a stylograph-pen filler,
but the water he evidently did not need or relish.
Fresh meat, and plenty of it, was his demand. And
we soon discovered that he liked game, such as
mice, squirrels, birds, much better than butcher's
meat.

Then began a lively campaign on the part of my
little boy against all the vermin and small game in
the neighborhood, to keep the hawk supplied. He
trapped and he hunted, he enlisted his mates in his
service, he even robbed the cats to feed the hawk.
His usefulness as a boy of all work was seriously
impaired. "Where is J—— ?" "Gone after a squirrel for his hawk." And often the day would be half
gone before his hunt was successful. The premises
were very soon cleared of mice, and the vicinity of
chipmunks and squirrels. Farther and farther he
was compelled to hunt the surrounding farms and
woods to keep up with the demands of the hawk.
By the time the hawk was ready to fly, he had consumed twenty-one chipmunks, fourteen red squirrels, sixteen mice, and twelve English sparrows,
besides a lot of butcher's meat.

His plumage very soon began to show itself,
crowding off tufts of the down. The quills on his
great wings sprouted and grew apace. What a ragged, uncanny appearance he presented! but his look
of extreme age gradually became modified. What

a lover of the sunlight he was! We would put him out upon the grass in the full blaze of the morning sun, and he would spread his wings and bask in it with the most intense enjoyment. In the nest the young must be exposed to the full power of the midday sun during our first heated terms in June and July, the thermometer often going up to ninety-three or ninety-five degrees, so that sunshine seemed to be a need of his nature. He liked the rain equally well, and when put out in a shower would sit down and take it as if every drop did him good.

His legs developed nearly as slowly as his wings. He could not stand steadily upon them till about ten days before he was ready to fly. The talons were limp and feeble. When we came with food, he would hobble along toward us like the worst kind of a cripple, drooping and moving his wings, and treading upon his legs from the foot back to the elbow, the foot remaining closed and useless. Like a baby learning to stand, he made many trials before he succeeded. He would rise up on his trembling legs only to fall back again.

One day, in the summer-house, I saw him for the first time stand for a moment squarely upon his legs with the feet fully spread beneath them. He looked about him as if the world suddenly wore a new aspect.

His plumage now grew quite rapidly. One red squirrel a day, chopped fine with an axe, was his

ration. He began to hold his game with his foot
while he tore it. The study was full of his shed
down. His dark brown mottled plumage began to
grow beautiful. The wings drooped a little, but
gradually he got control of them, and held them in
place.

It was now the 20th of July, and the hawk was
about five weeks old. In a day or two he was walking or jumping about the ground. He chose a position under the edge of a Norway spruce, where he
would sit for hours dozing, or looking out upon the
landscape. When we brought him game, he would
advance to meet us with wings slightly lifted, and
uttering a shrill cry. Toss him a mouse or sparrow,
and he would seize it with one foot and hop off to
his cover, where he would bend above it, spread his
plumage, look this way and that, uttering all the
time the most exultant and satisfied chuckle.

About this time he began to practice striking with
his talons, as an Indian boy might begin practicing
with his bow and arrow. He would strike at a dry
leaf in the grass, or at a fallen apple, or at some
imaginary object. He was learning the use of his
weapons. His wings also, — he seemed to feel them
sprouting from his shoulders. He would lift them
straight up and hold them expanded, and they would
seem to quiver with excitement. Every hour in the
day he would do this. The pressure was beginning to centre there. Then he would strike play-

fully at a leaf or a bit of wood, and keep his wings lifted.

The next step was to spring into the air and beat his wings. He seemed now to be thinking entirely of his wings. They itched to be put to use.

A day or two later he would leap and fly several feet. A pile of brush ten or twelve feet below the bank was easily reached. Here he would perch in true hawk fashion, to the bewilderment and scandal of all the robins and catbirds in the vicinity. Here he would dart his eye in all directions, turning his head over and glancing up into the sky.

He was now a lovely creature, fully fledged, and as tame as a kitten. But he was not a bit like a kitten in one respect, — he could not bear to have you stroke or even touch his plumage. He had a horror of your hand, as if it would hopelessly defile him. But he would perch upon it, and allow you to carry him about. If a dog or cat appeared, he was ready to give battle instantly. He rushed up to a little dog one day, and struck him with his foot savagely. He was afraid of strangers, and of any unusual object.

The last week in July he began to fly quite freely, and it was necessary to clip one of his wings. As the clipping embraced only the ends of his primaries, he soon overcame the difficulty, and by carrying his broad, long tail more on that side, flew with considerable ease. He made longer and longer excursions into the surrounding fields and vineyards, and did not always return. On such occasions we would go find him and fetch him back.

Late one rainy afternoon he flew away into the vineyard, and when, an hour later, I went after him, he could not be found, and we never saw him again. We hoped hunger would soon drive him back, but we have had no clew to him from that day to this.

VIII

THE CHIPMUNK

THE first chipmunk in March is as sure a token of the spring as the first bluebird or the first robin; and it is quite as welcome. Some genial influence has found him out there in his burrow, deep under the ground, and waked him up, and enticed him forth into the light of day. The red squirrel has been more or less active all winter; his track has dotted the surface of every new-fallen snow throughout the season. But the chipmunk retired from view early in December, and has passed the rigorous months in his nest, beside his hoard of nuts, some feet underground, and hence, when he emerges in March, and is seen upon his little journeys along the fences, or perched upon a log or rock near his hole in the woods, it is another sign that spring is at hand. His store of nuts may or may not be all consumed; it is certain that he is no sluggard, to sleep away these first bright warm days.

Before the first crocus is out of the ground, you may look for the first chipmunk. When I hear the little downy woodpecker begin his spring drumming, then I know the chipmunk is due. He cannot sleep after that challenge of the woodpecker reaches his ear.

Apparently the first thing he does on coming forth, as soon as he is sure of himself, is to go courting. So far as I have observed, the love-making of the chipmunk occurs in March. A single female will attract all the males in the vicinity. One early March day I was at work for several hours near a stone fence, where a female had apparently taken up her quarters. What a train of suitors she had that day! how they hurried up and down, often giving each other a spiteful slap or bite as they passed. The young are born in May, four or five at a birth.

The chipmunk is quite a solitary creature; I have never known more than one to occupy the same den. Apparently no two can agree to live together. What a clean, pert, dapper, nervous little fellow he is ! How fast his heart beats, as he stands up on the wall by the roadside, and, with hands spread out upon his breast, regards you intently! A movement of your arm, and he darts into the wall with a saucy *chip-r-r*, which has the effect of slamming the door behind him.

On some still day in autumn, the nutty days, the woods will often be pervaded by an undertone of sound, produced by their multitudinous clucking, as they sit near their dens. It is one of the characteristic sounds of fall.

The chipmunk has many enemies, such as cats,

weasels, black snakes, hawks, and owls. One season one had his den in the side of the bank near my study. As I stood regarding his goings and comings, one October morning, I saw him, when a few yards away from his hole, turn and retreat with all speed. As he darted beneath the sod, a shrike swooped down and hovered a moment on the wing just over the hole where he had disappeared. I doubt if the shrike could have killed him, but it certainly gave him a good fright.

It was amusing to watch this chipmunk carry nuts and other food into his den. He had made a well-defined path from his door out through the weeds and dry leaves into the territory where his feeding-ground lay. The path was a crooked one; it dipped under weeds, under some large, loosely piled stones, under a pile of chestnut posts, and then followed the remains of an old wall. Going and coming, his motions were like clockwork. He always went by spurts and sudden sallies. He was never for one moment off his guard. He would appear at the mouth of his den, look quickly about, take a few leaps to a tussock of grass, pause a breath with one foot raised, slip quickly a few yards over some dry leaves, pause again by a stump beside a path, rush across the path to the pile of loose stones, go under the first and over the second, gain the pile of posts, make his way through that, survey his course a half moment from the other side of it, and then dart on to some other cover, and presently beyond my range, where I think he gathered acorns, as there were no other nut-bearing trees than oaks near. In four or five minutes I would see him coming back, always keeping rigidly to the course he took going out, pausing at the same spots, darting over or under the same objects, clearing at a bound the same pile of leaves. There was no variation in his manner of proceeding all the time I observed him.

He was alert, cautious, and exceedingly methodical. He had found safety in a certain course, and he did not at any time deviate a hair's breadth from it. Something seemed to say to him all the time, "Beware, beware!" The nervous, impetuous ways of these creatures are no doubt the result of the life of fear which they lead.

My chipmunk had no companion. He lived all by himself in true hermit fashion, as is usually the case with this squirrel. Provident creature that he is, one would think that he would long ago have discovered that heat, and therefore food, is economized by two or three nesting together.

One day in early spring, a chipmunk that lived near me met with a terrible adventure, the memory of which will probably be handed down through many generations of its family. I was sitting in the summer-house with Nig the cat upon my knee, when the chipmunk came out of its den a few feet away, and ran quickly to a pile of chestnut posts about twenty yards from where I sat. Nig saw it, and was off my lap upon the floor in an instant. I spoke sharply to the cat, when she sat down and folded her paws under her, and regarded the squirrel, as I thought, with only a dreamy kind of interest. I fancied she thought it a hopeless case there amid that pile of posts. "That is not your game, Nig," I said, "so spare yourself any anxiety." Just then I was called to the house, where I was detained about five minutes. As I returned, I met Nig coming to the house with the chipmunk in her mouth. She had the air of one who had won a wager. She carried the chipmunk by the throat, and its body hung limp from her mouth. I quickly took the squirrel from her, and reproved her sharply. It lay in my hand as if dead, though I saw no marks of the cat's teeth upon it. Presently it gasped for its breath, then again and again. I saw that the cat had simply choked it. Quickly the film passed off its eyes, its heart began visibly to beat, and slowly the breathing became regular. I carried it back, and laid it down in the door of its den. In a moment it crawled or kicked itself in. In the afternoon I placed a handful of corn there, to express my sympathy, and as far as possible make amends for Nig's cruel treatment.

Not till four or five days had passed did my little neighbor emerge again from its den, and then only for a moment. That terrible black monster with the large green-yellow eyes, — it might be still lurking

near. How the black monster had captured the alert
and restless squirrel so quickly, under the circumstances, was a great mystery to me. Was not its
eye as sharp as the cat's, and its movements as
quick? Yet cats do have the secret of catching squirrels, and birds, and mice, but I have never yet had
the luck to see it done.

It was not very long before the chipmunk was
going to and from its den as usual, though the dread
of the black monster seemed ever before it, and
gave speed and extra alertness to all its movements.
In early summer four young chipmunks emerged
from the den, and ran freely about. There was nothing to disturb them, for, alas! Nig herself was
now dead.

One summer day I watched a cat for nearly a half
hour trying her arts upon a chipmunk that sat upon
a pile of stone. Evidently her game was to stalk
him. She had cleared half the distance, or about
twelve feet, that separated the chipmunk from a
dense Norway spruce, when I chanced to become
a spectator of the little drama. There sat the cat
crouched low on the grass, her big yellow eyes fixed
upon the chipmunk, and there sat the chipmunk
at the mouth of his den, motionless, with his eye
fixed upon the cat. For a long time neither moved.
"Will the cat bind him with her fatal spell?" I
thought. Sometimes her head slowly lowered and
her eyes seemed to dilate, and I fancied she was

160

about to spring. But she did not. The distance was too great to be successfully cleared in one bound. Then the squirrel moved nervously, but kept his eye upon the enemy. Then the cat evidently grew tired and relaxed a little and looked behind her. Then she crouched again and riveted her gaze upon the squirrel. But the latter would not be hypnotized; it shifted its position a few times and finally quickly entered its den, when the cat soon slunk away.

In digging his hole, it is evident that the chipmunk carries away the loose soil. Never a grain of it is seen in front of his door. Those pockets of his probably stand him in good stead on such occasions. Only in one instance have I seen a pile of earth before the entrance to a chipmunk's den, and that was where the builder had begun his house late in November, and was probably too much hurried to remove this ugly mark from before his door. I used to pass his place every morning in my walk, and my eye always fell upon that little pile of red, freshly dug soil. A little later I used frequently to surprise the squirrel furnishing his house, carrying in dry leaves of the maple and plane tree. He would seize a large leaf and with both hands stuff it into his cheek pockets, and then carry it into his den. I saw him on several different days occupied in this way. I trust he had secured his winter stores, though I am a little doubtful. He was hurriedly making himself a new home, and the cold of December was upon us while he was yet at work. It may be that he had moved the stores from his old quarters, wherever they were, and again it may be that he had been dispossessed of both his house and provender by some other chipmunk.

When nuts or grain are not to be had, these thrifty little creatures will find some substitute to help them over the winter. Two chipmunks near my study were occupied many days in carrying in cherry pits which they gathered beneath a large cherry-tree that stood ten or twelve rods away. As Nig was no longer about to molest them, they grew very fearless, and used to spin up and down the garden path to and from their source of supplies in a way quite unusual with these timid creatures. After they had got enough cherry pits, they gathered the seed of a sugar maple that stood near. Many of the keys remained upon the tree after the leaves had fallen, and these the squirrels harvested. They would run swiftly out upon the ends of the small branches, reach out for the maple keys, snip off the wings, and deftly slip the nut or samara into their cheek pockets. Day after day in late autumn, I used to see them thus occupied.

As I have said, I have no evidence that more than one chipmunk occupies the same den. One March morning, after a light fall of snow, I saw where one had come up out of his hole, which was in the side of our path to the vineyard, and after a moment's survey of the surroundings had started off on his travels. I followed the track to see where he had gone. He had passed through my woodpile, then under the beehives, then around the study and under some spruces and along the slope to the hole of a friend of his, about sixty yards from his own. Apparently he had gone in here, and then his friend had come forth with him, for there were two tracks leading from this doorway. I followed them to a third humble entrance, not far off, where the tracks were so numerous that I lost the trail. It was pleasing to see the evidence of their morning sociability written there upon the new snow.

One of the enemies of the chipmunk, as I discovered lately, is the weasel. I was sitting in the woods one autumn day when I heard a small cry, and a rustling amid the branches of a tree a few rods beyond me. Looking thither, I saw a chipmunk fall through the air, and catch on a limb twenty or more feet from the ground. He appeared to have dropped from near the top of the tree.

He secured his hold upon the small branch that had luckily intercepted his fall, and sat perfectly still. In a moment more I saw a weasel — one of the smaller red varieties — come down the trunk of the tree, and begin exploring the branches on a level with the chipmunk.

I saw in a moment what had happened. The weasel had driven the squirrel from his retreat in the rocks and stones beneath, and had pressed him so closely that he had taken refuge in the top of a tree. But weasels can climb trees, too, and this one had tracked the frightened chipmunk to the topmost branch, where he had tried to seize him. Then the squirrel had, in horror, let go his hold, screamed, and fallen through the air, till he struck the branch as just described. Now his bloodthirsty enemy was looking for him again, apparently relying entirely upon his sense of smell to guide him to the game.

How did the weasel know the squirrel had not fallen clear to the ground? He certainly did know, for when he reached the same tier of branches, he began exploring them. The chipmunk sat transfixed with fear, frozen with terror, not twelve feet away, and yet the weasel saw him not.

Round and round, up and down, he went on the branches, exploring them over and over. How he hurried, lest the trail get cold! How subtle and cruel and fiendish he looked! His snakelike movements, his tenacity, his speed!

He seemed baffled; he knew his game was near, but he could not strike the spot. The branch, upon the extreme end of which the squirrel sat, ran out and up from the tree seven or eight feet, and then, turning a sharp elbow, swept down and out at right angles with its first course.

The weasel would pause each time at this elbow and turn back. It seemed as if he knew that particular branch held his prey, and yet its crookedness each time threw him out. He would not give it up, but went over his course again and again.

One can fancy the feelings of the chipmunk, sitting there in plain view a few feet away, watching its deadly enemy hunting for the clew. How its little heart must have fairly stood still each time the fatal branch was struck! Probably as a last resort it would again have let go its hold and fallen to the ground, where it might have eluded its enemy awhile longer.

In the course of five or six minutes the weasel gave over the search, and ran hurriedly down the tree to the ground. The chipmunk remained motionless for a long time; then he stirred a little as if hope was reviving. Then he looked nervously about him; then he had recovered himself so far as to change his position. Presently he began to move cautiously along the branch to the bole of the tree; then, after a few moments' delay, he plucked up courage to descend to the ground, where I hope no weasel has disturbed him since.

IX

SPRING JOTTINGS

FOR ten or more years past I have been in the habit of jotting down, among other things in my note-book, observations upon the seasons as they passed, — the complexion of the day, the aspects of nature, the arrival of the birds, the opening of the flowers, or any characteristic feature of the passing moment or hour which the great open-air panorama presented. Some of these notes and observations touching the opening and the progress of the spring season follow herewith.

I need hardly say they are off-hand and informal; what they have to recommend them to the general reader is mainly their fidelity to actual fact. The sun always crosses the line on time, but the seasons which he makes are by no means so punctual; they loiter or they hasten, and the spring tokens are three or four weeks earlier or later some seasons than others. The ice often breaks up on the river early in March, but I have crossed upon it as late as the 10th of April. My journal presents many samples of both early and late springs.

But before I give these extracts, let me say a word

or two in favor of the habit of keeping a journal of
one's thoughts and days. To a countryman, especially of a meditative turn, who likes to preserve the
flavor of the passing moment, or to a person of leisure anywhere, who wants to make the most of life,
a journal will be found a great help. It is a sort
of deposit account wherein one saves up bits and
fragments of his life that would otherwise be lost
to him.

What seemed so insignificant in the passing, or as
it lay in embryo in his mind, becomes a valuable
part of his experiences when it is fully unfolded and
recorded in black and white. The process of writing
develops it; the bud becomes the leaf or flower;
the one is disentangled from the many and takes
definite form and hue. I remember that Thoreau
says in a letter to a friend, after his return from a
climb to the top of Monadnock, that it is not till he
gets home that he really goes over the mountain;
that is, I suppose, sees what the climb meant to
him when he comes to write an account of it to his
friend. Every one's experience is probably much
the same; when we try to tell what we saw and felt,
even to our journals, we discover more and deeper
meanings in things than we had suspected.

The pleasure and value of every walk or journey
we take may be doubled to us by carefully noting
down the impressions it makes upon us. How much
of the flavor of Maine birch I should have missed

had I not compelled that vague, unconscious being within me, who absorbs so much and says so little, to unbosom himself at the point of the pen! It was not till after I got home that I really went to Maine, or to the Adirondacks, or to Canada. Out of the chaotic and nebulous impressions which these expeditions gave me, I evolved the real experience. There is hardly anything that does not become much more in the telling than in the thinking or in the feeling.

I see the fishermen floating up and down the river above their nets, which are suspended far out of sight in the water beneath them. They do not know what fish they have got, if any, till after a while they lift the nets up and examine them. In all of us there is a region of subconsciousness above which our ostensible lives go forward, and in which much comes to us, or is slowly developed, of which we are quite ignorant until we lift up our nets and inspect them.

Then the charm and significance of a day are so subtle and fleeting! Before we know it, it is gone past all recovery. I find that each spring, that each summer and fall and winter of my life, has a hue and quality of its own, given by some prevailing mood, a train of thought, an event, an experience, — a color or quality of which I am quite unconscious at the time, being too near to it, and too completely enveloped by it. But afterward some mood or circumstance, an odor, or fragment of a tune, brings it back as by a flash; for one brief second the adamantine door of the past swings open and gives me a glimpse of my former life. One's journal, dashed off without any secondary motive, may often preserve and renew the past for him in this way.

These leaves from my own journal are not very good samples of this sort of thing, but they preserve for me the image of many a day which memory alone could never have kept.

March 3, 1879. The sun is getting strong, but winter still holds his own. No hint of spring in the earth or air. No sparrow or sparrow song yet. But on the 5th there was a hint of spring. The day warm and the snow melting. The first bluebird note this morning. How sweetly it dropped down from the blue overhead!

March 10. A real spring day at last, and a rouser! Thermometer between fifty and sixty degrees in the coolest spot; bees very lively about the hive, and working on the sawdust in the wood-yard; how they dig and wallow in the woody meal, apparently squeezing it, as if forcing it to yield up something to them! Here they get their first substitute for pollen. The sawdust of hickory and maple is preferred. The inner milky substance between the bark and the wood, called the cambium layer, is probably the source of their supplies.

In the growing tree it is in this layer or secretion

that the vital processes are the most active and potent. It has been found by experiment that this tender, milky substance is capable of exerting a very great force; a growing tree exerts a lifting and pushing force of more than thirty pounds to the square inch, and the force is thought to reside in the soft, fragile cells that make up the cambium layer. It is like the strength of Samson residing in his hair. Saw one bee enter the hive with pollen on his back, which he must have got from some open greenhouse; or had he found the skunk cabbage in bloom ahead of me?

The bluebirds! It seemed as if they must have been waiting somewhere close by for the first warm day, like actors behind the scenes, for they were here in numbers early in the morning; they rushed upon the stage very promptly when their parts were called. No robins yet. Sap runs, but not briskly. It is too warm and still; it wants a brisk day for sap, with a certain sharpness in the air, a certain crispness and tension.

March 12. A change to more crispness and coolness, but a delicious spring morning. Hundreds of snowbirds with a sprinkling of song and Canada sparrows are all about the house, chirping and lisping and chattering in a very animated manner. The air is full of bird voices; through this maze of fine sounds comes the strong note and warble of the robin, and the soft call of the bluebird. A few days ago, not a bird, not a sound; everything rigid and severe; then in a day the barriers of winter give way, and spring comes like an inundation. In a twinkling all is changed.

Under date of February 27, 1881, I find this note: "Warm; saw the male bluebird warbling and calling cheerily. The male bluebird spreads his tail as he flits about at this season, in a way to make him look very gay and dressy. It adds to his expression considerably, and makes him look alert and beau-like, and every inch a male. The grass is green under the snow, and has grown perceptibly. The warmth of the air seems to go readily through a covering of ice and snow. Note how quickly the ice lets go of the door-stones, though completely covered, when the day becomes warm."

The farmers say a deep snow draws the frost out of the ground. It is certain that the frost goes out when the ground is deeply covered for some time, though it is of course the warmth rising up from the depths of the ground that does it. A winter of deep snows is apt to prove fatal to the peach buds. The frost leaves the ground, the soil often becomes so warm that angle-worms rise to near the surface, the sap in the trees probably stirs a little; then there comes a cold wave, the mercury goes down to ten or fifteen below zero, and the peach buds are killed. It is not the cold alone that does it; it is the warmth at one end and the extreme cold at the other. When

172

the snow is removed so that the frost can get at the roots also, peach buds will stand fourteen or fifteen degrees below zero.

March 7, 1881. A perfect spring day at last, — still, warm, and without a cloud. Tapped two trees; the sap runs, the snow runs, everything runs. Bluebirds the only birds yet. Thermometer forty-two degrees in the shade. A perfect sap day. A perfect sap day is a crystalline day; the night must have a keen edge of frost, and the day a keen edge of air and sun, with wind north or northwest. The least film, the least breath from the south, the least suggestion of growth, and the day is marred as a sap day. Maple sap is maple frost melted by the sun. (9 P. M.) A soft, large-starred night; the moon in her second quarter; perfectly still and freezing; Venus throbbing low in the west. A crystalline night.

March 21, 1884. The top of a high barometric wave, a day like a crest, lifted up, sightly, sparkling. A cold snap without storm issuing in this clear, dazzling, sharp, northern day. How light, as if illuminated by more than the sun; the sky is full of light; light seems to be streaming up all around the horizon. The leafless trees make no shadows; the woods are flooded with light; everything shines; a day large and imposing, breathing strong masculine breaths out of the north; a day without a speck or film, winnowed through and through, all the windows and doors of the sky open. Day of crumpled rivers and lakes, of crested waves, of bellying sails, high-domed and lustrous day. The only typical March day of the bright heroic sort we have yet had.

March 24, 1884. Damp, still morning, much fog on the river. All the branches and twigs of the trees strung with drops of water. The grass and weeds beaded with fog drops. Two lines of ducks go up the river, one a few feet beneath the other. On second glance the under line proves to be the reflection of the other in the still water. As the ducks cross a large field of ice, the lower line is suddenly blotted out, as if the birds had dived beneath the ice. A train of cars across the river, — the train sunk beneath a solid stratum of fog, its plume of smoke and vapor unrolling above it and slanting away in the distance; a liquid morning; the turf buzzes as you walk over it.

Skunk cabbage on Saturday the 22d, probably in bloom several days. This plant always gets ahead of me. It seems to come up like a mushroom in a single night. Water newts just out, and probably piping before the frogs, though not certain about this.

March 25. One of the rare days that go before a storm; the flower of a series of days increasingly fair. To-morrow, probably, the flower falls, and days of rain and cold prepare the way for another fair day or days. The barometer must be high to-day; the birds fly high. I feed my bees on a rock, and sit long and watch them covering the combs, and rejoice in the multitudinous humming. The river is a great mirror dotted here and there by small cakes of ice. The first sloop comes lazily on up the flood tide, like the first butterfly of spring; the little steamer, our river omnibus, makes her first trip, and wakes the echoes with her salutatory whistle, her flags dancing in the sun.

April 1. Welcome to April, my natal month; the month of the swelling buds, the springing grass, the first nests, the first plantings, the first flowers, and, last but not least, the first shad! The door of the seasons first stands ajar this month, and gives us a peep beyond. The month in which to begin the world, in which to begin your house, in which to begin your courtship, in which to enter upon any new enterprise. The bees usually get their first pollen this month and their first honey. All hibernating creatures are out before April is past. The coon, the chipmunk, the bear, the turtles, the frogs, the snakes, come forth beneath April skies.

April 8. A day of great brightness and clearness, — a crystalline April day that precedes snow. In this sharp crisp air the flakes are forming. As in a warm streaming south wind one can almost smell the swelling buds, so a wind from the opposite quarter at this season as often suggests the crystalline snow. I go up in the sugar bush [this was up among the Catskills], and linger for an hour among the

175

old trees. The air is still, and has the property of being "hollow," as the farmers say; that is, it is heavy, motionless, and transmits sounds well. Every warble of a bluebird or robin, or caw of crow, or bark of dog, or bleat of sheep, or cackle of geese, or call of boy or man, within the landscape, comes distinctly to the ear. The smoke from the chimney goes straight up.

I walk through the bare fields; the shore larks run or flit before me; I hear their shuffling, gurgling, lisping, half-inarticulate song. Only of late years have I noticed the shore larks in this section. Now they breed and pass the summer on these hills, and I am told that they are gradually becoming permanent residents in other parts of the State. They are nearly as large as the English skylark, with conspicuous black markings about the head and throat; shy birds squatting in the sere grass, and probably taken by most country people who see them to be sparrows.

Their flight and manner in song is much like that of the skylark. The bird mounts up and up on ecstatic wing, till it becomes a mere speck against the sky, where it drifts to and fro, and utters at intervals its crude song, a mere fraction or rudiment of the skylark's song, a few sharp, lisping, unmelodious notes, as if the bird had a bad cold, and could only now and then make any sound, — heard a long distance, but insignificant, a mere germ of the true

lark's song; as it were the first rude attempt of nature in this direction. After due trial and waiting,
it develops the lark's song itself. But if the law
of evolution applies to bird-songs as well as to other
things, the shore lark should in time become a fine
songster. I know of no bird-song that seems so
obviously struggling to free itself and reach a fuller
expression. As the bird seems more and more inclined to abide permanently amid cultivated fields,
and to forsake the wild and savage north, let us
hope that its song is also undergoing a favorable
change.

How conspicuous the crows in the brown fields,
or against the lingering snow-banks, or in the clear
sky! How still the air! One could carry a lighted
candle over the hills. The light is very strong, and
the effect of the wall of white mountains rising up all
around from the checkered landscape, and holding
up the blue dome of the sky, is strange indeed.

April 14. A delicious day, warm as May. This
to me is the most bewitching part of the whole year.
One's relish is so keen, and the morsels are so few
and so tender. How the fields of winter rye stand
out! They call up visions of England. A perfect day
in April far excels a perfect day in June, because it
provokes and stimulates while the latter sates and
cloys. Such days have all the peace and geniality
of summer without any of its satiety or enervating
heat.

April 15. Not much cloud this morning, but much vapor in the air. A cool south wind with streaks of a pungent vegetable odor, probably from the willows. When I make too dead a set at it, I miss it; but when I let my nose have its own way, and take in the air slowly, I get it, an odor as of a myriad swelling buds. The long-drawn call of the high-hole comes up from the fields, then the tender rapid trill of the bush or russet sparrow, then the piercing note of the meadowlark, a flying shaft of sound.

April 21. The enchanting days continue without a break. One's senses are not large enough to take them all in. Maple buds just bursting, apple-trees full of infantile leaves. How the poplars and willows stand out! A moist, warm, brooding haze over all the earth. All day my little russet sparrow sings and trills divinely. The most prominent bird music in April is from the sparrows.

The yellowbirds (goldfinches) are just getting on their yellow coats. I saw some yesterday that had a smutty, unwashed look, because of the new yellow shining through the old drab-colored webs of the feathers. These birds do not shed their feathers in the spring, as careless observers are apt to think they do, but merely shed the outer webs of their feathers and quills, which peel off like a glove from the hand.

All the groves and woods lightly touched with new foliage. Looks like May; violets and dandelions in bloom. Sparrow's nest with two eggs. Maples hanging out their delicate fringe-like bloom. First barn swallows may be looked for any day after April 20.

This period may be called the vernal equipoise, and corresponds to the October calm called the Indian summer.

April 2, 1890. The second of the April days, clear as a bell. The eye of the heavens wide open at last. A sparrow day; how they sang! And the robins, too, before I was up in the morning. Now and then I could hear the rat-tat-tat of the downy at his drum. How many times I paused at my work to drink in the beauty of the day!

How I like to walk out after supper these days! I stroll over the lawn and stand on the brink of the hill. The sun is down, the robins pipe and call, and as the dusk comes on, they indulge in that loud chiding note or scream, whether in anger or in fun I never can tell. Up the road in the distance the multitudinous voice of the little peepers, — a thicket or screen of sound. An April twilight is unlike any other.

April 12. Lovely, bright day. We plow the ground under the hill for the new vineyard. In opening the furrow for the young vines I guide the team by walking in their front. How I soaked up the sunshine to-day! At night I glowed all over; my whole being had had an earth-bath; such a feeling of freshly plowed land in every cell of my brain. The furrow had struck in; the sunshine had photographed it upon my soul.

April 13. A warm, even hot April day. The air full of haze; the sunshine golden. In the afternoon J. and I walk out over the country north of town. Everybody is out, all the paths and byways are full of boys and young fellows. We sit on a wall a long time by a meadow and an orchard, and drink in the scene. April to perfection, such a sentiment of spring everywhere. The sky is partly overcast, the air moist, just enough so to bring out the odors, — a sweet perfume of bursting, growing things. One could almost eat the turf like a horse. All about the robins sang. In the trees the crow blackbird cackled and jingled. Athwart these sounds came every half minute the clear, strong note of the meadowlark. The larks were very numerous and were lovemaking. Then the high-hole called and the bush sparrow trilled. Arbutus days these, everybody wants to go to the woods for arbutus; it fairly calls one. The soil calls for the plow, too, the garden calls for the spade, the vineyard calls for the hoe. From all about the farm voices call, Come and do this, or do that. At night, how the "peepers" pile up the sound!

How I delight to see the plow at work such mornings! the earth is ripe for it, fairly lusts for it, and the freshly turned soil looks good enough to eat.

180

Plucked my first blood-root this morning, — a full blown flower with a young one folded up in a leaf beneath it, only the bud emerging, like the head of a pappoose protruding from its mother's blanket, — a very pretty sight. The blood-root always comes up with the leaf shielding the flower-bud, as one shields the flame of the candle in the open air with his hand half closed about it.

These days the song of the toad — *tr-r-r-r-r-r-r-r-r-r-r-r-r-r-r-r-r-r* — is heard in the land. At nearly all hours I hear it, and it is as welcome to me as the song of any bird. It is a kind of gossamer of sound drifting in the air. Mother toad is in the pools and puddles now depositing that long chain or raveling of eggs, while her dapper little mate rides upon her back and fertilizes them as they are laid. As I look toward the fields where the first brown thrasher is singing, I see emerald patches of rye. The unctuous, confident strain of the bird seems to make the fields grow greener hour by hour.

May 4. The perfection of early May weather. How green the grass, how happy the birds, how placid the river, how busy the bees, how soft the air! — that kind of weather when there seems to be dew in the air all day, — the day a kind of prolonged morning, — so fresh, so wooing, so caressing! The baby leaves on the apple-trees have doubled in size since last night.

March 12, 1891. Had positive proof this morning that at least one song sparrow has come back to his haunts of a year ago. One year ago to-day my attention was attracted, while walking over to the post-office, by an unfamiliar bird-song. It caught my ear while I was a long way off. I followed it up and found that it proceeded from a song sparrow. Its chief feature was one long, clear high note, very strong, sweet, and plaintive. It sprang out of the trills and quavers of the first part of the bird-song, like a long arc or parabola of sound. To my mental vision it rose far up against the blue, and turned sharply downward again and finished in more trills and quavers. I had never before heard anything like it. It was the usual long, silvery note in the sparrow's song greatly increased; indeed, the whole breath and force of the bird were put in this note, so that you caught little else than this silver loop of sound. The bird remained in one locality — the bushy corner of a field — the whole season. He indulged in the ordinary sparrow song, also. I had repeatedly had my eye upon him when he changed from one to the other.

And now here he is again, just a year after, in the same place, singing the same remarkable song, capturing my ear with the same exquisite lasso of sound. What would I not give to know just where he passed the winter, and what adventures by flood and field befell him!

(I will add that the bird continued in song the

Bloodroot

whole season, apparently confining his wanderings to a few acres of ground. But the following spring he did not return, and I have never heard him since, and if any of his progeny inherited this peculiar song, I have not heard them.)

X

GLIMPSES OF WILD LIFE

I

ANY glimpse of the wild and savage in nature, especially after long confinement indoors or in town, always gives a little fillip to my mind. Thus, when, in my walk from the city the other day, I paused, after a half hour, in a thick clump of red cedars crowning a little hill that arose amid a marshy and bushy bit of landscape, and found myself in the banqueting-hall of a hawk, something more than my natural history tastes stirred within me.

No hawk was there then, but the marks of his nightly presence were very obvious. The branch of a cedar about fifteen feet from the ground was his perch. It was worn smooth, with a feather or two adhering to it. The ground beneath was covered with large pellets and wads of mouse-hair; the leaves were white with his droppings, while the dried entrails of his victims clung here and there to the bushes. The bird evidently came here nightly to devour and digest its prey. This was its den, its retreat; all about lay its feeding-grounds. It revealed to me a new trait in the hawk, — its local attachments and habits; that it, too, had a home, and did not wander about like a vagabond. It had its domain, which it no doubt assiduously cultivated. Here it came to dine and meditate, and a most attractive spot it had chosen, a kind of pillared cave amid the cedars. It was such a spot as the pedestrian would be sure to direct his steps to, and, having reached it, would be equally sure to tarry and eat his own lunch there.

The winged creatures are probably quite as local as the four-footed. Sitting one night on a broad, gently rising hill, to see the darkness close in upon the landscape, my attention was attracted by a marsh hawk industriously working the fields about me. Time after time he made the circuit, varying but little in his course each time; dropping into the grass here and there, beating low over the bogs and bushes, and then disappearing in the distance. This was his domain, his preserve, and doubtless he had his favorite perch not far off.

All our permanent residents among the birds, both large and small, are comparatively limited in their ranges. The crow is nearly as local as the woodchuck. He goes farther from home in quest of food, but his territory is well defined, both winter and summer. His place of roosting remains the same year after year. Once, while spending a few days at a mountain lake nearly surrounded by deep woods, my attention was attracted each night, just at sundown, by an osprey that always came from the same direction, dipped into the lake as he passed over it for a sip of its pure water, and disappeared in the woods beyond. The routine of his life was probably as marked as that of any of us. He fished the waters of the Delaware all day, doubtless never going beyond a certain limit, and returned each night at sundown, as punctual as a day-laborer, to his retreat in the forest. The sip of water, too, from the lake he never failed to take.

All the facts we possess in regard to the habits of the song-birds in this respect point to the conclusion that the same individuals return to the same localities year after year, to nest and to rear their young. I am convinced that the same woodpecker occupies the same cavity in a tree winter after winter, and drums upon the same dry limb spring after spring. I like to think of all these creatures as capable of local attachments, and not insensible to the sentiment of home.

But I set out to give some glimpses of the wild life which one gets about the farm. Not of a startling nature are they, certainly, but very welcome for all that. The domestic animals require their lick of salt every week or so, and the farmer, I think, is equally glad to get a taste now and then of the wild life that has so nearly disappeared from the older and more thickly settled parts of the country.

Last winter a couple of bears, an old one and a young one, passed through our neighborhood. Their tracks were seen upon the snow in the woods, and the news created great excitement among the Nimrods. It was like the commotion in the water alongshore after a steamer had passed. The bears were probably safely in the Catskills by the time the hunters got dogs and guns ready and set forth. Country people are as eager to accept any rumor of a strange and dangerous creature in the woods as they are to believe in a ghost story. They want it to be true; it gives them something to think about and talk about. It is to their minds like strong drink to their palates. It gives a new interest to the woods, as the ghost story gives a new interest to the old house.

A few years ago, the belief became current in our neighborhood that a dangerous wild animal lurked in the woods about, now here, now there. It had been seen in the dusk. Some big dogs had encountered it in the night, and one of them was nearly killed. Then a calf and a sheep were reported killed and partly devoured. Women and children became afraid to go through the woods, and men avoided them after sundown. One day, as I passed an Irishman's shanty that stood in an opening in the woods, his wife came out with a pail, and begged leave to accompany me as far as the spring, which lay beside the road some distance into the woods. She was

188

afraid to go alone for water on account of the "wild baste." Then, to cap the climax of wild rumors, a horse was killed. One of my neighbors, an intelligent man and a good observer, went up to see the horse. He reported that a great gash had been eaten in the top of the horse's neck; that its back was bitten and scratched; and that he was convinced it was the work of some wild animal like a panther which had landed upon the horse's back, and fairly devoured it alive. The horse had run up and down the field trying to escape, and finally, in its desperation, had plunged headlong off a high stone wall by the barn and been killed. I was compelled to accept his story, but I pooh-poohed the conclusions. It was impossible that we should have a panther in the midst of us, or, if we had, that it would attack and kill a horse. But how eagerly the people believed it! It tasted good. It tasted good to me, too, but I could not believe it. It soon turned out that the horse was killed by another horse, a vicious beast that had fits of murderous hatred toward its kind. The sheep and calf were probably not killed at all, and the big dogs had had a fight among themselves. So the panther legend faded out, and our woods became as tame and humdrum as before. We cannot get up anything exciting that will hold, and have to make the most of such small deer as coons, foxes, and woodchucks. Glimpses of these and of the birds are all I have to report.

II

The day on which I have any adventure with a wild creature, no matter how trivial, has a little different flavor from the rest; as when, one morning in early summer, I put my head out of the back window and returned the challenge of a quail that sent forth his clear call from a fence-rail one hundred yards away. Instantly he came sailing over the field of raspberries straight toward me. When about fifteen yards away, he dropped into the cover and repeated his challenge. I responded, when in an instant he was almost within reach of me. He alighted under the window, and looked quickly around for his rival. How his eyes shone, how his form dilated, how dapper and polished and brisk he looked! He turned his eye up to me and seemed to say, " Is it you, then, who are mocking me? " and ran quickly around the corner of the house. Here he lingered some time amid the rosebushes, half persuaded that the call, which I still repeated, came from his rival. Ah, I thought, if with his mate and young he would only make my field his home! The call of the quail is a country sound that is becoming all too infrequent.

So fond am I of seeing Nature reassert herself that I even found some compensation in the loss of my chickens that bright November night when some wild creature, coon or fox, swept two of them out of the evergreens, and their squawking as they were hurried across the lawn called me from my bed to shout good-by after them. It gave a new interest to the hen-roost, this sudden incursion of wild nature. I feel bound to caution the boys about disturbing the wild rabbits that in summer breed in my currant-patch, and in autumn seek refuge under my study floor. The occasional glimpses I get of them about the lawn in the dusk, their cotton tails twinkling in the dimness, afford me a genuine pleasure. I have seen the time when I would go a good way to shoot a partridge, but I would not have killed, if I could, the one that started out of the vines that cover my rustic porch, as I approached that side of the house one autumn morning. How much of the woods, and of the untamable spirit of wild nature, she brought to my very door! It was tonic and exhilarating to see her whirl away toward the vineyard. I also owe a moment's pleasure to the gray squirrel that, finding my summer-house in the line of his travels one summer day, ran through it and almost over my feet as I sat idling with a book.

I am sure my power of digestion was improved that cold winter morning when, just as we were sitting down to breakfast about sunrise, a red fox loped along in front of the window, looking neither to the right nor to the left, and disappeared amid the currant-bushes. What of the wild and the cunning did he not bring! His graceful form and motion were

in my mind's eye all day. When you have seen a
fox loping along in that way, you have seen the
poetry there is in the canine tribe. It is to the eye
what a flowing measure is to the mind, so easy, so
buoyant ; the furry creature drifting along like a
large red thistledown, or like a plume borne by the
wind. It is something to remember with pleasure,
that a muskrat sought my door one December night
when a cold wave was swooping down upon us. Was
he seeking shelter, or had he lost his reckoning?
The dogs cornered him in the very doorway, and
set up a great hubbub. In the darkness, thinking
it was a cat, I put my hand down to feel it. The
creature skipped to the other corner of the doorway, hitting my hand with its cold, rope-like tail.
Lighting a match, I had a glimpse of him sitting
up on his haunches like a woodchuck, confronting
his enemies. I rushed in for the lantern, with the
hope of capturing him alive, but before I returned
the dogs, growing bold, had finished him.

I have had but one call from a coon, that I am
aware of, and I fear we did not treat him with due
hospitality. He took up his quarters for the day
in a Norway spruce, the branches of which nearly
brushed the house. I had noticed that the dog was
very curious about that tree all the forenoon. After
dinner his curiosity culminated in repeated loud and
confident barking. Then I began an investigation,
expecting to find a strange cat, or at most a red

squirrel. But a moment's scrutiny revealed his coon-ship. Then how to capture him became the problem. A long pole was procured, and I sought to dislodge him from his hold. The skill with which he maintained himself amid the branches excited our admiration. But after a time he dropped lightly to the ground, not in the least disconcerted, and at once on his guard against both man and beast. The dog was a coward, and dared not face him. When the coon's attention was diverted, the dog would rush in; then one of us would attempt to seize the coon's tail, but he faced about so quickly, his black eyes gleaming, that the hand was timid about seizing him. But finally in his skirmishing with the dog I caught him by the tail, and bore him safely to an open flour barrel, and he was our prisoner. Much amusement my little boy and I anticipated with him. He partook of food that same day, and on the second day would eat the chestnuts in our presence. Never did he show the slightest fear of us or of anything, but he was unwearied in his efforts to regain his freedom. After a few days we put a strap upon his neck and kept him tethered by a chain. But in the night, by dint of some hocus-pocus, he got the chain unsnapped and made off, and is now, I trust, a patriarch of his tribe, wearing a leather necktie.

The skunk visits every farm sooner or later. One night I came near shaking hands with one on my very door-stone. I thought it was the cat, and put down my hand to stroke it, when the creature, probably appreciating my mistake, moved off up the bank, revealing to me the white stripe on its body and the kind of cat I had saluted. The skunk is not easily ruffled, and seems to employ excellent judgment in the use of its terrible weapon.

Several times I have had calls from woodchucks. One looked in at the open door of my study one day, and, after sniffing awhile, and not liking the smell of such clover as I was compelled to nibble there, moved on to better pastures. Another one invaded the kitchen door while we were at dinner. The dogs promptly challenged him, and there was a lively scrimmage upon the door-stone. I thought the dogs were fighting, and rushed to part them. The incident broke in upon the drowsy summer noon, as did the appearance of the muskrat upon the frigid December night. The woodchuck episode that afforded us the most amusement occurred last summer. We were at work in a newly planted vineyard, when the man with the cultivator saw, a few yards in front of him, some large gray object that at first puzzled him. He approached it, and found it to be an old woodchuck with a young one in her mouth. She was carrying her kitten as does a cat, by the nape of the neck. Evidently she was moving her family to pastures new. As the man was in the line of her march, she stopped and considered what was to be

194

done. He called to me, and I approached slowly. As the mother saw me closing in on her flank, she was suddenly seized with a panic, and, dropping her young, fled precipitately for the cover of a large pile of grape-posts some ten or twelve rods distant. We pursued hotly, and overhauled her as she was within one jump of the house of refuge. Taking her by the tail, I carried her back to her baby; but she heeded it not. It was only her own bacon now that she was solicitous about. The young one remained where it had been dropped, keeping up a brave, reassuring whistle that was in ludicrous contrast to its exposed and helpless condition. It was the smallest woodchuck I had ever seen, not much larger than a large rat. Its head and shoulders were so large in proportion to the body as to give it a comical look. It could not walk about yet, and had never before been above ground. Every moment or two it would whistle cheerily, as the old one does when safe in its den, and the farm-dog is fiercely baying outside. We took the youngster home, and my little boy was delighted over the prospect of a tame woodchuck. Not till the next day would it eat. Then, getting a taste of the milk, it clutched the spoon that held it with great eagerness, and sucked away like a little pig. We were all immensely diverted by it. It ate eagerly, grew rapidly, and was soon able to run about. As the old one had been killed, we became curious as to the fate of the rest of her family, for no doubt there were more. Had she moved them, or had we intercepted her on her first trip? We knew where the old den was, but not the new. So we would keep a lookout. Near the end of the week, on passing by the old den, there were three young ones, creeping about a few feet from its mouth. They were starved out, and had come forth to see what could be found. We captured them all, and the young family was again united. How these poor, half-famished creatures did lay hold of the spoon when they got a taste of the milk! One could not help laughing. Their little shining black paws were so handy and so smooth; they seemed as if encased in kid gloves. They throve well upon milk, and then upon milk and clover. But after the novelty of the thing had worn off, the boy found he had encumbered himself with serious duties in assuming the position of foster-mother to this large family; so he gave them all away but one, the first one captured, which had outstripped all the others in growth. This soon became a very amusing pet, but it always protested when handled, and always objected to confinement. I should mention that the cat had a kitten about the age of the chuck, and as she had more milk than the kitten could dispose of, the chuck, when we first got him, was often placed in the nest with the kitten, and was regarded by the cat as tenderly as her own, and allowed to nurse freely. Thus a friendship sprang up between the kitten and the woodchuck, which lasted as long as the latter lived. They would play together precisely like two kittens: clinch and tumble about and roll upon the grass in a very amusing way. Finally the woodchuck took up his abode under the floor of the kitchen, and gradually relapsed into a half-wild state. He would permit no familiarities from any one save the kitten, but each day they would have a turn or two at their old games of rough-and-tumble. The chuck was now over half grown, and procured his own living. One day the dog, who had all along looked upon him with a jealous eye, encountered him too far from cover, and his career ended then and there.

In July the woodchuck was forgotten in our interest in a little gray rabbit which we found nearly famished. It was so small that it could sit in the hollow of one's hand. Some accident had probably befallen its mother. The tiny creature looked spiritless and forlorn. We had to force the milk into its mouth. But in a day or two it began to revive, and would lap the milk eagerly. Soon it took to grass and clover, and then to nibbling sweet apples and early pears. It grew rapidly, and was one of the softest and most harmless-looking pets I had ever seen. For a month or more the little rabbit was the only company I had, and it helped to beguile the time immensely. In coming in from the field

197

or from my work, I seldom failed to bring it a handful of red clover blossoms, of which it became very fond. One day it fell slyly to licking my hand, and I discovered it wanted salt. I would then moisten my fingers, dip them into the salt, and offer them to the rabbit. How rapidly the delicate little tongue would play upon them, darting out to the right and left of the large front incisors, the slender paws being pressed against my hand as if to detain it! But the rabbit proved really untamable; its wild nature could not be overcome. In its large box-cage or prison, where it could see nothing but the tree above it, it was tame, and would at times frisk playfully about my hand and strike it gently with its forefeet; but the moment it was liberated in a room or let down in the grass with a string about its neck, all its wild nature came forth. In the room it would run and hide; in the open it would make desperate efforts to escape, and leap and bound as you drew in the string that held it. At night, too, it never failed to try to make its escape from the cage, and finally, when two thirds grown, succeeded, and we saw it no more.

III

How completely the life of a bird revolves about its nest, its home! In the case of the wood thrush, its life and joy seem to mount higher and higher as the nest prospers. The male becomes a fountain

198

of melody; his happiness waxes day by day; he makes little triumphal tours about the neighborhood, and pours out his pride and gladness in the ears of all. How sweet, how well-bred, is his demonstration! But let any accident befall that precious nest, and what a sudden silence falls upon him! Last summer a pair of wood thrushes built their nest within a few rods of my house, and when the enterprise was fairly launched and the mother bird was sitting upon her four blue eggs, the male was in the height of his song. How he poured forth his rich melody, never in the immediate vicinity of the nest, but always within easy hearing distance! Every morning, as promptly as the morning came, between five and six, he would sing for half an hour from the top of a locust-tree that shaded my roof. I came to expect him as much as I expected my breakfast, and I was not disappointed till one morning I seemed to miss something. What was it? Oh, the thrush had not sung this morning. Something is the matter; and recollecting that yesterday I had seen a red squirrel in the trees not far from the nest, I at once inferred that the nest had been harried. Going to the spot, I found my fears were well grounded; every egg was gone. The joy of the thrush was laid low. No more songs from the treetop, and no more songs from any point, till nearly a week had elapsed, when I heard him again under the hill, where the pair had started a new nest, cautiously

199

tuning up, and apparently with his recent bitter experience still weighing upon him.

After a pair of birds have been broken up once or twice during the season, they become almost desperate, and will make great efforts to outwit their enemies. The past season my attention was attracted by a pair of brown thrashers. They first built their nest in a pasture-field under a low, scrubby apple-tree which the cattle had browsed down till it spread a thick, wide mass of thorny twigs only a few inches above the ground. Some blackberry briers had also grown there, so that the screen was perfect. My dog first started the bird, as I was passing by. By stooping low and peering intently, I could make out the nest and eggs. Two or three times a week, as I passed by, I would pause to see how the nest was prospering. The mother bird would keep her place, her yellow eyes never blinking. One morning, as I looked into her tent, I found the nest empty. Some night-prowler, probably a skunk or a fox, or maybe a black snake or a red squirrel by day, had plundered it. It would seem as if it was too well screened; it was in such a spot as any depredator would be apt to explore. "Surely," he would say, "this is a likely place for a nest." The birds then moved over the hill a hundred rods or more, much nearer the house, and in some rather open bushes tried again. But again they came to grief. Then, after some delay, the mother bird made a bold stroke. She seemed to reason with herself thus: "Since I have fared so disastrously in seeking seclusion for my nest, I will now adopt the opposite tactics, and come out fairly in the open. What hides me hides my enemies: let us try greater publicity." So she came out and built her nest by a few small shoots that grew beside the path that divides the two vineyards, and where we passed to and fro many times daily. I discovered her by chance early in the morning as I proceeded to my work. She started up at my feet and flitted quickly along above the plowed ground, almost as red as the soil. I admired her audacity. Surely no prowler by night or day would suspect a nest in this open and exposed place. There was no cover by which they could approach, and no concealment anywhere. The nest was a hasty affair, as if the birds' patience at nest-building had been about exhausted. Presently an egg appeared, and then the next day another, and on the fourth day a third. No doubt the bird would have succeeded this time had not man interfered. In cultivating the vineyards the horse and cultivator had to pass over this very spot. Upon this the bird had not calculated. I determined to assist her. I called my man, and told him there was one spot in that vineyard, no bigger than his hand, where the horse's foot must not be allowed to fall, nor tooth of cultivator to touch. Then I showed him the nest, and charged him to avoid it. Probably if I had kept the secret to myself, and let the bird run her own risk, the nest would have escaped. But the result was that the man, in elaborately trying to avoid the nest, overdid the matter; the horse plunged, and set his foot squarely upon it. Such a little spot, the chances were few that the horse's foot would fall exactly there; and yet it did, and the birds' hopes were again dashed. The pair then disappeared from my vicinity, and I saw them no more.

The summer just gone I passed at a farmhouse on the skirts of the Northern Catskills. How could I help but see what no one else of all the people about seemed to notice, — a little bob-tailed song sparrow building her nest in a pile of dry brush very near the kitchen door. It was late in July, and she had doubtless reared one brood in the earlier season. Her toilet was decidedly the worse for wear. I noted her day after day, very busy about the fence and quince bushes between the house and milk house, with her beak full of coarse straw and hay. To a casual observer, she seemed flitting about aimlessly, carrying straws from place to place just to amuse herself. When I came to watch her closely to learn the place of her nest, she seemed to suspect my intention, and made many little feints and movements calculated to put me off the track. But I would not be misled, and presently had her secret. The male did not assist her at all, but sang much of the time in an apple-tree or upon the fence, on the other

side of the house. Those artists who paint pictures
of devoted male birds singing from the branch that
holds the nest, or in its immediate vicinity, do not
give the birds credit for all the wit they possess.
They do not advertise the place where their treasures are hid in this way. See yonder indigo-bird
shaking out its happy song from the topmost twig
of the maple or oak; its nest is many yards away,
in a low bush not more than three feet from the
ground.

And so with nearly all the birds. The one thing
to which they bend all their wits is the concealment of their nests. When you come upon the sitting bird, she will almost let you touch her rather
than start up before you, and thus betray her
secret. The bobolink begins to scold and to circle
about you as soon as you enter the meadow where
his nest is so well hidden. He does not wait to
show his anxiety till you are almost upon it. By
no action of his can you get a clew as to its exact
whereabouts.

The song sparrow nearly always builds upon the
ground, but my little neighbor of last July laid the
foundations of her domicile a foot or more above the
soil. And what a mass of straws and twigs she did
collect together! How coarse and careless and aim-
less at first, — a mere lot of rubbish dropped upon
the tangle of dry limbs; but presently how it began
to refine and come into shape in the centre! till there

was the most exquisite hair-lined cup set about by a chaos of coarse straws and branches. What a process of evolution! The completed nest was foreshadowed by the first stiff straw; but how far off is yet that dainty casket with its complement of speckled eggs! The nest was so placed that it had for canopy a large, broad, drooping leaf of yellow dock. This formed a perfect shield against both sun and rain, while it served to conceal it from any curious eyes from above, — from the cat, for instance, prowling along the top of the wall. Before the eggs had hatched, the docken leaf wilted and dried and fell down upon the nest. But the mother bird managed to insinuate herself beneath it, and went on with her brooding all the same.

Then I arranged an artificial cover of leaves and branches, which shielded her charge till they had flown away. A mere trifle was this little bob-tailed bird with her arts and her secrets, and the male with his song, and yet the pair gave a touch of something to those days and to that place which I would not willingly have missed.

I have spoken of nature as a stage whereon the play, more or less interrupted and indirect, constantly goes on. An amusing actor on that stage one season, on my own premises, was a certain male bluebird. To the spectator it was a comedy, but to the actor himself I imagine it was quite serious business. The bird and his mate had a nest in a box upon an outhouse. In this outhouse was a window with one pane broken out. At almost any hour in the day from spring to early summer, the male bird could be seen fluttering and pecking against this window from the outside. Did he want to get in ? Apparently so, and yet he would now and then pause in his demonstrations, alight in the frame of the broken pane, look intently inside, and after a moment resume his assault upon the window. The persons who saw the actions of the bird were at a loss how to interpret them. But I could see at once what was the matter. The bird saw its image in the mirror of the glass (the dark interior helped the reflection), and was making war, as he supposed, upon a rival. Only the unyielding glass kept him from tweaking out every saucy blue feather upon the spot! Then he would peep in through the vacant pane and try to determine where his rival had so suddenly disappeared. How it must have puzzled his little poll! And he learned nothing from experience. Hundreds of times did he perch in the broken pane and sharply eye the interior. And for two months there did not seem to be an hour when he was not assaulting the window. He never lost faith in the reality of the bird within, and he never abated one jot his enmity toward him. If the glass had been a rough surface, he would certainly have worn his beak and claws and wings to mere stubs. The incident shows the pugnacious disposition of the bluebird, and it shows how shallow a bird's wit is when new problems or conditions confront it. I have known a cock-robin to assault an imaginary rival in a garret window, in the same manner, and keep up the warfare for weeks.

On still another occasion similar antics of a male bluebird greatly disturbed the sleep of my hired man in the early morning. The bird with its mate had a nest in a box near the house, and after the manner of the bluebirds was very inquisitive and saucy about windows; one morning it chanced to discover its reflected image in the windows of the hired man's room. The shade, of some dark stuff, was down on the inside, which aided in making a kind of looking-glass of the window. Instantly the bird began an assault upon his supposed rival in the window, and made such a clattering that there was no more sleep inside that room. Morning after morning the bird kept this up, till the tired plowman complained bitterly, and declared his intention to kill the bird. In an unlucky moment — unlucky for me, who had morning work to be done — I suggested that he leave the shade up and try the effect. He did so, and his morning sleep was henceforth undisturbed.

A Western correspondent writes me that she once put a looking-glass down on the floor in front of the canary bird's cage. The poor canary had not had any communion with his own kind for years. "He used often to watch the ugly sparrows — the little plebeians — from his aristocratic gilded palace. I opened his cage and he walked up to the looking-glass, and it was not long before he made up his mind. He collected dead leaves, twigs, bits of paper, and all sorts of stray bits, and began a nest right off. Several days after in his lonely cage he would take bits of straw and arrange them when they were given him."

XI

A LIFE OF FEAR

AS I sat looking from my window the other
morning at a red squirrel gathering hickory
nuts from a small hickory, and storing them up in
his den in the bank, I was forcibly reminded of the
state of constant fear and apprehension in which the
wild creatures live, and I tried to picture to myself
what life would be to me, or to any of us, hedged
about by so many dangers, real or imaginary.

The squirrel would shoot up the tree, making only
a brown streak from the bottom to the top; would
seize his nut and rush down again in the most precipitate manner. Halfway to his den, which was not
over three rods distant, he would rush up the trunk
of another tree for a few yards to make an observation. No danger being near, he would dive into
his den and reappear again in a twinkling.

Returning for another nut, he would mount the
second tree again for another observation. Satisfied
that the coast was clear, he would spin along the top
of the ground to the tree that bore the nuts, shoot
up it as before, seize the fruit, and then back again
to his retreat.

Never did he fail, during the half hour or more that I watched him, to take an observation on his way both to and from his nest. It was "snatch and run" with him. Something seemed to say to him all the time: "Look out! look out!" "The cat!" "The hawk!" "The owl!" "The boy with the gun!"

It was a bleak December morning; the first fine flakes of a cold, driving snowstorm were just beginning to sift down, and the squirrel was eager to finish harvesting his nuts in time. It was quite touching to see how hurried and anxious and nervous he was. I felt like going out and lending a hand. The nuts were small, poor pig-nuts, and I thought of all the gnawing he would have to do to get at the scanty meat they held. My little boy once took pity on a squirrel that lived in the wall near the gate, and cracked the nuts for him, and put them upon a small board shelf in the tree where he could sit and eat them at his ease.

The red squirrel is not so provident as the chipmunk. He lays up stores irregularly, by fits and starts; he never has enough put up to carry him over the winter; hence he is more or less active all the season. Long before the December snow, the chipmunk has for days been making hourly trips to his den with full pockets of nuts or corn or buckwheat, till his bin holds enough to carry him through to April. He need not, and I believe does not, set foot out of doors during the whole winter. But the red squirrel trusts more to luck.

As alert and watchful as the red squirrel is, he is frequently caught by the cat. My Nig, as black as ebony, knows well the taste of his flesh. I have known him to be caught by the black snake and successfully swallowed. The snake, no doubt, lay in ambush for him.

This fear, this ever present source of danger of the wild creatures, we know little about. Probably the only person in the civilized countries who is no better off than the animals in this respect is the Czar of Russia. He would not even dare gather nuts as openly as my squirrel. A blacker and more terrible cat than Nig would be lying in wait for him, and would make a meal of him. The early settlers in this country must have experienced something of this dread of apprehension from the Indians. Many African tribes now live in the same state of constant fear of the slave-catchers or of other hostile tribes. Our ancestors, back in prehistoric times, or back of that in geologic times, must have known fear as a constant feeling. Hence the prominence of fear in infants and children when compared with the youth or the grown person. Babies are nearly always afraid of strangers.

In the domestic animals also, fear is much more active in the young than in the old. Nearly every farm boy has seen a calf but a day or two old, which its mother has secreted in the woods or in a remote field, charge upon him furiously with a wild bleat, when first discovered. After this first ebullition of fear, it usually settles down into the tame humdrum of its bovine elders.

Eternal vigilance is the price of life with most of the wild creatures. There is only one among them whose wildness I cannot understand, and that is the common water turtle. Why is this creature so fearful? What are its enemies? I know of nothing that preys upon it. Yet see how watchful and suspicious these turtles are as they sun themselves upon a log or a rock. Before you are fairly in gunshot of them, they slide down into the water and are gone.

The land turtle, or terrapin, on the other hand, shows scarcely a trace of fear. He will indeed pause in his walk when you are very near him, but he will not retreat into his shell till you have poked him with your foot or your cane. He appears to have no enemies; but the little spotted water turtle is as shy as if he were the delicate titbit that every creature is searching for. I did once find one which a fox had dug out of the mud in winter, and carried a few rods and dropped on the snow, as if he had found he had no use for it.

One can understand the fearlessness of the skunk. Nearly every creature but the farm-dog yields to him the right of way. All dread his terrible weapon. If you meet one in your walk in the twilight fields,

the chances are that you will turn out for him, not
he for you. He may even pursue you, just for the
fun of seeing you run. He comes waltzing toward
you, apparently in the most hilarious spirits.

The coon is probably the most courageous creature among our familiar wild animals. Who ever
saw a coon show the white feather? He will face
any odds with perfect composure. I have seen a coon
upon the ground, beset by four men and two dogs,
and never for a moment losing his presence of mind,
or showing a sign of fear. The raccoon is clear grit.

The fox is a very wild and suspicious creature,
but curiously enough, when you suddenly come face
to face with him, when he is held by a trap, or driven
by the hound, his expression is not that of fear, but
of shame and guilt. He seems to diminish in size
and to be overwhelmed with humiliation. Does he
know himself to be an old thief, and is that the reason of his embarrassment? The fox has no enemies
but man, and when he is fairly outwitted, he looks
the shame he evidently feels.

In the heart of the rabbit fear constantly abides.
How her eyes protrude! She can see back and front
and on all sides as well as a bird. The fox is after
her, the owls are after her, the gunners are after
her, and she has no defense but her speed. She always keeps well to cover. The northern hare keeps
in the thickest brush. If the hare or rabbit crosses
a broad open exposure, it does so hurriedly, like a

mouse when it crosses the road. The mouse is in danger of being pounced upon by a hawk, and the hare or rabbit by the snowy owl, or else the great horned owl.

A friend of mine was following one morning a fresh rabbit track through an open field. Suddenly the track came to an end, as if the creature had taken wings, — as it had after an unpleasant fashion. There, on either side of its last foot imprint, were several parallel lines in the snow, made by the wings of the great owl that had swooped down and carried it off. What a little tragedy was seen written there upon the white, even surface of the field!

The rabbit has not much wit. I once, when a boy, saw one, that had been recently caught, liberated in an open field in the presence of a dog that was being held a few yards away. But the poor thing lost all presence of mind and was quickly caught by the clumsy dog.

A hunter once saw a hare running upon the ice along the shore of one of the Rangeley lakes. Presently a lynx appeared in hot pursuit; as soon as the hare found it was being pursued, it began to circle, foolish thing. This gave the lynx greatly the advantage, as it could follow in a much smaller circle. Soon the hare was run down and seized.

I saw the same experiment tried with a red squirrel with quite opposite results. The boy who had caught the squirrel in his wire trap had a very bright and nimble dog about the size of a fox, that seemed to be very sure he could catch a red squirrel under any circumstances if only the trees were out of the way. So the boy went to the middle of an open field with his caged squirrel, the dog, 'who seemed to know what was up, dancing and jumping about him. It was in midwinter; the snow had a firm crust that held boy and dog alike. The dog was drawn back a few yards and the squirrel liberated. Then began one of the most exciting races I have witnessed for a long time. It was impossible for the lookers-on not to be convulsed with laughter, though neither dog nor squirrel seemed to regard the matter as much of a joke. The squirrel had all his wits about him, and kept them ready for instant use. He did not show the slightest confusion. He was no match for the dog in fair running, and he discovered this fact in less than three seconds; he must win, if at all, by strategy. Not a straight course for the nearest tree, but a zigzag course ; yea, a double or treble zigzag course. Every instant the dog was sure the squirrel was his, and every instant he was disappointed. It was incredible and bewildering to him. The squirrel dodged this way and that. The dog looked astonished and vexed.

Then the squirrel issued from between his hind legs and made three jumps toward the woods before he was discovered. Our sides ached with laughter, cruel as it may seem.

It was evident the squirrel would win. The dog seemed to redouble his efforts. He would overshoot the game, or shoot by it to the right or the left. The squirrel was the smaller craft, and could out-tack him easily. One more leap and the squirrel was up a tree, and the dog was overwhelmed with confusion and disgust.

He could not believe his senses. "Not catch a squirrel in such a field as that? Go to, I will have him yet!" and he bounded up the tree as high as one's head, and then bit the bark of it in his anger and chagrin.

The boy says his dog has never bragged since about catching red squirrels "if only the trees were out of reach!"

When any of the winged creatures are engaged in a life and death race in that way, or in any other race, the tactics of the squirrel do not work; the pursuer never overshoots nor shoots by his mark. The flight of the two is timed as if they were parts of one whole. A hawk will pursue a sparrow or a robin through a zigzag course and not lose a stroke or half a stroke of the wing by reason of any darting to the right or left. The clew is held with fatal precision. No matter how quickly nor how often the sparrow or the finch changes its course, its enemy changes, simultaneously, as if every move was known to it from the first.

The same thing may be noticed among the birds

in their love chasings; the pursuer seems to know perfectly the mind of the pursued. This concert of action among birds is very curious. When they are on the alert, a flock of sparrows, or pigeons, or cedar-birds, or snow buntings, or blackbirds, will all take flight as if there was but one bird, instead of a hundred. The same impulse seizes every individual bird at the same instant, as if they were sprung by electricity.

Or when a flock of birds is in flight, it is still one body, one will; it will rise, or circle, or swoop with a unity that is truly astonishing.

A flock of snow buntings will perform their aerial evolutions with a precision that the best-trained soldiery cannot equal. Have the birds an extra sense which we have not? A brood of young partridges in the woods will start up like an explosion, every brown particle and fragment hurled into the air at the same instant. Without word or signal, how is it done?

XII

LOVERS OF NATURE

I

WE love nature with a different love at different periods of our lives. In youth our love is sensuous. It is not so much a conscious love as it is an irresistible attraction. The senses are keen and fresh, and they crave a field for their exercise. We delight in the color of flowers, the perfume of meadows and orchards, the moist, fresh smell of the woods. We eat the pungent roots and barks, we devour the wild fruits, we slay the small deer. Then nature also offers a field of adventure; it challenges and excites our animal spirits. The woods are full of game, the waters of fish; the river invites the oar, the breeze, the sail, the mountain-top promises a wide prospect. Hence the rod, the gun, the boat, the tent, the pedestrian club. In youth we are nearer the savage taste, the primitive condition of mankind, and wild nature is our proper home. The transient color of the young bird points its remote ancestry, and the taste of youth for rude nature in like manner is the survival of an earlier race instinct.

Later in life we go to nature as an escape from
the tension and turmoil of business, or for rest and
recreation from study, or seeking solace from grief
and disappointment, or as a refuge from the frivolity
and hypocrisies of society. We lie under trees, we
stroll through lanes, or in meadows and pastures,
or muse on the shore. Nature "salves" our worst
wounds; she heals and restores us.

Or we cultivate an intellectual pleasure in nature,
and follow up some branch of natural science, as
botany, or ornithology, or mineralogy.

Then there is the countryman's love of nature,
the pleasure in cattle, horses, bees, growing crops,
manual labor, sugar-making, gardening, harvesting,
and the rural quietness and repose.

Lastly, we go to nature for solitude and for communion with our own souls. Nature attunes us to
a higher and finer mood. This love springs from
our religious needs and instincts. This was the love
of Thoreau, of Wordsworth, and has been the in-
spiration of much modern poetry and art.

Dr. Johnson said he had lived in London so long
that he had ceased to note the changes of the seasons.
But Dr. Johnson was not a lover of Nature. Of that
feeling for the country of which Wordsworth's
poetry, for instance, is so full, he probably had not
a vestige. Think of Wordsworth shut up year in and
year out — in the city! That lover of shepherds, of
mountains, of lonely tarns, of sounding waterfalls,

LOVERS OF NATURE

"Who looked upon the hills with tenderness,
And made dear friendships with the streams and groves."

Dr. Johnson's delight was in men and in verbal fisticuffs with them, but Wordsworth seems to have loved Nature more than men; at least he was drawn most to those men who lived closest to Nature and were more a part of her. Thus he says he loved shepherds, "dwellers in the valleys,"

"Not verily
For their own sakes, but for the fields and hills
Where was their occupation and abode."

Your real lover of nature does not love merely the beautiful things which he culls here and there; he loves the earth itself, the faces of the hills and mountains, the rocks, the streams, the naked trees no less than the leafy trees, — a plowed field no less than a green meadow. He does not know what it is that draws him. It is not beauty, any more than it is beauty in his father and mother that makes him love them. It is "something far more deeply interfused," — something native and kindred that calls to him. In certain moods, how good the earth, the soil, seems! One wants to feel it with his hands and smell it — almost taste it. Indeed, I never see a horse eat soil and sods without a feeling that I would like to taste it too. The rind of the earth, of this "round and delicious globe" which has hung so long upon the great Newtonian tree, ripening in the sun, must be sweet.

I recall an Irish girl lately come to this country, who worked for us, and who, when I dug and brought to the kitchen the first early potatoes, felt them, and stroked them with her hand, and smelled them, and was loath to lay them down, they were so full of suggestion of the dear land and home she had so lately left. I suppose it was a happy surprise to her to find that the earth had the same fresh, moist smell here that it had in Ireland, and yielded the same crisp tubers. The canny creature had always worked in the fields, and the love of the soil and of homely country things was deep in her heart. Another emigrant from over the seas, a laboring man, confined to the town, said to me in his last illness, that he believed he would get well if he could again walk in the fields. A Frenchman who fled the city and came to the country said, with an impressive gesture, that he wanted to be where he could see the blue sky over his head.

These little incidents are but glints or faint gleams of that love of Nature to which I would point, — an affection for the country itself, and not a mere passing admiration for its beauties. A great many people admire Nature; they write admiring things about her; they apostrophize her beauties; they describe minutely pretty scenes here and there; they climb mountains to see the sun set, or the sun rise, or

make long journeys to find waterfalls, but Nature's
real lover listens to their enthusiasm with coolness
and indifference. Nature is not to be praised or
patronized. You cannot go to her and describe her;
she must speak through your heart. The woods and
fields must melt into your mind, dissolved by your
love for them. Did they not melt into Wordsworth's
mind? They colored all his thoughts; the solitude
of those green, rocky Westmoreland fells broods
over every page. He does not tell us how beautiful
he finds Nature, and how much he enjoys her; he
makes us share his enjoyment.

Richard Jefferies was probably as genuine a lover
of Nature as was Wordsworth, but he had not the
same power to make us share his enjoyment. His
page is sometimes wearisome from mere description
and enumeration. He is rarely interpretative; the
mood, the frame of mind, which Nature herself
begets, he seldom imparts to us. What we finally
love in Nature is ourselves, some suggestion of the
human spirit, and no labored description or careful
enumeration of details will bring us to this.

"Nor do words
Which practiced talent readily affords,
Prove that her hand has touched responsive chords."

It has been aptly said that Jefferies was a reporter
of genius, but that he never (in his nature books)
got beyond reporting. His "Wild Life" reads like

223

a kind of field newspaper; he puts in everything, he is diligent and untiring, but for much of it one cares very little after he is through. For selecting and combining the things of permanent interest so as to excite curiosity and to impart charm, he has but little power.

The passion for Nature is by no means a mere curiosity about her, or an itching to portray certain of her features; it lies deeper, and is probably a form of, or closely related to, our religious instincts. When you go to Nature, bring us good science or else good literature, and not a mere inventory of what you have seen. One demonstrates, the other interprets.

Observation is selective and detective. A real observation begets warmth and joy in the mind. To see things in detail as they lie about you and enumerate them is not observation; but to see the significant things, to seize the quick movement and gesture, to disentangle the threads of relation, to know the nerves that thrill from the cords that bind, or the typical and vital from the commonplace and mechanical, — that is to be an observer. In Thoreau's "Walden" there is observation; in the Journals published since his death there is close and patient scrutiny, but only now and then anything that we care to know. Considering that Thoreau spent half of each day for upward of twenty years in the open air, bent upon spying out Nature's ways and doings, it is remarkable that he made so few real observations.

Yet how closely he looked! He even saw that mysterious waving line which one may sometimes note in little running brooks. "I see stretched from side to side of this smooth brook where it is three or four feet wide what seems to indicate an invisible waving line, like a cobweb, against which the water is heaped up a very little. This line is constantly swayed to and fro, as if by the current or wind, bellying forward here and there. I try repeatedly to catch and break it with my hand and let the water run free, but still to my surprise I clutch nothing but fluid, and the imaginary line keeps its place."

A little closer scrutiny would have shown him that this waving water-line was probably caused in some way by the meeting of two volumes or currents of water.

The most novel and interesting observation I can now recall is his discovery of how the wild apple-tree in the pastures triumphs over the browsing cattle, namely, by hedging itself about by a dense thorny growth, keeping the cows at arm's length, as it were, and then sending up a central shoot beyond their reach.

One of the most acute observations Thoreau's Journals contain is not upon nature at all, but upon the difference between men and women "in respect to the adornment of their heads:" "Do you ever see an old or jammed bonnet on the head of a woman at a public meeting? But look at any assembly of men with their hats on; how large a proportion of the hats will be old, weather-beaten, and indented; but, I think, so much more picturesque and interesting. One farmer rides by my door in a hat which it does me good to see, there is so much character in it, so much independence, to begin with, and then affection for his old friends, etc., etc. I should not wonder if there were lichens on it. . . . Men wear their hats for use, women theirs for ornament. I have seen the greatest philosopher in the town with what the traders would call a 'shocking bad hat' on, but the woman whose bonnet does not come up to the mark is at best a blue-stocking."

So clever an observation upon anything in nature as that is hard to find in the Journals.

To observe is to discriminate and to take note of all the factors.

One day, while walking in my vineyard, lamenting the damage the storm of yesterday had wrought in it, my ear caught, amid the medley of other sounds and songs, an unfamiliar bird-note from the air overhead. Gradually it dawned upon my consciousness that this was not the call of any of our native birds, but of a stranger. Looking steadily in the direction the sound came, after some moments I made out the form of a bird flying round and round in a large circle high in air, and momentarily uttering its loud sharp call. The size, the shape, the manner, and the voice of the bird were all strange. In a moment I knew it to be an English skylark, apparently adrift and undecided which way to go. Finally it seemed to make up its mind, and then bore away to the north. My ear had been true to its charge.

The man who told me that some of our birds took an earth bath, and some of them a water bath, and a few of them took both, had looked closer into this matter than I had. The sparrows usually earth their plumage, but the English sparrow does both. The farm boy who told a naturalist a piece of news about the turtles, namely, that the reason why we never see any small turtles about the fields is because for two or three years the young turtles bury themselves in the ground and keep quite hidden from sight, had used his eyes to some purpose. This was a real observation.

Just as a skilled physician, in diagnosing a case, picks out the significant symptoms and separates them from the rest, so the real observer, with eye and ear, seizes what is novel and characteristic in the scenes about him. His attention goes through the play at the surface and reaches the rarer incidents beneath or beyond.

Richard Jefferies was not strictly an observer; he was a living and sympathetic spectator of the nature about him, a poet, if you please, but he tells

us little that is memorable or suggestive. His best
books are such as the " Gamekeeper at Home," and
the "Amateur Poacher," where the human element
is brought in, and the descriptions of nature are
relieved by racy bits of character drawing. By far
the best thing of all is a paper which he wrote
shortly before his death, called "My Old Village."
It is very beautiful and pathetic, and reveals the
heart and soul of the man as nothing else he has
written does. I must permit myself to transcribe
one paragraph of it. It shows how he, too, was
under the spell of the past, and such a recent past,
too: —

"I think I have heard that the oaks are down.
They may be standing or down, it matters nothing
to me; the leaves I last saw upon them are gone for
evermore, nor shall I ever see them come there
again, ruddy in spring. I would not see them again,
even if I could; they could never look again as they
used to do. There are too many memories there.
The happiest days become the saddest afterward;
let us never go back, lest we, too, die. There are no
such oaks anywhere else, none so tall and straight,
and with such massive heads, on which the sun used
to shine as if on the globe of the earth, one side in
shadow, the other in bright light. How often I have
looked at oaks since, and yet have never been able
to get the same effect from them! Like an old author
printed in another type, the words are the same,

but the sentiment is different. The brooks have ceased to run. There is no music now at the old hatch where we used to sit, in danger of our lives, happy as kings, on the narrow bar over the deep water. The barred pike that used to come up in such numbers are no more among the flags. The perch used to drift down the stream and then bring up again. The sun shone there for a very long time, and the water rippled and sang, and it always seemed to me that I could feel the rippling and the singing and the sparkling back through the centuries. The brook is dead, for where man goes, nature ends. I dare say there is water there still, but it is not the brook; the brook is gone, like John Brown's soul [not our John Brown]. There used to be clouds over the fields, white clouds in blue summer skies. I have lived a good deal on clouds; they have been meat to me often; they bring something to the spirit which even the trees do not. I see clouds now sometimes when the iron gripe of hell permits for a minute or two; they are very different clouds and speak differently. I long for some of the old clouds that had no memories. There were nights in those times over those fields, not darkness, but Night, full of glowing suns and glowing richness of life that sprang up to meet them. The nights are there still; they are everywhere, nothing local in the night ; but it is not the Night to me seen through the window."

In the literature of nature I know of no page so pathetic and human.

Moralizing about nature or through nature is tedious enough, and yet, unless the piece has some moral or emotional background, it does not touch us. In other words, to describe a thing for the mere sake of describing it, to make a dead set at it like a reporter, whatever may be the case in painting, will not do in literature. The object must be informed with meaning, and to do this the creative touch of the imagination is required. Take this passage from Whitman on the night, and see if there is not more than mere description there: —

"A large part of the sky seemed just laid in great splashes of phosphorus. You could look deeper in, farther through, than usual; the orbs thick as heads of wheat in a field. Not that there was any special brilliancy either, — nothing near as sharp as I have seen of keen winter nights, but a curious general luminousness throughout to sight, sense, and soul. The latter had much to do with it. . . . Now, indeed, if never before, the heavens declared the glory of God. It was to the full the sky of the Bible, of Arabia, of the prophets, and of the oldest poems."

Or this touch of a January night on the Delaware River: —

"Overhead, the splendor indescribable; yet something haughty, almost supercilious, in the night; never did I realize more latent sentiment, almost

230

passion, in the silent interminable stars up there. One can understand on such a night why, from the days of the Pharaohs or Job, the dome of heaven, sprinkled with planets, has supplied the subtlest, deepest criticism on human pride, glory, ambition."

Matthew Arnold quotes this passage from Obermann as showing a rare feeling for nature: —

"My path lay beside the green waters of the Thiele. Feeling inclined to muse, and finding the night so warm that there was no hardship in being all night out of doors, I took the road to Saint Blaise. I descended a steep bank, and got upon the shore of the lake where its ripple came up and expired. The air was calm; every one was at rest; I remained there for hours. Toward morning the moon shed over the earth and waters the ineffable melancholy of her last gleams. Nature seems unspeakably grand, when, plunged in a long reverie, one hears the rippling of the waters upon a solitary strand, in the calm of a night still enkindled and luminous with the setting moon.

"Sensibility beyond utterance, charm and torment of our vain years; vast consciousness of a nature everywhere greater than we are, and everywhere impenetrable; all-embracing passion, ripened wisdom, delicious self-abandonment — everything that a mortal heart can contain of life-weariness and yearning, I felt it all. I experienced it all, in this

231

memorable night. I have made a grave step toward
the age of decline. I have swallowed up ten years of
life at once. Happy the simple whose heart is always
young!"

The moral element is behind this also, and is the
source of its value and charm. In literature never
Nature for her own sake, but for the sake of the soul
which is over and above all.

II

One of the most desirable things in life is a fresh
impression of an old fact or scene. One's love of
nature may be a constant factor, yet it is only now
and then that he gets a fresh impression of the
charm and meaning of nature; only now and then
that the objects without and the mood within so fit
together that we have a vivid and original sense of
the beauty and significance that surround us. How
often do we really see the stars? Probably a great
many persons never see them at all, — that is, never
look upon them with any thrill of emotion. If I see
them a few times a year, I think myself in luck.
If I deliberately go out to see them, I am quite sure
to miss them; but occasionally, as one glances up to
them in his lonely night walk, the mind opens, or
the heaven opens — which is it? — and he has a mo-
mentary glimpse of their ineffable splendor and significance. How overwhelming, how awe-inspiring!
His thought goes like a lightning flash into that

serene abyss, and then the veil is drawn again. One's science, one's understanding, tells him he is a voyager on the celestial deep, that the earth beneath his feet is a star among stars, that we can never be any more in the heavens than we are now, or any more within reach of the celestial laws and forces; but how rare the mood in which we can realize this astounding fact, in which we can get a fresh and vivid impression of it! To have it ever present with one in all its naked grandeur would perhaps be more than we could bear.

The common and the familiar, — how soon they cease to impress us! The great service of genius, speaking through art and literature, is to pierce through our callousness and indifference and give us fresh impressions of things as they really are; to present things in new combinations, or from new points of view, so that they shall surprise and delight us like a new revelation. When poetry does this, or when art does it, or when science does it, it recreates the world for us, and for the moment we are again Adam in paradise.

Herein lies one compensation to the lover of nature who is an enforced dweller in the town: the indifference which familiarity breeds is not his. His weekly or monthly sallies into the country yield him a rare delight. To his fresh, eager senses the charm of novelty is over all. Country people look with a kind of pitying amusement upon the delight of their newly arrived city friends; but would we not, after all, give something if we could exchange eyes with them for a little while?

We who write about Nature pick out, I suspect, only the rare moments when we have had glimpses of her, and make much of them. Our lives are dull, and our minds crusted over with rubbish like those of other people. Then writing about Nature, as about most other subjects, is an expansive process; we are under the law of evolution; we grow the germ into the tree; a little original observation goes a good way. Life is a compendium. The record in our minds and hearts is in shorthand. When we come to write it out, we are surprised at its length and significance. What we feel in a twinkling, it takes a long time to tell to another.

When I pass along by a meadow in June, where the bobolinks are singing and the daisies dancing in the wind, and the scent of the clover is in the air, and where the boys and girls are looking for wild strawberries in the grass, I take it all in in a glance, it enters swiftly through all my senses; but if I set about writing an account of my experience for my reader, how long and tedious the process, how I must beat about the bush! And then, if I would have him see and feel it, I must avoid a point-blank description and bring it to him, or him to it, by a kind of indirection, so as to surprise him and give him more than I at first seemed to promise.

LOVERS OF NATURE

To a countryman like myself the presence of natural objects, the open face of the country, sheds a cheering and soothing influence at all times; but it is only at rare intervals that he experiences the thrill of a fresh impression. I find that a kind of preoccupation, as the farmer with his work, the angler with his rod, the sportsman with his gun, the walker with his friend, the lounger with his book, affords conditions that are not to be neglected. So much will steal in at the corners of your eyes; the unpremeditated glance, when the mind is passive and receptive, often stirs the soul. Upon whom does the brook make such an impression as upon the angler? How he comes to know its character! how he studies its every phase! how he feels it through that rod and line as if they were a part of himself! I pity the person who does not get at least one or two fresh impressions of the charm and sweetness of nature in the spring. Later in the season it gets to be more of an old story; but in March, when the season is early, and in April, when the season is late, there occasionally come days which awaken a new joy in the heart. Every recurring spring one experiences this fresh delight. There is nothing very tangible yet in awakening nature, but there is something in the air, some sentiment in the sunshine and in the look of things, a prophecy of life and renewal, that sends a thrill through the frame. The first sparrow's song, the first robin's call, the first bluebird's warble, the first phœbe's note — who can hear it without emotion? Or the first flock of migrating geese or ducks, — how much they bring north with them! When the red-shouldered starlings begin to gurgle in the elms or golden willows along the marshes and water-courses, you will feel spring then; and if you look closely upon the ground beneath them, you will find that sturdy advanced guard of our floral army, the skunk cabbage, thrusting his spear-point up through the ooze, and spring will again quicken your pulse.

One seems to get nearer to nature in the early spring days : all screens are removed, the earth everywhere speaks directly to you; she is not hidden by verdure and foliage; there is a peculiar delight in walking over the brown turf of the fields that one cannot feel later on. How welcome the smell of it, warmed by the sun; the first breath of the reviving earth. How welcome the full, sparkling water-courses, too, everywhere drawing the eye; by and by they will be veiled by the verdure and shrunken by the heat. When March is kind, for how much her slightest favors count! The other evening, as I stood on the slope of a hill in the twilight, I heard a whistling of approaching wings, and presently a woodcock flying low passed near me. I could see his form and his long curved wings dimly against the horizon; his whistling slowly vanished in the gathering night, but his passage made something stir and respond within me. March was on the wing, she was abroad in the soft still twilight searching out the moist, springy places where the worms first come to the surface and where the grass first starts; and her course was up the valley from the south. A day or two later I sat on a hillside in the woods late in the day, amid the pines and the hemlocks, and heard the soft, elusive spring call of the little owl, — a curious musical undertone hardly separable from the silence; a bell, muffled in feathers, tolling in the twilight of the woods and discernible only to the most alert ear. But it was the voice of spring, the voice of the same impulse that sent the woodcock winging his way through the dusk, that was just beginning to make the pussy-willows swell and the grass to freshen in the spring runs.

Occasionally, of a bright, warm, still day in March, such as we have had the present season, the little flying spider is abroad. It is the most delicate of all March tokens, but very suggestive. Its long, waving threads of gossamer, invisible except when the sunlight falls upon them at a particular angle, stream out here and there upon the air, a filament of life, reaching and reaching as if to catch and detain the most subtle of the skyey influences.

Nature is always new in the spring, and lucky are we if it finds us new also.

XIII

A TASTE OF KENTUCKY BLUE–GRASS

HOW beautiful is fertility! A landscape of
fruitful and well-cultivated fields; an unbroken expanse of grass; a thick, uniform growth of
grain, — how each of these fills and satisfies the eye!
And it is not because we are essentially utilitarian
and see the rich loaf and the fat beef as the outcome
of it all, but because we read in it an expression of
the beneficence and good-will of the earth. We love
to see harmony between man and nature; we love
peace and not war; we love the adequate, the complete. A perfect issue of grass or grain is a satisfaction to look upon, because it is a success. These
things have the beauty of an end exactly fulfilled,
the beauty of perfect fitness and proportion. The
barren in nature is ugly and repels us, unless it be on
such a scale and convey such a suggestion of power
as to awaken the emotion of the sublime. What can
be less inviting than a neglected and exhausted Virginia farm, the thin red soil showing here and there
through the ragged and scanty turf? and what,
on the other hand, can please the eye of a countryman more than the unbroken verdancy and fertility

of a Kentucky blue-grass farm? I find I am very apt to take a farmer's view of a country. That long line of toiling and thrifty yeomen back of me seems to have bequeathed something to my blood that makes me respond very quickly to a fertile and well-kept landscape, and that, on the other hand, makes me equally discontented in a poor, shabby one. All the way from Washington till I struck the heart of Kentucky, the farmer in me was unhappy; he saw hardly a rood of land that he would like to call his own. But that remnant of the wild man of the woods, which most of us still carry, saw much that delighted him, especially down the New River, where the rocks and the waters and the steep forest-clad mountains were as wild and as savage as anything he had known in his early Darwinian ages. But when we emerged upon the banks of the Great Kanawha, the man of the woods lost his interest, and the man of the fields saw little that was comforting.

When we cross the line into Kentucky, I said, we shall see a change. But no, we did not. The farmer still groaned in spirit; no thrifty farms, no substantial homes, no neat villages, no good roads anywhere, but squalor and sterility on every hand. Nearly all the afternoon we rode through a country like the poorer parts of New England, unredeemed by anything like New England thrift. It was a country of coal, a very new country, geologically speaking, and the top-soil did not seem to have had time

240

to become deepened and enriched by vegetable mould. Near sundown, as I glanced out of the window, I thought I began to see a change. Presently I was very sure I did. It began to appear in the more grassy character of the woods. Then I caught sight of peculiarly soft and uniform grassy patches here and there in the open. Then in a few moments more the train had shot us fairly into the edge of the blue-grass region, and the farmer in me began to be on the alert. We had passed in a twinkling from a portion of the earth's surface which is new, which is of yesterday, to a portion which is of the oldest, from the carboniferous to the lower silurian. Here, upon this lower silurian, the earth that saw and nourished the great monsters and dragons, was growing the delicate blue-grass. It had taken all these millions upon millions of years to prepare the way for this little plant to grow to perfection. I thought I had never seen fields and low hills look so soft in the twilight; they seemed clad in greenish gray fur. As we neared Mount Sterling, how fat and smooth the land looked; what long, even, gently flowing lines against the fading western sky, broken here and there by herds of slowly grazing or else reposing and ruminating cattle! What peace and plenty it suggested! From a land raw and crude and bitter like unripe fruit, we had suddenly been transported into the midst of one ripe and mellow with the fullness of time. It was sweet to look upon.

I was seized with a strong desire to go forth and taste it by a stroll through it in the twilight.

In the course of the ten days that followed, the last ten days of May, I had an opportunity to taste it pretty well, and my mind has had a grassy flavor ever since. I had an opportunity to see this restless and fitful American nature of ours in a more equable and beneficent mood than I had ever before seen it; all its savageness and acridness gone, no thought now but submission to the hand and wants of man. I afterward saw the prairies of Illinois, and the vast level stretches of farming country of northern Ohio and Indiana, but these lands were nowhere quite so human, quite so beautiful, or quite so productive as the blue-grass region. One likes to see the earth's surface lifted up and undulating a little, as if it heaved and swelled with emotion; it suggests more life, and at the same time that the sense of repose is greater. There is no repose in a prairie; it is stagnation, it is a *dead* level. Those immense stretches of flat land pain the eye, as if all life and expression had gone from the face of the earth. There is just unevenness enough in the blue-grass region to give mobility and variety to the landscape. From almost any given point one commands broad and extensive views — of immense fields of wheat or barley, or corn or hemp, or grass or clover, or of woodland pastures.

With Professor Proctor I drove a hundred miles

or more about the country in a buggy. First from Frankfort to Versailles, the capital of Woodford County; then to Lexington, where we passed a couple of days with Major McDowell at Ashland, the old Henry Clay place; then to Georgetown in Scott County; thence back to Frankfort again. The following week I passed three days on the great stock farm of Colonel Alexander, where I saw more and finer blooded stock in the way of horses, cattle, and sheep than I had ever seen before. From thence we went south to Colonel Shelby's, where we passed a couple of days on the extreme edge of the blue-grass circle in Boyle County. Here we strike the rim of sharp low hills that run quite around this garden of the State, from the Ohio River on the west to the Ohio again on the north and east. Kentucky is a great country for licks; there are any number of streams and springs that bear the names of licks. Probably the soil of no other State in the Union has been so much licked and smacked over as that of Kentucky. Colonel Shelby's farm is near a stream called Knob Lick, and within a few miles of a place called Blue Lick. I expected to see some sort of salt spring where the buffalo and deer used to come to lick; but instead of that saw a raw, naked spot of earth, an acre or two in extent, which had apparently been licked into the shape of a clay model of some scene in Colorado or the Rocky Mountains. There were gullies and chasms and sharp knobs and

peaks as blue and barren as could be, and no sign
of a spring or of water visible. The buffalo had
licked the clay for the saline matter it held, and had
certainly made a deep and lasting impression.

From Shelby City we went west sixty or more
miles, skirting the blue-grass region, to Lebanon
Junction, where I took the train for Cave City. The
blue-grass region is as large as the State of Massachusetts, and is, on the whole, the finest bit of the
earth's surface, with the exception of parts of England, I have yet seen. In one way it is more pleasing
than anything one sees in England, on account of
the greater sense of freedom and roominess which
it gives one. Everything is on a large, generous scale.
The fields are not so cut up, nor the roadways so
narrow, nor the fences so prohibitory. Indeed, the
distinguishing feature of this country is its breadth:
one sees fields of corn or wheat or clover of from
fifty to one hundred acres each. At Colonel Alexander's I saw three fields of clover lying side by side
which contained three hundred acres: as the clover
was just in full bloom, the sight was a very pleasing one. The farms are larger, ranging from several hundred to several thousand acres. The farmhouses are larger, with wide doors, broad halls, high
ceilings, ample grounds, and hospitality to match.
There is nothing niggardly or small in the people
or in their country. One sees none of the New York
or New England primness and trimness, but the

ample, flowing Southern way of life. It is common
to see horses and cattle grazing in the grounds
immediately about the house; there is nothing but
grass, and the great forest trees, which they cannot
hurt. The farmhouses rarely stand near the highway, but are set after the English fashion from a
third to half a mile distant, amid a grove of primitive forest trees, and flanked or backed up by the
many lesser buildings that the times of slavery made
necessary. Educated gentlemen farmers are probably the rule more than in the North. There are not
so many small or so many leased farms. The pro-
prietors are men of means, and come the nearest to
forming a landed gentry of any class of men we have
in this country. They are not city men running a
brief and rapid career on a fancy farm, but genuine
countrymen, who love the land and mean to keep
it. I remember with pleasure one rosy-faced young
farmer, whose place we casually invaded in Lincoln
County. He was a graduate of Harvard University
and of the Law School, but here he was with his
trousers tucked into his boot-legs, helping to cultivate his corn, or looking after his herds upon his
broad acres. He was nearly the ideal of a simple,
hearty, educated country farmer and gentleman.

But the feature of this part of Kentucky which
struck me the most forcibly, and which is perhaps
the most unique, is the immense sylvan or woodland pastures. The forests are simply vast grassy

orchards of maple and oak, or other trees, where the herds graze and repose. They everywhere give a look to the land as of royal parks and commons. They are as clean as a meadow, and as inviting as long, grassy vistas and circles of cool shade can make them. All the saplings and bushy undergrowths common to forests have been removed, leaving only the large trees scattered here and there, which seem to protect rather than occupy the ground. Such a look of leisure, of freedom, of amplitude, as these forest groves give to the landscape!

What vistas, what aisles, what retreats, what depths of sunshine and shadow! The grass is as uniform as a carpet, and grows quite up to the boles of the trees. One peculiarity of the blue-grass is that it takes complete possession of the soil; it suffers no rival; it is as uniform as a fall of snow. Only one weed seems to hold its own against it, and that is ironweed, a plant like a robust purple aster five or six feet high. This is Kentucky's one weed, so far as I saw. It was low and inconspicuous while I was there, but before fall it gets tall and rank, and its masses of purple flowers make a very striking spectacle. Through these forest glades roam the herds of cattle or horses. I know no prettier sight than a troop of blooded mares with their colts slowly grazing through these stately aisles, some of them in sunshine, and some in shadow. In riding along the highway there was hardly an hour when such a scene was not in view. Very often the great farm-house stands in one of these open forests and is approached by a graveled road that winds amid the trees. At Colonel Alexander's the cottage of his foreman, as well as many of the farm buildings and stables, stands in a grassy forest, and the mares with their colts roam far and wide. Sometimes when they were going for water, or were being started in for the night, they would come charging along like the wind, and what a pleasing sight it was to see their glossy coats glancing adown the long sun-flecked vistas! Sometimes the more open of these forest lands are tilled; I saw fine crops of hemp growing on them, and in one or two cases corn. But where the land has never been under cultivation it is re-markably smooth, — one can drive with a buggy with perfect ease and freedom anywhere through these woods. The ground is as smooth as if it had been rolled. In Kentucky we are beyond the south-ern limit of the glacial drift; there are no surface boulders and no abrupt knolls or gravel-banks. An-other feature which shows how gentle and uniform the forces which have moulded this land have been is the beautiful depressions which go by the ugly name of "sink-holes." They are broad, turf-lined bowls sunk in the surface here and there, and as smooth and symmetrical as if they had been turned out by a lathe. Those about the woodlands of Colo-nel Alexander were from one to two hundred feet

across and fifteen or twenty feet deep. The green
turf sweeps down into them without a break, and
the great trees grow from their sides and bottoms
the same as elsewhere. They look as if they might
have been carved out by the action of whirling
water, but are probably the result of the surface
water seeking a hidden channel in the underlying
rock, and thus slowly carrying away the soil with it.
They all still have underground drainage through
the bottom. By reason of these depressions this
part of the State has been called "goose-nest land,"
their shape suggesting the nests of immense geese.
On my way southward to the Mammoth Cave, over
the formation known as the subcarboniferous, they
formed the most noticeable feature of the landscape.
An immense flock of geese had nested here, so that
in places the rims of their nests touched one another.
As you near the great cave, you see a mammoth
depression, nothing less than a broad, oval valley
which holds entire farms, and which has no outlet
save through the bottom. In England these depressions would be called punch-bowls; and though they
know well in Kentucky what punch is made of, and
can furnish the main ingredient of superb quality,
and in quantity that would quite fill some of these
grassy basins, yet I do not know that they apply
this term to them. But in the good old times before
the war, when the spirit of politics ran much higher
than now, these punch-bowls and the forests about

them were the frequent scene of happy and convivial gatherings. Under the great trees the political orators held forth; a whole ox would be roasted to feed the hungry crowd, and something stronger than punch flowed freely. One farmer showed us in our walk where Crittenden and Breckinridge had frequently held forth, but the grass had long been growing over the ashes where the ox had been roasted.

What a land for picnics and open-air meetings! The look of it suggested something more large and leisurely than the stress and hurry of our American life. What was there about it that made me think of Walter Scott and the age of romance and chivalry? and of Robin Hood and his adventurous band under the greenwood tree? Probably it was those stately, open forests, with their clear, grassy vistas where a tournament might be held, and those superb breeds of horses wandering through them, upon which it was so easy to fancy knights and ladies riding. The land has not the mellow, time-enriched look of England; it could not have it under our harder, fiercer climate; but it has a sense of breadth and a roominess which one never sees in England except in the great royal parks.

The fences are mainly posts and rails, which fall a little short of giving the look of permanence which a hedge or a wall and dike afford.

The Kentuckians have an unhandsome way of

treating their forests when they want to get rid of them ; they girdle the trees and let them die, instead of cutting them down at once. A girdled tree dies hard; the struggle is painful to look upon; inch by inch, leaf by leaf, it yields, and the agony is protracted nearly through the whole season. The land looked accursed when its noble trees were all dying or had died, as if smitten by a plague. One hardly expected to see grass or grain growing on it. The girdled trees stand for years, their gaunt skeletons blistering in the sun or blackening in the rain. Through southern Indiana and Illinois I noticed this same lazy, ugly custom of getting rid of the trees.

The most noticeable want of the blue-grass region is water. The streams bore underground through the limestone rock so readily that they rarely come to the surface. With plenty of sparkling streams and rivers like New England, it would indeed be a land of infinite attractions. The most unsightly feature the country afforded was the numerous shallow basins, scooped out of the soil and filled with stagnant water, where the flocks and herds drank. These, with the girdled trees, were about the only things the landscape presented to which the eye did not turn with pleasure. Yet when one does chance upon a spring, it is apt to be a strikingly beautiful one. The limestone rock, draped with dark, dripping moss, opens a cavernous mouth from which in most instances a considerable stream flows. I saw three or four such springs, about which one wanted to linger long. The largest was at Georgetown, where a stream ten or twelve feet broad and three or four feet deep came gliding from a cavernous cliff without a ripple. It is situated in the very edge of the town, and could easily be made a feature singularly attractive. As we approached its head, a little colored girl rose up from its brink with a pail of water. I asked her name. "Venus, sir; Venus." It was the nearest I had ever come to seeing Venus rising from the foam.

There are three hard things in Kentucky, only one of which is to my taste; namely, hard bread, hard beds, and hard roads. The roads are excellent, macadamized as in England, and nearly as well kept; but that "beat-biscuit," a sort of domestic hardtack, in the making of which the flour or dough is beaten long and hard with the rolling-pin, is, in my opinion, a poor substitute for Yankee bread; and those mercilessly hard beds, — the macadamizing principle is out of place there, too. It would not be exact to call Kentucky butter bad; but with all their fine grass and fancy stock, they do not succeed well in this article of domestic manufacture. But Kentucky whiskey is soft, seductively so, and I caution all travelers to beware how they suck any iced preparation of it through a straw of a hot day; it is not half so innocent as it tastes.

The blue-grass region has sent out, and continues

to send out, the most famous trotting-horses in the world. Within a small circle not half a dozen miles across were produced all the more celebrated horses of the past ten years; but it has as yet done nothing of equal excellence in the way of men. I could but ask myself why this ripe and mellow geology, this stately and bountiful landscape, these large and substantial homesteads, have not yet produced a crop of men to match. Cold and sterile Massachusetts is far in the lead in this respect. Granite seems a better nurse of genius than the lime-rock. The one great man born in Kentucky, Abraham Lincoln, was not a product of this fertile region. Henry Clay was a Virginian. The two most eminent native blue-grass men were John C. Breckinridge and John J. Crittenden. It seems that it takes something more than a fertile soil to produce great men; a deep and rich human soil is much more important. Kentucky has been too far to one side of the main current of our national life; she has felt the influence of New England but very little; neither has she been aroused by the stir and enterprise of the great West. Her schoolhouses are too far apart, even in this rich section, and she values a fast trotter or racer more than she does a fine scholar.

What gives the great fertility to the blue-grass region is the old limestone rock, laid down in the ancient Silurian seas, which comes to the surface over all this part of the State and makes the soil by

its disintegration. The earth's surface seems once to
have bulged up here like a great bubble, and then
to have been planed or ground off by the elements.
This wearing away process removed all the more
recent formations, the coal beds and the conglomerate or other rocks beneath them, and left this ancient
limestone exposed. Its continued decay keeps up
the fertility of the soil. Wheat and corn and clover
are rotated for fifty years upon the same fields without manure, and without any falling off in their
productiveness. Where the soil is removed, the
rock presents that rough, honeycombed appearance
which surfaces do that have been worm-eaten instead of worn. The tooth which has gnawed, and
is still gnawing it, is the carbonic acid carried into
the earth by rain-water. Hence, unlike the prairies of the West, the fertility of this soil perpetually
renews itself. The blue-grass seems native to this region; any field left to itself will presently be covered
with blue-grass. It is not cut for hay, but is for
grazing alone. Fields which have been protected
during the fall yield good pasturage even in winter.
And a Kentucky winter is no light affair, the mercury often falling fifteen or twenty degrees below
zero.

I saw but one new bird in Kentucky, namely, the
lark finch, and but one pair of those. This is a
Western bird of the sparrow kind which is slowly
making its way eastward, having been found as far

east as Long Island. I was daily on the lookout for it, but saw none till I was about leaving this part of the State. Near old Governor Shelby's place in Boyle County, as we were driving along the road, my eye caught a grayish brown bird like the sky-lark, but with a much more broad and beautifully marked tail. It suggested both a lark and a sparrow, and I knew at once it was the lark finch I had been looking for. It alighted on some low object in a plowed field, and with a glass I had a good view of it, — a very elegant, distinguished-appearing bird for one clad in the sparrow suit, the tail large and dark, with white markings on the outer web of the quills. Much as I wanted to hear his voice, he would not sing, and it was not till I reached Adams County, Illinois, that I saw another one and heard the song. Driving about the country here — which, by the way, reminded me more of the blue-grass region than anything I saw outside of Kentucky — with a friend, I was again on the lookout for the new bird, but had begun to think it was not a resident, when I espied one on the fence by the roadside. It failed to sing, but farther on we saw another one, which alighted upon a fruit tree near us. We paused to look and to listen, when instantly it struck up and gave us a good sample of its musical ability. It was both a lark and a sparrow song; or, rather, the notes of a sparrow uttered in the continuous and rapid manner of the skylark, — a pleasing per-

formance, but not meriting the praise I had heard
bestowed upon it.

In Kentucky and Illinois, and probably throughout the West and Southwest, certain birds come to
the front and are conspicuous which we see much
less of in the East. The blue jay seems to be a garden and orchard bird, and to build about dwellings
as familiarly as the robin does with us. There must
be dozens of these birds in this part of the country
where there is but one in New England. And the
brown thrashers, — in Illinois they were as common
along the highways as song sparrows or chippies are
with us, and nearly as familiar. So also were the turtle doves and meadowlarks. That the Western birds
should be more tame and familiar than the same
species in the East is curious enough. From the
semi-domestication of so many of the English birds,
when compared with our own, we infer that the
older the country, the more the birds are changed
in this respect; yet the birds of the Mississippi Valley are less afraid of man than those of the valley of
the Hudson or the Connecticut. Is it because the
homestead, with its trees and buildings, affords the
birds on the great treeless prairies their first and
almost only covert? Where could the perchers perch
till trees and fences and buildings offered? For this
reason they would at once seek the vicinity of man
and become familiar with him.

In Kentucky the summer redbird everywhere

attracted my attention. Its song is much like that
of its relative the tanager, and its general habits and
manners are nearly the same.

The oriole is as common in Kentucky as in New
York or New England. One day we saw one weave
into her nest unusual material. As we sat upon the
lawn in front of the cottage, we had noticed the bird
just beginning her structure, suspending it from a
long, low branch of the Kentucky coffee-tree that
grew but a few feet away. I suggested to my host
that if he would take some brilliant yarn and scatter it about upon the shrubbery, the fence, and the
walks, the bird would probably avail herself of it,
and weave a novel nest. I had heard of it being
done, but had never tried it myself. The suggestion was at once acted upon, and in a few moments a
handful of zephyr yarn, crimson, orange, green, yellow, and blue, was distributed about the grounds.
As we sat at dinner a few moments later, I saw the
eager bird flying up toward her nest with one of
these brilliant yarns streaming behind her. They
had caught her eye at once, and she fell to work
upon them with a will; not a bit daunted by their
brilliant color, she soon had a crimson spot there
amid the green leaves. She afforded us rare amusement all the afternoon and the next morning. How
she seemed to congratulate herself over her rare
find! How vigorously she knotted those strings to
her branch and gathered the ends in and sewed them

through and through the structure, jerking them spitefully like a housewife burdened with many cares! How savagely she would fly at her neighbor, an oriole that had a nest just over the fence a few yards away, when she invaded her territory! The male looked on approvingly, but did not offer to lend a hand. There is something in the manner of the female on such occasions, something so decisive and emphatic, that one entirely approves of the course of the male in not meddling or offering any suggestions. It is the wife's enterprise, and she evidently knows her own mind so well that the husband keeps aloof, or plays the part of an approving spectator.

The woolen yarn was ill-suited to the Kentucky climate. This fact the bird seemed to appreciate, for she used it only in the upper part of her nest, in attaching it to the branch and in binding and compacting the rim, making the sides and bottom of hemp, leaving it thin and airy, much more so than are the same nests with us. No other bird would, perhaps, have used such brilliant material; their instincts of concealment would have revolted, but the oriole aims more to make its nest inaccessible than to hide it. Its position and depth insure its safety.

The red-headed woodpecker was about the only bird of this class I saw, and it was very common. Almost any moment, in riding along, their conspicuous white markings as they flew from tree to tree were to be seen festooning the woods. Yet I was told that they were far less numerous than formerly. Governor Knott said he believed there were ten times as many when he was a boy as now. But what beautiful thing is there in this world that was not ten times more abundant when one was a boy than he finds it on becoming a man? Youth is the principal factor in the problem. If one could only have the leisure, the alertness, and the freedom from care that he had when a boy, he would probably find that the world had not deteriorated so much as he is apt to suspect.

The field or meadow bird, everywhere heard in Kentucky and Illinois, is the black-throated bunting, a heavy-beaked bird the size and color of an English sparrow, with a harsh, rasping song, which it indulges in incessantly. Among bird-songs it is like a rather coarse weed among our wild flowers.

I could not find the mockingbird in song, though it breeds in the blue-grass counties. I saw only two specimens of the bird in all my wanderings. The Virginia cardinal was common, and in places the yellow-breasted chat was heard. Once I heard from across a broad field a burst of bobolink melody from a score or more of throats, — a flock of the birds probably pausing on their way north. In Chicago I was told that the Illinois bobolink had a different song from the New England species, but I could detect no essential difference. The song of certain birds, notably that of the bobolink, seems to vary slightly in different localities, and also to change during a series of years. I no longer hear the exact bobolink song which I heard in my boyhood, in the localities where I then heard it. Not a season passes but I hear marked departures in the songs of our birds from what appears to be the standard song of a given species.

XIV

IN MAMMOTH CAVE

SOME idea of the impression which Mammoth Cave makes upon the senses, irrespective even of sight, may be had from the fact that blind people go there to see it, and are greatly struck with it. I was assured that this is a fact. The blind seem as much impressed by it as those who have their sight. When the guide pauses at the more interesting point, or lights the scene up with a great torch or with Bengal lights, and points out the more striking features, the blind ·exclaim, " How wonderful! how beautiful!" They can feel it, if they cannot see it. They get some idea of the spaciousness when words are uttered. The voice goes forth in these colossal chambers like a bird. When no word is spoken, the silence is of a kind never experienced on the surface of the earth, it is so profound and abysmal. This, and the absolute darkness, to a person with eyes makes him feel as if he were face to face with the primordial nothingness. The objective universe is gone; only the subjective remains; the sense of hearing is inverted, and reports only the murmurs from within. The blind miss much, but much remains to them.

The great cave is not merely a spectacle to the eye; it is a wonder to the ear, a strangeness to the smell and to the touch. The body feels the presence of unusual conditions through every pore.

For my part, my thoughts took a decidedly sepulchral turn; I thought of my dead and of all the dead of the earth, and said to myself, the darkness and the silence of their last resting-place is like this; to this we must all come at last. No vicissitudes of earth, no changes of seasons, no sound of storm or thunder penetrate here; winter and summer, day and night, peace or war, it is all one; a world beyond the reach of change, because beyond the reach of life. What peace, what repose, what desolation! The marks and relics of the Indian, which disappear so quickly from the light of day above, are here beyond the reach of natural change. The imprint of his moccasin in the dust might remain undisturbed for a thousand years. At one point the guide reaches his arm beneath the rocks that strew the floor and pulls out the burnt ends of canes, which were used, probably, when filled with oil or grease, by the natives to light their way into the cave doubtless centuries ago.

Here in the loose soil are ruts worn by cartwheels in 1812, when, during the war with Great Britain, the earth was searched to make saltpetre. The guide kicks corn-cobs out of the dust where the oxen were fed at noon, and they look nearly as fresh as ever they did. In those frail corn-cobs and in those wheel-tracks as if the carts had but just gone along, one seemed to come very near to the youth of the century, almost to overtake it.

At a point in one of the great avenues, if you stop and listen, you hear a slow, solemn ticking like a great clock in a deserted hall; you hear the slight echo as it fathoms and sets off the silence. It is called the clock, and is caused by a single large drop of water falling every second into a little pool. A ghostly kind of clock there in the darkness, that is never wound up and that never runs down. It seemed like a mockery where time is not, and change does not come, — the clock of the dead. This sombre and mortuary cast of one's thoughts seems so natural in the great cave, that I could well understand the emotions of a lady who visited the cave with a party a few days before I was there. She went forward very reluctantly from the first; the silence and the darkness of the huge mausoleum evidently impressed her imagination, so that when she got to the spot where the guide points out the " Giant's Coffin," a huge, fallen rock, which in the dim light takes exactly the form of an enormous coffin, her fear quite overcame her, and she begged · piteously to be taken back. Timid, highly imaginative people, especially women, are quite sure to have a sense of fear in this strange underground world. The guide told me of a lady in one of the parties he was conducting through, who wanted to linger behind a little all alone; he suffered her to do so, but presently heard a piercing scream. Rushing back, he found her lying prone upon the ground in a dead faint. She had accidentally put out her lamp, and was so appalled by the darkness that instantly closed around her that she swooned at once.

Sometimes it seemed to me as if I were threading the streets of some buried city of the fore-world. With your little lantern in your hand, you follow your guide through those endless and silent avenues, catching glimpses on either hand of what appears to be some strange antique architecture, the hoary and crumbling walls rising high up into the darkness. Now we turn a sharp corner, or turn down a street, which crosses our course at right angles; now we come out into a great circle, or spacious court, which the guide lights up with a quick-paper torch, or a colored chemical light. There are streets above you and streets below you. As this was a city where day never entered, no provision for light needed to be made, and it is built one layer above another to the number of four or five, or on the plan of an enormous ant-hill, the lowest avenues being several hundred feet beneath the uppermost. The main avenue leading in from the entrance is called the Broadway, and if Broadway, New York, were arched over and reduced to utter darkness and silence, and its roadway blocked with mounds of earth and fragments of rock, it would, perhaps, only lack that gray, cosmic, elemental look, to make it resemble this. A mile or so from the entrance we pass a couple of rude stone houses, built forty or more years ago by some consumptives, who hoped to prolong their lives by a residence in this pure, antiseptic air. Five months they lived here, poor creatures, a half dozen of them, without ever going forth into the world of light. But the long entombment did not arrest the disease; the mountain did not draw the virus out, but seemed to draw the strength and vitality out, so that when the victims did go forth into the light and air, bleached as white as chalk, they succumbed at once, and nearly all died before they could reach the hotel, a few hundred yards away.

Probably the prettiest thing they have to show you in Mammoth Cave is the Star Chamber. This seems to have made an impression upon Emerson when he visited the cave, for he mentions it in one of his essays, "Illusions." The guide takes your lantern from you and leaves you seated upon a bench by the wayside, in the profound cosmic darkness. He retreats along a side alley that seems to go down to a lower level, and at a certain point shades his lamp with his hat, so that the light falls upon the ceiling over your head. You look up, and the first thought is that there is an opening just there that permits you to look forth upon the midnight skies. You see the darker horizon line where the sky ends and the mountains begin. The sky is blue-black and is thickly studded with stars, rather small stars, but apparently genuine. At one point a long, luminous streak simulates exactly the form and effect of a comet. As you gaze, the guide slowly moves his hat, and a black cloud gradually creeps over the sky, and all is blackness again. Then you hear footsteps retreating and dying away in the distance. Presently all is still, save the ringing in your own ears. Then after a few moments, during which you have sat in silence like that of the interstellar spaces, you hear over your left shoulder a distant flapping of wings, followed by the crowing of a cock. You turn your head in that direction and behold a faint dawn breaking on the horizon. It slowly increases till you hear footsteps approaching, and your dusky companion, playing the part of Apollo, with lamp in hand ushers in the light of day. It is rather theatrical, but a very pleasant diversion nevertheless.

Another surprise was when we paused at a certain point, and the guide asked me to shout or call in a loud voice. I did so without any unusual effect following. Then he spoke in a very deep bass, and instantly the rocks all about and beneath us became like the strings of an Æolian harp. They seemed transformed as if by enchantment. Then I tried, but did not strike the right key; the rocks were dumb; I tried again, but got no response; flat and dead the sounds came back as if in mockery; then

266

I struck a deeper bass, the chord was hit, and the
solid walls seemed to become as thin and frail as a
drum-head or as the frame of a violin. They fairly
seemed to dance about us, and to recede away from
us. Such wild, sweet music I had never before heard
rocks discourse. Ah, the magic of the right key!
"Why leap ye, ye high hills?" why, but that they
had been spoken to in the right voice? Is not the
whole secret of life to pitch our voices in the right
key? Responses come from the very rocks when
we do so. I thought of the lines of our poet of Demo-
cracy: —

"Surely, whoever speaks to me in the right voice, him or
      her I shall follow,
As the water follows the moon, silently, with fluid steps,
      anywhere around the globe."

Where we were standing was upon an arch over
an avenue which crossed our course beneath us. The
reverberations on Echo River, a point I did not reach,
can hardly be more surprising, though they are described as wonderful.

There are four or five levels in the cave, and a
series of avenues upon each. The lowest is some
two hundred and fifty feet below the entrance. Here
the stream which has done all this carving and tun-
neling has got to the end of its tether. It is here
on a level with Green River in the valley below,
and flows directly into it. I say the end of its tether,

though if Green River cuts its valley deeper, the stream will, of course, follow suit. The bed of the river has probably, at successive periods, been on a level with each series of avenues of the cave. The stream is now doubtless but a mere fraction of its former self. Indeed, every feature of the cave attests the greater volume and activity of the forces which carved it, in the earlier geologic ages. The waters have worn the rock as if it were but ice. The domes and pits are carved and fluted in precisely the way dripping water flutes snow or ice. The rainfall must have been enormous in those early days, and it must have had a much stronger and sharper tooth of carbonic acid gas than now. It has carved out enormous pits with perpendicular sides, two or three hundred feet deep. Goring Dome I remember particularly. You put your head through an irregularly shaped window in the wall at the side of one of the avenues, and there is this huge shaft or well, starting from some higher level and going down two hundred feet below you. There must have been such wells in the old glaciers, worn by a rill of water slowly eating its way down. It was probably ten feet across, still moist and dripping. The guide threw down a lighted torch, and it fell and fell, till I had to crane my neck far out to see it finally reach the bottom. Some of these pits are simply appalling, and where the way is narrow, have been covered over to prevent accidents.

IN MAMMOTH CAVE

No part of Mammoth Cave was to me more impressive than its entrance, probably because here its gigantic proportions are first revealed to you, and can be clearly seen. That strange colossal underworld here looks out into the light of day, and comes in contrast with familiar scenes and objects. When you are fairly in the cave, you cannot see it; that is, with your aboveground eyes; you walk along by the dim light of your lamp as in a huge wood at night; when the guide lights up the more interesting portions with his torches and colored lights, the effect is weird and spectral; it seems like a dream; it is an unfamiliar world; you hardly know whether this is the emotion of grandeur which you experience, or of mere strangeness. If you could have the light of day in there, you would come to your senses, and could test the reality of your impressions. At the entrance you have the light of day, and you look fairly in the face of this underground monster, yea, into his open mouth, which has a span of fifty feet or more, and down into his contracting throat, where a man can barely stand upright, and where the light fades and darkness begins. As you come down the hill through the woods from the hotel, you see no sign of the cave till you emerge into a small opening where the grass grows and the sunshine falls, when you turn slightly to the right, and there at your feet yawns this terrible pit; and you feel indeed as if the mountain had opened its mouth and was lying in wait to swallow you down, as a whale might swallow a shrimp. I never grew tired of sitting or standing here by this entrance and gazing into it. It had for me something of the same fascination that the display of the huge elemental forces of nature have, as seen in thunder-storms, or in a roaring ocean surf. Two phœbe-birds had their nests in little niches of the rocks, and delicate ferns and wild flowers fringed the edges.

Another very interesting feature to me was the behavior of the cool air which welled up out of the mouth of the cave. It simulated exactly a fountain of water. It rose up to a certain level, or until it filled the depression immediately about the mouth of the cave, and then flowing over at the lowest point, ran down the hill toward Green River, along a little water-course, exactly as if it had been a liquid. I amused myself by wading down into it as into a fountain. The air above was muggy and hot, the thermometer standing at about eighty-six degrees, and this cooler air of the cave, which was at a temperature of about fifty-two degrees, was separated in the little pool or lakelet which is formed from the hotter air above it by a perfectly horizontal line. As I stepped down into it I could feel it close over my feet, then it was at my knees, then I was immersed to my hips, then to my waist, then I stood neck-deep in it, my body almost chilled, while my face and head were bathed by a sultry, oppressive air. Where the two bodies of air came in contact, a slight film of vapor was formed by condensation; I waded in till I could look under this as under a ceiling. It was as level and as well defined as a sheet of ice on a pond. A few moments' immersion into this aerial fountain made one turn to the warmer air again. At the depression in the rim of the basin one had but to put his hand down to feel the cold air flowing over like water. Fifty yards below you could still wade into it as into a creek, and at a hundred yards it was still quickly perceptible, but broader and higher; it had begun to lose some of its coldness, and to mingle with the general air; all the plants growing on the margin of the water-course were in motion, as well as the leaves on the low branches of the trees near by. Gradually this cool current was dissipated and lost in the warmth of the day.

XV

HASTY OBSERVATION

WHEN Boswell told Dr. Johnson that while
in Italy he had several times seen the experiment tried of placing a scorpion within a circle
of burning coals, and that in every instance the scorpion, after trying to break through the fiery circle,
retired to the centre and committed suicide by darting its sting into its head, the doctor showed the true
scientific spirit by demanding further proof of the
fact. The mere testimony of the eye under such
circumstances was not enough; appearances are
often deceptive. "If the great anatomist Morgagni,"
said the doctor, "after dissecting a scorpion on
which the experiment had been tried, should certify
that its sting had penetrated its head, that would
be convincing." For almost the only time in his life
the superstitious doctor showed himself, I say, a
true scientist, a man refusing to accept the truth of
appearances.

But this frame of mind was not habitual to him,
for the next moment he said that swallows sleep all
winter in the bed of a river or pond, "conglobu-
lated" into a ball. The scientific spirit would have

required him to insist upon the proof of the alleged fact in this case the same as in the other. Has any competent observer verified this statement? Have swallows been taken out of the mud, or been seen to throw themselves into the water?

Albertus Magnus (1193–1280), in his book on animals, says that the eel leaves the water in the night-time, and invades the fields and gardens to feed upon peas and lentils. A scientific man makes this statement, and probably upon no stronger proof than that some eels dropped by poachers in their hasty retreat had been found in a pea-patch. If peas had been found, and found in many cases, in the stomachs of eels, that would have been pretty conclusive proof that eels eat peas.

The great thing in observation is not to be influenced by our preconceived notions, or by what we want to be true, or by our fears, hopes, or any personal element, and to see the thing just as it is. A person who believes in ghosts and apparitions cannot be depended upon to investigate an alleged phenomenon of this sort, because he will not press his inquiry far enough, and will take for granted the very fact we want proof of.

The eye does not always see what is in front of it. Indeed, it might almost be said, it sees only what is back of it, in the mind. Whenever I have any particular subject in mind, every walk gives me new material. If I am thinking about tree-toads, I find

274

tree-toads. If I am dwelling upon birds'-nests, I find plenty of nests which otherwise I should have passed by. If bird-songs occupy me, I am bound to hear some new or peculiar note.

Every one has observed how, after he has made the acquaintance of a new word, that word is perpetually turning up in his reading, as if it had suddenly become the fashion. When you have a thing in mind, it is not long till you have it in hand. Torrey and Drummond, the botanists, were one day walking in the woods near West Point. "I have never yet found so and so," said Drummond, naming a rare kind of moss. "Find it anywhere," said Torrey, and stooped and picked it up at their feet. Thoreau could pick up arrow-heads with the same ease. Many people have the same quick eye for a four-leaved clover. I may say of myself without vanity, that I see birds with like ease. It is no effort, I cannot help it. Either my eye or my ear is on duty quite unbeknown to me. When I visit my friends, I leave a trail of birds behind me, as old Amphion left a plantation of trees wherever he sat down and played.

The scientific habit of mind leads a man to take into account all possible sources of error in such observations. The senses are all so easily deceived. People of undoubted veracity tell you of the strange things they have known to rain down, or of some strange bird or beast they have seen. But if you question them closely, you are pretty sure to find some flaw in the observation, or some link of evidence wanting. We are so apt to jump to conclusions; we take one or two steps in following up the evidence, and then leap to the result that seems to be indicated. If you find a trout in the milk, you may be justified in jumping to a conclusion not flattering to your milkman, but if you find angle-worms in the barrel of rain-water after a shower, you are not to conclude that therefore they rained down, as many people think they do.

Or if after a shower in summer you find the ground swarming with little toads, you are not to infer that the shower brought them down. I have frequently seen large numbers of little toads hopping about after a shower, but only in particular localities. Upon a small, gravelly hill in the highway along which I was in the habit of walking, I have seen them several seasons, but in no other place upon that road. Just why they come out on such occasions is a question; probably to get their jackets wet. There was a pond and marshy ground not far off where they doubtless hatched. Because the frogs are heard in the marshes in spring as soon as the ice and snow are gone, it is a popular belief that they hibernate in these places. But the two earliest frogs, I am convinced, pass the winter in the ground in the woods, and seek the marshes as soon as the frost and ice are gone. I have heard the hyla pipe in a feeble, tentative manner in localities where the ground was

free from frost, while the marshes near by were yet
covered with solid ice; and in spring I have dug
out another species from beneath the leaf mould in
the woods. Both these species are properly land-
frogs, and only take to the water to breed, returning again to the woods later in the season. The
same is true of the tree-frog, which passes the winter
in the ground or in hollow trees, and takes to the
marshes in May to deposit its eggs. The common
bullfrog and the pickerel frog doubtless pass the
winter in the beds of ponds and streams. I think
it is quite certain that hibernating animals in the
ground do not freeze, though by no means beyond
the reach of frost. The frogs, ants, and crickets are
probably protected by some sort of acid which their
bodies secrete, though this is only a guess of my
own. The frog I dug out of the leaves one spring
day, while the ground above and below him was
frozen hard, was entirely free from frost, though his
joints were apparently very stiff. A friend of mine,
in felling some trees in winter, cut through a den
of field crickets; the ground was frozen about their
galleries, but the crickets themselves, though motionless, were free from frost. Cut the large, black tree
ants out of a pine log in winter, and though apparently lifeless, they are not frozen.

There is something in most of us that welcomes
a departure from the ordinary routine of natural
causes; we like to believe that the impossible hap-

pens; we like to see the marvelous and the mysterious crop out of ordinary occurrences. We like to believe, for instance, that snakes can charm their prey; can exert some mysterious influence over bird or beast at a distance of many feet, which deprives it of power to escape. But there is probably little truth in this popular notion. Fear often paralyzes, and doubtless this is the whole secret of the power of snakes and cats to charm their prey. It is what is called a subjective phenomenon; the victim is fascinated or spellbound by the sudden and near appearance of its enemy. A sportsman, in whose veracity I have full confidence, told me that his pointer dog had several times worked up to a woodcock or partridge and seized it in his mouth. Of course the dog brought no mysterious power to bear upon the bird. He could hardly have seen the bird till he came plump upon it; he was wholly intent upon unraveling its trail. The bird, in watching the eager motions and the gradual approach of the dog, must have been thrown into such a state of fear or consternation as to quite paralyze its powers, and suffered the dog to pick it up. In the case of snakes, they doubtless in most instances approach and seize their prey unawares. I have seen a little snake in the woods pursue and overtake a lizard that was trying to escape from it. There was no attempt at charming; superior speed alone gave the victory to the snake. I have known a red squirrel to be caught and swallowed by a black snake, but I have no belief that the squirrel was charmed; it was more probably seized from some ambush.

One can hardly understand how a mouse can be caught by a hawk except upon the theory that the mouse is suddenly paralyzed by fear. The meadow mouse when exposed to view is very wary and quick in its movements; it is nibbling grass in the meadow bottom, or clearing its runway, or shaping its nest, when the hawk poises on wing high in the air above it. When the hawk discovers its victim, it descends with extended talons to the earth and seizes it. It does not drop like a bolt from heaven; its descent, on the contrary, is quite deliberate, and must be attended by a sound of rushing wings that ought to reach the mouse's ear, if the form escapes its eye.

There is doubtless just as much "charming" in this case as in any other, or when a fish hawk falls through the air and seizes a fish near the surface in perfectly clear water, — what hinders the fish from seeing and avoiding its enemy? Apparently nothing; apparently it allows itself to be seized. Every fisherman knows how alert most fish are, how quickly they discover him and dart away, even when he is immediately above them. All I contend for is that the snake, the cat, the hawk, does not exert some mysterious power over its prey, but that its prey in many cases loses its power to escape through

279

fear. It is said that a stuffed snake's skin will charm a bird as well as the live snake.

I came near reaching a hasty conclusion the other day with regard to a chickadee's nest. The nest is in a small cavity in the limb of a pear-tree near my study, and the birds and I are on very friendly terms. As the nest of a pair of chickadees had been broken up here a few seasons ago by a mouse or squirrel, I was apprehensive lest this nest share the same fate. Hence when, one morning, the birds were missing, and I found on inspection what appeared to be the hair of some small animal adhering to the edges of the hole that leads to the nest, I concluded that the birds had been cleaned out again. Later in the day I examined the supposed hair with my pocket glass, and found it was not hair, but some vegetable fibre. My next conclusion was that the birds had not been molested, but that they were furnishing their apartment, and some of the material had stuck to the door jambs. This proved to be the correct inference. The chickadee makes a little felt-like mat or carpet with which it covers the bottom of the nest-cavity. A day or two later, in my vineyard near by, I found where a piece of heavy twine that held a young grapevine to a stake had been pulled down to the ground and picked and beaten, and parts of it reduced to its original tow. Here, doubtless, the birds had got some of their carpeting material.

HASTY OBSERVATION

I recently read in a work on ornithology that the rings of small holes which we see in the trunks and limbs of perfectly sound apple-trees are made by woodpeckers in search of grubs and insects. This is a hasty inference. These holes are made by woodpeckers, but the food they obtain at the bottom of them is not the flesh of worm or insect, but the flesh of the apple-tree,—the soft, milky inner bark. The same writer says these holes are not hurtful to the tree, but conducive to its health. Yet I have seen the limbs of large apple-trees nearly killed by being encompassed by numerous rings of large, deep holes made by the yellow-bellied woodpecker. This bird drills holes in the sugar maple in the spring for the sap. I have known him to spend the greater part of a bright March day on the sunny side of a maple, indulging in a tipple of maple sap every four or five minutes. As fast as his well holes filled up, he would sip them dry.

A lady told me that a woodpecker drilled holes in the boards that form the eaves of her house, for the grubs of the carpenter bumblebee. This also seemed to me a hasty conclusion, because the woodpeckers made holes so large that the next season the blue-birds nested there. The woodpeckers were probably drilling for a place to nest. A large ice-house stands on the river-bank near me, and every season the man in charge has to shoot or drive away the high-holes that cut numerous openings through the outer

sheathing of hemlock boards into the spaces filled
with sawdust, where they find the digging easy and
a nesting-place safe and snug.

My neighbor caught a small hawk in his shad-net,
and therefore concluded the hawk ate fish. He put
him in a cage, and offered him fragments of shad.
The little hawk was probably in pursuit of a bird
which took refuge under the net as it hung upon
the drying-poles ; or he may have swooped down
upon the net in the spirit of pure bluster and bra-
vado, and thus come to grief in a hurry. The fine,
strong threads of the net defied his murderous beak
and talons. He was engulfed as completely as is
a fly in a spider's web, and the more he struggled,
the more hopeless his case became. It was a pigeon
hawk, and these little marauders are very saucy.

My neighbor says that in the city of Brooklyn he
has known kingbirds to nest in boxes like martins
and bluebirds. I question this observation, though
it may be true. The cousin of the kingbird, the
great crested flycatcher, builds in cavities in trees,
and its relative, the phœbe-bird, nests under bridges
and hay-sheds. Hence there is this fact to start with
in favor of my neighbor's observation.

But when a lady from Pennsylvania writes me
that she has seen "swallows rolling and dabbling in
the mud in early spring, their breasts so covered
with it that it would take but little stretch of imagination to believe they had just emerged from the bot-

Sapsucker

Louis Agassiz Fuertes.

tom of the pond beside which they were playing,"
I am more than skeptical. The lady has not seen
straight. The swallows were not rolling in the mud;
there was probably not a speck of mud upon their
plumage, but a little upon their beaks and feet. The
red of their breasts was their own proper color.
They were building their nests, as my correspondent
knew, but they did not carefully mix and knead the
mud, as she thought they did; they had selected
mortar already of the proper sort.

The careful observer is not long in learning that
there is truth in the poet's remark, that "things are
not what they seem." Everywhere on the surface
of nature things seem one thing, and mean quite
another. The hasty observer is misled by the seeming, and thus misses the real truth.

The little green snake that I saw among the
"live-for-evers" the other day, how nearly it escaped
detection by the close resemblance of its color to that
of the plant! And when, a few days later, I saw
one carelessly disposed across the top of the bending
grass and daisies, but a few feet from where I sat,
my eye again came near being baffled.

The little snake was probably lying in wait for
some insect. Presently it slid gently down into the
grass, moving so slowly as to escape any but the most
watchful eye. After its head and a part of its body
were upon the ground, its tail still pointed straight
up and exactly resembled some fresh vegetable

growth. The safeguard of this little snake is in his protective coloring; hence his movements are slower and more deliberate than those of the other snakes.

This simulation is very common in nature. Every creature has its enemy, and pretends to be that which it is not, in order to escape detection. The tree-frog pretends to be a piece of bark, or a lichen upon a tree; the wood frog is the color of the dry leaves upon which it hops, though when spawning in the little black pools and tarns in spring, its color is very dark, like the element it inhabits.

One day, in my walk in the woods, I disturbed a whip-poor-will where she sat upon her eggs on the ground. When I returned to the spot some hours afterward, and tried to make out the bird upon her nest, my eye was baffled for some moments, so successful was she in pretending to be only a mottled stick or piece of fallen bark.

Only the most practiced eye can detect the partridge (ruffed grouse) when she sits or stands in full view upon the ground in the woods. How well she plays her part, rarely moving, till she suddenly bursts up before you, and is gone in a twinkling! How well her young are disciplined always to take their cue from her! Not one will stir till she gives the signal.

One day in my walk, as I paused on the side of a steep hill in the edge of the woods, my eye chanced to fall upon a partridge, sitting upon the leaves beside a stump scarcely three paces from me. "Can she have a nest there?" was my first thought. Then I remembered it was late in the summer, and she certainly could not be incubating. Then why is she sitting there in that exposed manner? Keeping my eye upon her, I took a step forward, when, quick as a flash, she sprang into the air and went humming away. At the same moment, all about me, almost from under my feet, her nearly grown young sprang up and went booming through the woods after her. Not one of them had moved or showed fear till their mother gave the word.

To observe Nature and to know her secrets, one needs not only a sharp eye, but a steady and patient eye. You must look again and again, and not be misled by appearances. All the misinformation about the objects and phenomena of nature afloat among country people is the result of hasty and incomplete observation.

In parts of the country where wheat is grown, there is quite a prevalent belief among the farmers that if the land is poor or neglected, the wheat will turn into chess or cheat grass. Have they not seen it, have they not known the wheat to disappear entirely, and the chess to be there in its place?

But like so many strange notions that are current in the rural districts, this notion is the result of incomplete observation. The cheat grass was there all the while, feebler and inconspicuous, but biding its time; when the wheat failed and gave up possession of the soil, the grass sprang forward and took its place.

Nature always has a card to play in that way. There is no miracle nor case of spontaneous generation about the curious succession of forest trees, — oak succeeding pine, or poplar succeeding birch or maple, — if we could get at the facts. Nature only lets loose germs which the winds or the birds and animals have long since stored there, and which have only been waiting their opportunity to grow.

A great many people are sure there is such a creature as a glass snake, a snake which breaks up into pieces to escape its enemies, and then when danger is past gets itself together again and goes its way.

Not long since a man published an account in a scientific journal of a glass snake which he had encountered in a hay-field, and which, when he attempted to break its head, had broken itself up into five or six pieces. He carefully examined the pieces and found them of regular lengths of three or four inches, and that they dovetailed together by a nice and regular process. He left the fragments in the grass, and when he returned from dinner they were all gone. He therefore inferred the snake had reconstructed itself and traveled on. If he had waited to see this process, his observation would have been complete. On another occasion he cut one in two with his scythe, when the snake again made small

change of itself. Again he went to his
at the critical time, and when he returned,
ments of the reptile had disappeared.

This will not do. We must see the play o
we can report upon the last act.

There is, of course, a small basis of fact
superstition of the glass snake. The creature is no
snake at all, but a species of limbless lizard quite
common in the West. And it has the curious power
of voluntarily breaking itself up into regular pieces
when disturbed, but it is only the tail which is so
broken up; the body part remains intact. Break
this up and the snake is dead. The tail is dispro-
portionately long, and is severed at certain points,
evidently to mislead its enemies. It is the old trick
of throwing a tub to a whale. The creature sacrifices its tail to secure the safety of its body. These
fragments have no power to unite themselves again,
but a new tail is grown in place of the part lost.
When a real observer encountered the glass or joint
snake, these facts were settled.

The superstition of the hair-snake is founded upon
a like incomplete observation. Everywhere may be
found intelligent people who will tell you they know
that a horsehair, if put into the spring, will turn into
a snake, and that all hair-snakes have this origin.
But a hair never turns into a snake any more than
wheat is transformed into chess. The so-called hair-
snake is a parasitical worm which lives in the bodies

sects, and which at maturity takes to
lay its eggs.

, while trout-fishing in July and August,
grasshoppers for bait, has not been vexed
the body of the insect, when snapped at by
ut, yielding a long, white, brittle thread,
...en clogged his hook, and spoiled the attractive-
ness of the bait? This thread is the hair-worm.
How the germ first gets into the body of the grasshopper, I do not know. After the creature leaves
the insect, it becomes darker in color, and harder
and firmer in texture, and more closely resembles a
large hair.

See what pains the trapper will take to outwit the
fox; see what art the angler will practice to deceive
the wary trout. One must pursue the truth with like
patience and diligence.

The farmers all think, or used to think, that the
hen-hawk was their enemy, but one spring the Agri-
cultural Department procured three hundred hen-
hawks, and examined the craw of each of them, and
made the valuable discovery that this hawk sub-
sisted almost entirely upon meadow mice, thus prov-
ing it to be one of the farmer's best friends. The
crow, also, when our observations upon his food
habits are complete, is found to be a friend, and not
an enemy. The smaller hawks do prey upon birds
and chickens, though the pretty little sparrow hawk
lives largely upon insects.

Gilbert White quotes the great Linnæus as saying that "hawks make a truce with other birds as long as the cuckoo is heard." This is also a superstition. Watch closely, and you will see the small hawks in pursuit of birds at all seasons ; and when a hawk pursues a bird, or when one bird pursues another, it has the power to tack and turn, and to time its movements to that of the bird pursued, which is quite marvelous. The sparrow might as well dodge its own shadow as to dodge the sharp-shinned hawk. It escapes, if at all, by rushing into a bush or tree, where the movements of its enemy are impeded by the leaves and branches.

Speaking of hawks reminds me that I read the other day in one of the magazines a very pretty poem, in which a hawk was represented poised in midair, on motionless wing, during the calm of a midsummer day. Now of a still day this is an impossible feat for a hawk or any other bird. The poet had not observed quite closely enough. She had noted (as who has not?) the hawk stationary in the air on motionless wing, but she failed to note, or she had forgotten, that the wind was blowing. He cannot do it on a calm day; the blowing wind furnishes the power necessary to buoy him up. He so adjusts his wings to the moving currents that he hangs stationary upon them. When the hawk hovers in the air of a still day, he is compelled to beat his wings rapidly. He must expend upon the air the power er just

he frag-

ut before

the

which, in the former case, is expended upon him. Thus does hasty and incomplete observation mislead one.

One day in early April, as I was riding along the road, I heard the song of the brown thrasher. The thrasher is not due yet, I said to myself, but there was its song, and no mistake, with all its quips and quirks and interludes, being repeated in a treetop a few yards in advance of me. Let us have a view of the bird, I said, as I approached the tree upon which I fancied he was perched. The song ceased and no thrasher was visible, but there sat a robin, which, as I paused, flew to a lower tree in a field at some distance from the road. Then I moved on, thinking the songster had eluded me. On looking back, I chanced to see the robin fly back to the top of the tree where I had first disturbed it, and in a moment or two more forth came the thrasher's song again. Then I went cautiously back and caught the robin in the very act of reproducing perfectly the song of the brown thrasher. A bolder plagiarist I had never seen; not only had he got the words, as it were correctly, but he delivered them in the same self-conscious manner. His performance would probably have deceived the brown thrasher himself. How did the robin come by this song? I can suggest no other explanation than that he must have learned it from the brown thrasher. Probably the latter bird sang near the nest of the robin, so that the young heard this song and not that of their own kind. If so, it would be interesting to know if all the young males learned the song.

Close attention is the secret of learning from nature's book, as from every other. Most persons only look at the pictures, but the real student studies the text; he alone knows what the pictures really mean. There is a great deal of by-play going on in the life of nature about us, a great deal of variation and outcropping of individual traits, that we entirely miss unless we have our eyes and ears open.

It is not like the play at the theatre, where everything is made conspicuous and aims to catch the eye, and where the story clearly and fully unfolds itself. On nature's stage many dramas are being played at once, and without any reference to the lookers-on, unless it be to escape their notice. The actors rush or strut across the stage, the curtain rises or falls, the significant thing happens, and we heed it not, because our wits are dull, or else our minds are preoccupied. We do not pay strict attention. Nature will not come to you; you must go to her; that is, you must put yourself in communication with her; you must open the correspondence; you must train your eye to pick out the significant things. A quick open sense and a lively curiosity like that of a boy are necessary. Indeed, the sensitiveness and alertness of youth and the care and patience of later years are what make the successful observer.

The other morning my little boy and I set out to find the horse, who had got out of the pasture and gone off. Had he gone up the road or down? We did not know, but we imagined we could distinguish his track going down the road, so we began our search in that direction. The road presently led through a piece of woods. Suddenly my little boy stopped me.

"Papa, see that spider's web stretched across the road: our horse has not gone this way."

My face had nearly touched the web or cable of the little spider, which stretched completely across the road, and which certainly would have been swept away had the horse or any other creature passed along there in the early morning. The boy's eye was sharper than my own. He had been paying stricter attention to the signs and objects about him. We turned back, and soon found the horse in the opposite direction.

This same little boy, by looking closely, has discovered that there are certain stingless wasps. When he sees one which bears the marks, he boldly catches him in his hand. The wasp goes through the motions of stinging so perfectly, so works and thrusts with its flexible body, that nearly every hand to which it is offered draws back. The mark by which the boy is guided is the light color of the wasp's face. Most country boys know that white-faced bumblebees are stingless, but I have not before known a boy bold enough to follow the principle out and apply it to wasps as well. These white-faces are the males, and answer to the drones in the bee-hive; though the drones have not a white face.

We cannot all find the same things in Nature. She is all things to all men. She is like the manna that came down from heaven. "He made manna to descend for them, in which were all manner of tastes; and every Israelite found in it what his palate was chiefly pleased with. If he desired fat in it, he had it. In it the young men tasted bread; the old men, honey; and the children, oil." But all found in it substance and strength. So with Nature. In her are "all manner of tastes," science, art, poetry, utility, and good in all. The botanist has one pleasure in her, the ornithologist another, the explorer another, the walker another, and the sportsman another; what all may have is the refreshment and the exhilaration which come from a loving and intelligent scrutiny of her manifold works.

XVI

BIRD LIFE IN AN OLD APPLE–TREE

NEAR my study there used to stand several old apple-trees that bore fair crops of apples, but better crops of birds. Every year these old trees were the scenes of bird incidents and bird histories that were a source of much interest and amusement. Young trees may be the best for apples, but old trees are sure to bear the most birds. If they are very decrepit, and full of dead and hollow branches, they will bear birds in winter as well as summer. The downy woodpecker wants no better place than the brittle, dozy trunk of an apple-tree in which to excavate his winter home. My old apple-trees are all down but one, and this one is probably an octogenarian, and I am afraid cannot stand another winter. Its body is a mere shell not much over one inch thick, the heart and main interior structure having turned to black mould long ago. An old tree, unlike an old person, as long as it lives at all, always has a young streak, or rather ring, in it. It wears a girdle of perpetual youth.

My old tree has never yet failed to yield me a bushel or more of gillyflowers, and it has turned out at least a dozen broods of the great crested flycatcher, and robins and bluebirds in proportion. It carries up one large decayed trunk, which some one sawed off at the top before my time, and in this a downy woodpecker is now, January 12, making a home. Several years ago, a downy woodpecker excavated a retreat in this branch, which the following season was appropriated by the bluebirds, and has been occupied by them nearly every season since. When the bluebirds first examined the cavity in the spring, I suppose they did not find the woodpecker at home, as he is a pretty early riser.

I happened to be passing near the tree when, on again surveying the premises one afternoon, they found him in. The male bluebird was very angry, and I suppose looked upon the innocent downy as an intruder. He seized on him, and the two fell to the ground, the speckled woodpecker quite covered by the blue coat of his antagonist. Downy screamed vigorously, and got away as soon as he could, but not till the bluebird had tweaked out a feather or two. He is evidently no fighter, though one would think that a bird that had an instrument with which it could drill a hole into a tree could defend itself against the soft-billed bluebird.

Two seasons the English sparrows ejected the bluebirds and established themselves in it, but were in turn ejected by me, their furniture of hens' feathers and straws pitched out, and the bluebirds invited to return, which later in the season they did.

The new cavity which downy is now drilling is just above the old one and near the top of the stub. Its wells are usually sunk to a depth of six or eight inches, but in the present case it cannot be sunk more than four inches without breaking through into the old cavity. Downy seems to have considered the situation, and is proceeding cautiously. As she passed last night in her new quarters, I am inclined to think it is about finished, and there must be at least one inch of wood beneath her. She worked vigorously the greater part of the day, her yellow chips strewing the snow beneath. I paused several times to observe her proceedings. After her chips accumulate, she stops her drilling and throws them out. This she does with her beak, shaking them out very rapidly with a flirt of her head. She did not disappear from sight each time to load her beak, but withdrew her head, and appeared to seize the fragments as if from her feet. If she had had a companion, I should have thought he was handing them up to her from the bottom of the cavity. Maybe she had them piled up near the doorway.

The woodpeckers, both the hairy and the downy, usually excavate these winter retreats in the fall. They pass the nights and the stormy days in them. So far as I have observed, they do not use them as nesting-places the following season. Last night when I rapped on the trunk of the old apple-tree near sundown, downy put out her head with a surprised and inquiring look, and then withdrew it again as I passed on.

I have spoken of the broods of the great crested flycatchers that have been reared in the old apple-tree. This is by no means a common bird, and as it destroys many noxious insects, I look upon it with a friendly eye, though it is the most uncouth and unmusical of the flycatchers. Indeed, among the other birds of the garden and orchard it seems quite like a barbarian. It has a harsh, froglike scream, form and manners to suit, and is clad in a suit of butternut brown. It seeks a cast-off snakeskin to weave into its nest, and not finding one, will take an onion skin, a piece of oiled paper, or large fish scales. It builds in a cavity in a tree, rears one brood, and is off early in the season. I never see or hear it after August 1.

A pair have built in a large, hollow limb in my old apple-tree for many years. Whether it is the same pair or not, I do not know. Probably it is, or else some of their descendants. I looked into the cavity one day while the mother bird was upon the nest, but before she had laid any eggs. A sudden explosive sound came up out of the dark depths of the limb, much like that made by an alarmed cat. It made me jerk my head back, when out came the bird and hurried off. For several days I saw no more of the pair, and feared they had deserted the spot. But they had not; they were only more sly than usual. I soon discovered an egg in the nest, and then another and another.

One day, as I stood near by, a male bluebird came along with his mate, prospecting for a spot for a second nest. He alighted at the entrance of this hole and peeped in. Instantly the flycatcher was upon him. The blue was enveloped by the butter-nut brown. The two fell to the ground, where the bluebird got away, and in a moment more came back and looked in the hole again, as much as to say, "I will look into that hole now at all haz-ards." The barbarian made a dash for him again, but he was now on his guard and avoided her.

Not long after, the bluebirds decided to occupy the old cavity of the downy woodpecker from which I had earlier in the season expelled the English sparrows. After they had established themselves here, a kind of border war broke out between the male bluebird and the flycatchers, and was kept up for weeks. The bluebird is very jealous and very bold. He will not even tolerate a house wren in the vicinity of his nest. Every bird that builds in a cavity he looks upon as his natural rival and en-emy. The flycatchers did not seek any quarrel with him as long as he kept to his own domicile, but he could not tolerate them in the same tree. It was a pretty sight to see this little blue-coat charging the butternut through the trees. The beak of the latter would click like a gunlock, and its harsh, savage voice was full of anger, but the bluebird never flinched, and was always ready to renew the fight.

The English sparrow will sometimes worst the bluebird by getting possession of the box or cavity ahead of him. Once inside, the sparrow can hold the fort, and the bluebird will soon give up the siege; but in a fair field and no favor, the native bird will quickly rout the foreigner.

Speaking of birds that build in cavities reminds me of a curious trait the high-hole has developed in my vicinity, one which I have never noticed or heard of elsewhere. It drills into buildings and steeples and telegraph poles, and in some instances makes itself a serious nuisance. One season the large imitation Greek columns of an unoccupied old-fashioned summer residence near me were badly marred by them. The bird bored into one column, and finding the cavity — a foot or more across — not just what it was looking for, cut into another one, and into still another. Then he bored into the ice-house on the premises, and in the sawdust filling between the outer and inner sheathing found a place to his liking. One bird seemed like a monomaniac, and drilled holes up and down and right and left, as if possessed of an evil spirit. It is quite probable that if a high-hole or other woodpecker should go crazy, it would take to just this sort of thing, drilling into seasoned timber till it used its strength up. The one I refer to would cut through a dry hemlock board in a very short time, making the slivers fly. The sound was like that of a carpenter's hammer. It may have been that he was an unmated bird, a bachelor, whose suit had not prospered that season, and who was giving vent to his outraged instincts in drilling these mock nesting-places.

XVII

THE WAYS OF SPORTSMEN

I HAVE often had occasion to notice how much more intelligence the bird carries in its eye than do any of the quadrupeds. The animal will see you, too, if you are moving, but if you stand quite still, even the wary fox will pass within a few yards of you and not know you from a stump, unless the wind brings him your scent. But a crow or a hawk will discern you when you think yourself quite hidden. His eye is as keen as the fox's sense of smell, and seems fairly to penetrate veils and screens. Most of the water-fowl are equally sharp-eyed. The chief reliance of the animals for their safety, as well as for their food, is upon the keenness of their scent, while the fowls of the air depend mainly upon the eye.

A hunter out in Missouri relates how closely a deer approached him one day in the woods. The hunter was standing on the top of a log, about four feet from the ground, when the deer bounded playfully into a glade in the forest, a couple of hundred yards away. The animal began to feed and to move slowly toward the hunter. He was on the alert, but did not see or scent his enemy. He never took a bite

of grass, says the sportsman, without first putting
his nose to it, and then instantly raising his head
and looking about.

In about ten minutes the deer had approached
within fifty yards of the gunner; then the murderous instinct of the latter began to assert itself. His
gun was loaded with fine shot, but he dared not
make a move to change his shells lest the deer see
him. He had one shell loaded with No. 4 shot in
his pocket. Oh! if he could only get that shell into
his gun.

The unsuspecting deer kept approaching; presently he passed behind a big tree, and his head was
for a moment hidden. The hunter sprang to his
work; he took one of the No. 8 shells out of his
gun, got his hand into his pocket, and grasped the
No. 4. Then the shining eyes of the deer were in
view again. The hunter stood in this attitude five
minutes. How we wish he had been compelled to
stand for five hundred!

Then another tree shut off the buck's gaze for a
moment; in went the No. 4 shell into the barrel and
the gun was closed quickly, but there was no time to
bring it to the shoulder. The animal was now only
thirty yards away. His hair was smooth and glossy,
and every movement was full of grace and beauty.
Time after time he seemed to look straight at the
hunter, and once or twice a look of suspicion seemed
to cross his face.

THE WAYS OF SPORTSMEN

The man began to realize how painful it was to stand perfectly still on the top of a log for fifteen minutes. Every muscle ached and seemed about to rebel against his will. If the buck held to his course, he would pass not more than fifteen feet to one side of the gun, and the man that held it thought he might almost blow his heart out.

There was one more tree for him to pass behind, when the gun could be raised. He approached the tree, rubbed his nose against it, and for a moment was half hidden behind it. When his head appeared on the other side, the gun was pointed straight at his eye, — and with only No. 4 shot, which could only wound him, but could not kill him.

The deer stops; he does not expose his body back of the fore leg, as the hunter had wished. The latter begins to be ashamed of himself, and has about made up his mind to let the beautiful creature pass unharmed, when the buck suddenly gets his scent, his head goes up, his nostrils expand, and a look of terror comes over his face. This is too much for the good resolutions of the hunter. Bang! goes the gun, the deer leaps into the air, wheels around a couple of times, recovers himself, and is off in a twinkling, no doubt carrying, the narrator says, a hundred No. 4 shot in his face and neck. The man says: "I've always regretted shooting at him."

I should think he would. But a man in the woods, with a gun in his hand, is no longer a man, — he is a brute. The devil is in the gun to make brutes of us all.

If the game on this occasion had been, say a wild turkey or a grouse, its discriminating eye would have figured out the hunter there on that log very quickly. This manly exploit of the Western hunter reminds me of an exploit of a Brooklyn man, who last winter killed a bull moose in Maine. It was a more sportsmanlike proceeding, but my sympathies were entirely with the moose. The hero tells his story in a New York paper. With his guides, all armed with Winchester rifles, he penetrated far into the wilderness till he found a moose yard. It was near the top of a mountain. They started one of the animals and then took up its trail. As soon as the moose found it was being followed, it led right off in hopes of outwalking its enemies. But they had snow-shoes and he did not; they had food and he did not. On they went, pursued and pursuers, through the snow-clogged wilderness, day after day. The moose led them the most difficute route he could find.

At night the men would make camp, build a fire, eat and smoke, and roll themselves in their blankets and sleep. In the morning they would soon come up to the camping-place of the poor moose, where the imprint of his great body showed in the snow, and where he had passed a cold, supperless night.

On the fifth day the moose began to show signs of fatigue; he rested often, he also tried to get around and behind his pursuers and let them pass on. Think how inadequate his wit was to cope with the problem, — he thought they would pass by him if he went to one side.

On the morning of the sixth day he had made up his mind to travel no farther, but to face his ene- mies and have it out with them. As he heard them approach, he rose up from his couch of snow, mane erect, his look fierce and determined. Poor crea- ture, he did not know how unequal the contest was. How I wish he could at that moment have had a Winchester rifle, too, and known how to use it. There would have been fair play then. With such weapons as God had given him he had determined to meet the foe, and if they had had only such weap- ons as God had given them, he would have been safe. But they had weapons which the devil had given them, and their deadly bullets soon cut him down, and now probably his noble antlers decorate the hall of his murderer.

XVIII

TALKS WITH YOUNG OBSERVERS

I

TO teach young people or old people how to observe nature is a good deal like trying to teach them how to eat their dinner. The first thing necessary in the latter case is a good appetite; this given, the rest follows very easily. And in observing nature, unless you have the appetite, the love, the spontaneous desire, you will get little satisfaction. It is the heart that sees more than the mind. To love Nature is the first step in observing her. If a boy had to learn fishing as a task, what slow progress he would make; but as his heart is in it, how soon he becomes an adept.

The eye sees quickly and easily those things in which we are interested. A man interested in horses sees every fine horse in the country he passes through; the dairyman notes the cattle; the bee culturist counts the skips of bees; the sheep-grower notes the flocks. Is it any effort for the ladies to note the new bonnets and the new cloaks upon the street? We all see and observe easily in the line of our business, our tasks, our desires.

If one is a lover of the birds, he sees birds everywhere, plenty of them. I think I seldom miss a bird
in my walk if he is within eye or ear shot, even
though my mind be not intent upon that subject.
Walking along the road this very day, feeling a cold,
driving snow-storm, I saw some large birds in the
top of a maple as I passed by. I do not know how
I came to see them, for I was not in an ornitholo-
gical frame of mind. But I did. There were three
of them feeding upon the buds of the maple. They
were nearly as large as robins, of a dark ash-color,
very plump, with tails much forked. What were
they? My neighbor did not know; had never seen
such birds before. I instantly knew them to be pine
grosbeaks from the far north. I had not seen them
before for ten years. A few days previously I had
heard one call from the air as it passed over ; I
recognized the note, and hence knew that the birds
were about. They come down from the north at
irregular intervals, and are seen in flocks in various
parts of the States. They seem just as likely to
come mild winters as severe ones. Later in the day
the birds came about my study. I sat reading with
my back to the window, when I was advised of their
presence by catching a glimpse of one reflected in
my eye-glasses as it flew up from the ground to the
branch of an apple-tree only a few feet away. I
only mention the circumstance to show how quick
an observer is to take the hint. I was absorbed in

my reading, but the moment that little shadow flitted athwart that luminous reflection of the window in the corner of my glasses, something said, "That was a bird." Approaching the window, I saw several of them sitting not five feet away. I could inspect them perfectly. They were a slate-color, with a tinge of bronze upon the head and rump. In full plumage the old males are a dusky red. Hence these were all either young males or females. Occasionally among these flocks an old male may be seen. It would seem as if only a very few of the older and wiser birds accompanied these younger birds in their excursions into more southern climes.

Presently the birds left the apple-bough that nearly brushed my window, and, with a dozen or more of their fellows that I had not seen, settled in a Norway spruce a few yards away, and began to feed upon the buds. They looked very pretty there amid the driving snow. I was flattered that these visitants from the far north should find entertainment on my premises. How plump, contented, and entirely at home they looked. But they made such havoc with the spruce buds that after a while I began to fear not a bud would be left upon the trees; the spruces would be checked in their growth the next year. So I presently went out to remonstrate with them and ask them to move on. I approached them very slowly, and when beside the tree within a few feet of several of them, they heeded me not. One bird kept its position and went on snipping off the buds till I raised my hand ready to seize it, before it moved a yard or two higher up. I think it was only my white, uncovered hand that disturbed it. Indeed,

> "They were so unacquainted with man,
> Their tameness was shocking to me."

The snow was covered with the yellow chaffy scales of the buds, and still the birds sifted them down, till I was compelled to "shoo" them away, when they moved to a tree nearer the house, beneath which they left more yellow chaff upon the snow.

The mind of an observer is like a gun with a hair trigger, — it goes at a touch, while the minds of most persons require very vigorous nudging. You must take the hint, and take it quickly, if you would get up any profitable intimacy with nature. Above all, don't jump to conclusions; look again and again; verify your observations. Be sure the crow is pulling corn, and not probing for grubs, before you kill him. Be sure it is the oriole purloining your grapes, and not the sparrows, before you declare him your enemy. I one day saw hummingbirds apparently probing the ripe yellow cheeks of my finest peaches, but I was not certain till I saw a bird hovering over a particular peach, and then mounting upon a ladder I examined it, when sure enough, the golden cheek was full of pin-holes. The orioles destroy many of my earliest pears, but it required much watching to catch them in the very act. I once saw a phœbe-bird swoop down upon a raspberry bush and carry a berry to a rail on a near fence, but I did not there-fore jump to the conclusion that the phœbe was a berry-eater. What it wanted was the worm in the berry. How do I know? Because I saw it extract something from the berry and fly away.

A French missionary, said to have been a good naturalist, writing in this country in 1634, makes this curious statement about our hummingbird: "This bird, as one might say, dies, or, to speak more correctly, puts itself to sleep in the month of October, living fastened to some little branchlet of a tree by the feet, and wakes up in the month of April when the flowers are in abundance, and some-times later, and for that cause is called in the Mexi-can tongue the 'Revived.'" How could the good missionary ever have been led to make such a state-ment? The actual finding of the bird wintering in that way would have been the proof science demands, and nothing short of that.

A boy in the interior of the State wrote to me the other day that while in the field looking after Indian arrow-heads he had seen a brown and gray bird with a black mark running through the eye, and that the bird walked instead of hopped. He said it had a high, shrill whistle and flew like a meadowlark.

313

This boy is a natural observer; he noted that the bird was a walker. Most of the birds hop or jump, keeping both feet together. This boy heard his bird afterward in the edge of the evening, and "followed it quite a ways, but could not get a glimpse of it." He had failed to note the crest on its head and the black spot on its breast, for doubtless his strange bird was the shore lark, a northern bird, that comes to us in flocks in the late fall or early winter, and in recent years has become a permanent resident of certain parts of New York State. I have heard it in full song above the hills in Delaware County, after the manner of the English skylark, but its song was a crude, feeble, broken affair compared with that of the skylark. These birds thrive well in confinement. I had one seven months in a cage while living in Washington. It was disabled in the wing by a gunner, who brought it to me. Its wound soon healed; it took food readily; it soon became tame, and was an object of much interest and amusement. The cage in which I had hastily put it was formerly a case filled with stuffed birds. Its front was glass. As it was left out upon the porch over night, a strange cat discovered the bird through this glass, and through the glass she plunged and captured the bird. In the morning there was the large hole in this glass, and the pretty lark was gone. I have always indulged a faint hope that the glass was such a surprise to the cat, and made such a racket about

314

her eyes and ears as she sprang against it, that she beat a hasty retreat, and that the bird escaped through the break.

II

In May two boys in town wrote to me to explain to them the meaning of the egg-shells, mostly those of robins, that were to be seen lying about on the ground here and there. I supposed every boy knew where most of these egg-shells came from. As soon as the young birds are out, the mother bird removes the fragments of shells from the nest, carrying them in her beak some distance, and dropping them here and there. All our song-birds, so far as I know, do this.

Sometimes, however, these shells are dropped by blue jays after their contents have been swallowed. The jay will seize a robin's egg by thrusting his beak into it, and hurry off lest he be caught in the act by the owner. At a safe distance he will devour the contents at his leisure, and drop the shell.

The robins, however, have more than once caught the jay in the act. He has the reputation among them of being a sneak thief. Many and many a time during the nesting season you may see a lot of robins mob a jay. The jay comes slyly prowling through the trees, looking for his favorite morsel, when he is discovered by a vigilant robin, who instantly rushes at him crying, "Thief! thief!" at the top of his voice. All the robins that have nests within hearing gather to the spot and join in the pursuit of the jay, screaming and scolding.

The jay is hustled out of the tree in a hurry, and goes sneaking away with the robins at his heels. He is usually silent, like other thieves, but sometimes the birds make it so hot for him that he screams in anger and disgust.

Of the smaller birds, such as the vireos and the warblers, the jay will devour the young. My little boy one day saw a jay sitting beside a nest in a tree, probably that of the red-eyed vireo, and coolly swallowing the just hatched young, while the parent birds were powerless to prevent him. They flew at him and snapped their beaks in his face, but he heeded them not. A robin would have knocked him off his feet at her first dive.

One is sometimes puzzled by seeing a punctured egg lying upon the ground. One day I came near stepping upon one that was lying in the path that leads to the spring, — a fresh egg with a little hole in it carefully placed upon the gravel. I suspected it to be the work of the cowbird, and a few days later I had convincing proof that the cowbird is up to this sort of thing. I was sitting in my summer-house with a book, when I had a glimpse of a bird darting quickly down from the branches of the maple just above me toward the vineyard, with something in its beak. Following up my first glance with more deliberate scrutiny, I saw a female cowbird alight upon the ground and carefully deposit some small object there, and then, moving a few inches away, remain quite motionless. Without taking my eyes from the spot, I walked straight down there. The bird flew away, and I found the object she had dropped to be a little speckled bird's egg still warm. I saw that it was the egg of the red-eyed vireo. It was punctured with two holes where the bird had seized it; otherwise it had been very carefully handled. For some days I had been convinced that a pair of vireos had a nest in my maple, but much scrutiny had failed to reveal it to me.

Only a few moments before the cowbird appeared I had seen the happy pair leave the tree together, flying to a clump of trees lower down the slope of the hill. The female had evidently just deposited her egg, the cowbird had probably been watching near by, and had seized it the moment the nest was vacated. Her plan of course was to deposit one of her own in its place.

I now made a more thorough search for the nest, and soon found it, but it was beyond my reach on an outer branch, and whether or not the cowbird dropped one of her own eggs in place of the one she had removed, I do not know. Certain am I that the vireos soon abandoned the nest, though they do not always do this when hoodwinked in this way.

RIVERBY

I once met a gentleman on the train who told me about a brood of quails that had hatched out under his observation. He was convinced that the mother quail had broken the shells for the young birds. He sent me one of the shells to convince me that it had been broken from the outside. At first glance it did appear so. It had been cut around near the large end, with the exception of a small space, as if by regular thrusts or taps from a bird's beak, so that this end opened like the lid of a box on a hinge, and let the imprisoned bird escape. What convinced the gentleman that the force had been applied from the outside was that the edges of the cut or break were bent in.

If we wish rightly to interpret Nature, to get at the exact truth of her ways and doings, we must cultivate what is called the critical habit of mind; that is, the habit of mind that does not rest with mere appearances. One must sift the evidence, must cross-question the facts. This gentleman was a lawyer, but he laid aside the cunning of his craft in dealing with the question of these egg-shells.

The bending in or the indented appearance of the edge of the shells was owing to the fact that the thin, paper-like skin that lines the interior of the shell had dried and shrunken, and had thus drawn the edges of the shell inward. The cut was made by the beak of the young bird, probably by turning its head from right to left; one little point it could not reach, and this formed the hinge of the lid I have spoken of. Is it at all probable that if the mother bird had done this work she would have left this hinge, and left it upon every egg, since the hinge was of no use? The complete removal of the cap would have been just as well.

Neither is it true that the parent bird shoves its young from the nest when they are ready to fly, unless it be in the case of doves and pigeons. Our small birds certainly do not do this. The young birds will launch out of their own motion as soon as their wings will sustain them, and sometimes before. There is usually one of the brood a little more forward than its mates, and this one is the first to venture forth. In the case of the bluebird, chickadee, high-hole, nuthatch, and others, the young are usually a day or two in leaving the nest.

The past season I was much interested in seeing a brood of chickadees, reared on my premises, venture upon their first flight. Their heads had been seen at the door of their dwelling — a cavity in the limb of a pear-tree — at intervals for two or three days. Evidently they liked the looks of the great outside world ; and one evening, just before sundown, one of them came forth. His first flight was of several yards to a locust, where he alighted upon an inner branch, and after some chirping and calling proceeded to arrange his plumage and compose himself for the night. I watched him till it was nearly dark. He did not appear at all afraid there alone in the tree, but put his head under his wing and settled down for the night as if it were just what he had always been doing. There was a heavy shower a few hours later, but in the morning he was there upon his perch in good spirits.

I happened to be passing in the morning when another one came out. He hopped out upon a limb, shook himself, and chirped and called loudly. After some moments an idea seemed to strike him. His attitude changed, his form straightened up, and a thrill of excitement seemed to run through him. I knew what it all meant; something had whispered to the bird, "Fly!" With a spring and a cry he was in the air, and made good headway to a near hemlock. Others left in a similar manner during that day and the next, till all were out.

Some birds seem to scatter as soon as they are out of the nest. With others the family keeps together the greater part of the season. Among birds that have this latter trait may be named the chickadee, the bluebird, the blue jay, the nuthatch, the kingbird, the phœbe-bird, and others of the true flycatchers.

One frequently sees the young of the phœbe sitting in a row upon a limb, while the parents feed them in regular order. Twice I have come upon a brood of young but fully fledged screech owls in a dense hemlock wood, sitting close together upon a low branch. They stood there like a row of mummies, the yellow curtains of their eyes drawn together to a mere crack, till they saw themselves discovered. Then they all changed their attitudes as if an electric current had passed through the branch upon which they sat. Leaning this way and that, they stared at me like frightened cats till the mother took flight, when the young followed.

The family of chickadees above referred to kept in the trees about my place for two or three weeks. They hunted the same feeding-ground over and over, and always seemed to find an abundance. The parent birds did the hunting, the young did the calling and the eating. At any hour in the day you could find the troop slowly making their way over some part of their territory.

Later in the season one of the parent birds seemed smitten with some fatal malady. If birds have leprosy, this must have been leprosy. The poor thing dropped down through a maple-tree close by the house, barely able to flit a few feet at a time. Its plumage appeared greasy and filthy, and its strength was about gone. I placed it in the branches of a spruce-tree, and never saw it afterward.

III

A boy brought me a dead bird the other morning which his father had picked up on the railroad. It had probably been killed by striking the telegraph wires. As it was a bird the like of which he had never seen before, he wanted to know its name. It was a wee bird, mottled gray and brown like nearly all our ground birds, as the sparrow, the meadow-lark, the quail: a color that makes the bird practically invisible to its enemies in the air above. Unlike the common sparrows, its little round wings were edged with yellow, with a tinge of yellow on its shoulders; hence its name, the yellow-winged sparrow. It has also a yellowish line over the eye. It is by no means a common bird, though there are probably few farms in the Middle and Eastern States upon which one could not be found. It is one of the birds to be looked for. Ordinary observers do not see it or hear it.

It is small, shy, in every way inconspicuous. Its song is more like that of an insect than that of any other of our birds. If you hear in the fields in May and June a fine, stridulous song like that of a big grasshopper, it probably proceeds from this bird. Move in the direction of it and you will see the little brown bird flit a few yards before you. For several mornings lately I have heard and seen one on a dry, gravelly hillock in a field. Each time he has been near the path where I walk. Unless your ear is on the alert, you will miss his song. Amid the other bird-songs of May heard afield it is like a tiny, obscure plant amid tall, rank growths. The bird affords a capital subject for the country boy, or town boy, either, when he goes to the country, to exercise his powers of observation upon. If he finds this bird, he will find a good many other interesting things. He may find the savanna sparrow also, which closely resembles the bird he is looking for. It is a trifle larger, has more bay about the wings, and is more common toward the coast. Its yellow markings are nearly the same. A relative of both these birds is called Henslow's sparrow. Like the savanna sparrow, it is fonder of marshy land than the yellow-wing, and its song, though of the simplest, is much louder. It has an olive-green head and spotted breast.

I never see the yellow-wing without being reminded of a miniature meadowlark. Its short tail, its round wings, its long and strong legs and feet, its short beak, its mottled coat, the touch of yellow, as if he had just rubbed against a newly opened dandelion, but in this case on the wings instead of on the breast, the quality of its voice, and its general shape and habits, all suggest a tiny edition of this large emphatic walker of our meadows.

The song of this little sparrow is like the words "chick, chick-a-su-su," uttered with a peculiar buzzing sound. Its nest is placed upon the ground in the open field, with four or five speckled eggs. The eggs are rounder and their ground color whiter than the eggs of other sparrows.

I do not know whether this kind walks or hops.

This would be an interesting point for the young observer to determine. All the other sparrows known to me are hoppers, but from the unusually long and strong legs of this species, its short tail and erect manner, I more than half suspect it is a walker. If so, this adds another meadowlark feature.

Let the young observer follow up and identify any one bird, and he will be surprised to find how his love and enthusiasm for birds will kindle. He will not stop with the one bird. Carlyle wrote in a letter to his brother, "Attempt to explain what you do know, and you already know something more." Bring what powers of observation you already have to bear upon animate nature, and already your powers are increased. You can double your capital and more in a single season.

The first among the less common birds which I identified when I began the study of ornithology was the red-eyed vireo, the little gray bird with a line over its eye that moves about with its incessant cheerful warble all day, rain or shine, among the trees, and it so fired my enthusiasm that before the end of the season I had added a dozen or more (to me) new birds to my list. After a while the eye and ear become so sensitive and alert that they seem to see and hear of themselves, and like sleepless sentinels report to you whatever comes within their range. Driving briskly along the road the other day, I saw a phœbe-bird building her nest under a cliff of rocks. I had but a glimpse, probably two seconds, through an opening in the trees, but it was long enough for my eye to take in the whole situation: the gray wall of rock, the flitting form of the bird, and the half-finished nest into which the builder settled. Yesterday, May 7, I went out for an hour's walk looking for birds'-nests. I made a tour of some orchards, pastures, and meadows, but found nothing, and then came home and found a blue jay's nest by my very door. How did I find it? In the first place my mind was intent upon nest-finding: I was ripe for a bird's-nest. In the second place I had for some time suspected that a pair of jays were nesting or intending to nest in some of the evergreens about my house; a pair had been quite familiar about the premises for some weeks, and I had seen the male feed the female, always a sure sign that the birds are mated, and are building or ready to build. Many birds do this. I have even seen the crow feed its mate in April. Just at this writing, a pair of chickadees attracted my attention in a spruce-tree in front of my window. One of them, of course the male, is industriously feeding the other. The female hops about, imitating the voice and manner of a young bird, her wings quivering, her cry plaintive, while the male is very busy collecting some sort of fine food out of the just bursting buds of the tree. Every half minute or so he approaches her and delivers his morsel into her beak. I should know from this fact alone that the birds have a nest near by. The truth is, it is just on the other side of the study in a small cavity in a limb of a pear-tree. The female is laying her eggs, one each day, probably, and the male is making life as easy for her as possible, by collecting all her food for her.

Hence when, as I came down the drive, a blue jay alighted in a maple near me, I paused to observe him. He wiped his beak on a limb, changed his position a couple of times, then uttered a low mellow note. The voice as of a young jay, tender and appealing, came out of a Norway spruce near by. The cry was continued, when the bird I was watching flew in amid the top branches, and the cry became still more urgent and plaintive. I stepped along a few paces and saw the birds, the female standing up in her nest and the male feeding her. The nest was placed in a sort of basket formed by the whorl of up-curving branches at the top of the tree, the central shaft being gone.

It contained four eggs of a dirty brownish greenish color. As I was climbing up to it, a turtle dove threw herself out of the tree and fluttered to the ground as if mortally wounded. My little boy was looking on, and seeing the dove apparently so helpless and in such distress, ran to see "what in the world ailed it." It fluttered along before him for a few yards, and then its mate appearing upon the scene, the two flew away, much to the surprise of the boy. We soon found the doves' nest, a shelf of twigs on a branch about midway of the tree. It held two young birds nearly fledged. How they seemed to pant as they crouched there, a shapeless mass of down and feathers, regarding us! The doves had been so sly about their nesting that I had never suspected them for a moment. The next tree held a robin's nest, and the nest of a purple finch is probably near by. One usually makes a mistake in going away from home to look for birds'-nests. Search the trees about your door.

The blue jay is a cruel nest-robber, but this pair had spared the doves in the same tree, and I think they have made their peace with the robins, as I do not see the latter hustling them about any more. Probably they want to stand well with their neighbors, and so go away from home to commit their robberies.

IV

If a new bird appears in my neighborhood, my eye or ear reports it at once. One April several of those rare thrushes — Bicknell's or Slide Mountain thrush — stopped for two days in my currant-patch. How did I know? I heard their song as I went about the place, a fine elusive strain unlike that of any other thrush. To locate it exactly I found very difficult. It always seemed to be much farther off than it actually was. There is a hush and privacy about its song that makes it unique. It has a mild, fluty quality, very sweet, but in a subdued key. It is a bird of remote northern mountain-tops, and its song seems adjusted to the low, thick growths of such localities.

The past season a solitary great Carolina wren took up its abode in a bushy land near one corner of my vineyard. It came late in the season, near the end of August, the only one I had ever heard north of the District of Columbia. During my Washington days, many years ago, this bird was one of the most notable songsters observed in my walks. His loud, rolling whistle and warble, his jocund calls and salutations, — how closely they were blended with all my associations with nature on the Potomac. When, therefore, one morning my ear caught the same blithe, ringing voice on the Hudson, be assured I was quickly on the alert. How it brought up the past. How it reopened a chapter of my life that had long been closed. It stood out amid other bird songs and calls with a distinctness that attracted the dullest ears. Such a southern, Virginia air as it gave to that nook by the river's side!

I left my work amid the grapes and went down to interview the bird. He peeped at me inquisitively and suspiciously for a few moments from a little clump of weeds and bushes, then came out in fuller view, and finally hopped to the top of a grape-post, drooped his wings and tail, lifted up his head, and sang and warbled his best. If he had known exactly what I came for, and had been intent upon doing his best to please me, he could not have succeeded better.

The great Carolina wren is a performer like the mockingbird, and is sometimes called the mocking wren. He sings and acts as well. He seems bent on attracting the attention of somebody or something. A Southern poet has felicitously interpreted certain notes by the words, "Sweetheart, sweetheart, sweet."

Day after day and week after week, till the frosts of the late October came, the bird tarried in that spot, confining his wanderings to a very small area and calling and warbling at all hours. From my summer-house I could often hear his voice rise up from under the hill, seeming to fill all the space down there with sound. What brought this solitary bird there, so far from the haunts of his kind, I know not. Maybe he was simply spying out the land, and will next season return with his mate. Mockingbirds have wandered north as far as Connecticut, and were found breeding there by a collector, who robbed them of their eggs. The mocking wren would be a great acquisition to our northern river-banks and bushy streams. It is the largest of our wrens, and in the volume and variety of its notes and the length of its song season surpasses all others.

A lover of nature never takes a walk without

perceiving something new and interesting. All life in the winter woods or fields as revealed upon the snow, how interesting it is. I recently met a business man who regularly goes camping to the Maine woods every winter from the delight he has in various signs of wild life written upon the snow. His morning paper, he says, is the sheet of snow which he reads in his walk. Every event is chronicled, every new arrival registers his name, if you have eyes to read it!

In December my little boy and I took our skates and went a mile distant from home into the woods to a series of long, still pools in a wild, rocky stream for an hour's skating. There was a light skim of snow upon the ice, but not enough to interfere seriously with our sport, while it was ample to reveal the course of every wild creature that had passed the night before. Here a fox had crossed, there a rabbit or a squirrel or a muskrat.

Presently we saw a different track and a strange one. The creature that made it had come out of a hole in the ground about a yard from the edge of the long, narrow pool upon which we were skating, and had gone up the stream, leaving a track upon the snow as large as that of an ordinary-sized dog, but of an entirely different character.

We had struck the track of an otter, a rare animal in the Hudson River Valley; in fact, rare in any part of the State. We followed it with deep interest; it threw over the familiar stream the air of some remote pool or current in the depths of the Adirondacks or the Maine woods. Every few rods the otter had apparently dropped upon his belly and drawn himself along a few feet by his fore paws, leaving a track as if a log or bag of meal had been drawn along there. He did this about every three rods.

At the head of the pool, where the creek was open and the water came brawling down over rocks and stones, the track ended on the edge of the ice; the otter had taken to the water. A cold bath, one would say, in mid-December, but probably no colder to him than the air, as his coat is perfectly waterproof.

On another pool farther up the track reappeared, and was rubbed out here and there by the same heavy dragging in the snow, like a chain with a long solid bar at regular distances in place of links. At one point the otter had gone ashore and scratched a little upon the ground. He had gone from pool to pool, taking the open rapids wherever they appeared.

The otter is a large mink or weasel, three feet or more long and very savage. It feeds upon fish, which it seems to capture with ease. It is said that it will track them through the water as a hound tracks a fox on land. It will travel a long distance under the ice, on a single breath of air. Every now and then it will exhale this air, which will form a large bubble next the ice, where in a few moments it becomes purified and ready to be taken into the creature's lungs again. If by any accident the bubble were to be broken up and scattered, the otter might drown before he could collect it together again. A man who lived near the creek said the presence of the otter accounted for the scarcity of fish there.

V

The other day one of my farmer neighbors asked me if I had seen the new bird that was about. This man was an old hunter, and had a sharp eye for all kinds of game, but he had never before seen the bird, which was nearly as large as a robin, of a dull blue or slate color marked with white.

Another neighbor, who was standing by, said the bird had appeared at his house the day before. A cage with two canaries was hanging against the window, when suddenly a large bird swooped down as if to dash himself against it; but arresting himself when near the glass, he hovered a moment, eying the birds, and then flew to a near tree.

The poor canaries were so frightened that they fell from their perches and lay panting upon the floor of their cage.

No one had ever seen the bird before; what was it ? It was the shrike, who thought he was sure of a dinner when he saw those canaries.

If you see, in late autumn or winter, a slim, ashen-gray bird, in size a little less than the robin, having white markings, flying heavily from point to point, and always alighting on the topmost branch of a tree, you may know it is the shrike.

He is very nearly the size and color of the mockingbird, but with flight and manners entirely different. There is some music in his soul, though his murderous beak nearly spoils it in giving it forth.

One winter morning, just at sunrise, as I was walking along the streets of a city, I heard the shrike's harsh warble. Looking about me, I soon saw the bird perched upon the topmost twig of a near tree, saluting the sunrise. It was what the robin might have done, but the strain had none of the robin's melody.

Some have compared the shrike's song to the creaking of a rusty gate-hinge, but it is not quite so bad as that. Still, it is unmistakably the voice of a savage. None of the birds of prey have musical voices.

The shrike had probably come to town to try his luck with English sparrows. I do not know that he caught any, but in a neighboring city I heard of a shrike that made great havoc with the sparrows.

VI

When Nature made the flying squirrel, she seems to have whispered a hint or promise of the same gift to the red squirrel. At least there is a distinct suggestion of the same power in the latter. When hard

333

pressed, the red squirrel will trust himself to the air with the same faith that the flying squirrel does, but, it must be admitted, with only a fraction of the success of the latter. He makes himself into a rude sort of parachute, which breaks the force of his fall very much. The other day my dog ran one up the side of the house, through the woodbine, upon the roof. As I opened fire upon him with handfuls of gravel, to give him to understand he was not welcome there, he boldly launched out into the air and came down upon the gravel walk, thirty feet below, with surprising lightness and apparently without the least shock or injury, and was off in an instant beyond the reach of the dog. On another occasion I saw one leap from the top of a hickory-tree and fall through the air at least forty feet and alight without injury. During their descent upon such occasions their legs are widely extended, their bodies are broadened and flattened, the tail stiffened and slightly curved, and a curious tremulous motion runs through all. It is very obvious that a deliberate attempt is made to present the broadest surface possible to the air, and I think a red squirrel might leap from almost any height to the ground without serious injury. Our flying squirrel is in no proper sense a flyer. On the ground he is more helpless than a chipmunk, because less agile. He can only sail or slide down a steep incline from the top of one tree to the foot of another. The flying squirrel is active

334

only at night; hence its large, soft eyes, its soft fur, and its gentle, shrinking ways. It is the gentlest and most harmless of our rodents. A pair of them for two or three successive years had their nest behind the blinds of an upper window of a large, unoccupied country house near me. You could stand in the room inside and observe the happy family through the window-pane against which their nest pressed. There on the window-sill lay a pile of large, shining chestnuts, which they were evidently holding against a time of scarcity, as the pile did not diminish while I observed them. The nest was composed of cotton and wool which they filched from a bed in one of the chambers, and it was always a mystery how they got into the room to obtain it. There seemed to be no other avenue than the chimney flue.

There are always gradations in nature, or in natural life; no very abrupt departures. If you find any marked trait or gift in a species, you will find hints and suggestions of it, or, as it were, preliminary studies of it, in other allied species. I am not thinking of the law of evolution which binds together the animal life of the globe, but of a kind of overflow in nature which carries any marked endowment or characteristic of a species in lessened force or completion to other surrounding species. Or if looked at from the other way, a progressive series, the idea being more and more fully carried out in each succeeding type, — a kind of lateral and secondary evolution. Thus there are progressive series among our song-birds. The brown thrasher is an advance upon the catbird, and the mockingbird is an advance upon the brown thrasher in the same direction. Each one carries the special gift of song or mimicking some stages forward. The same among the larks, through the so-called meadowlark and the shore lark, up to the crowning triumph of the skylark. The nightingale also finishes a series which starts with the hedge warbler and includes the robin redbreast. Our ground-sparrow songs probably reach their highest perfection in the song of the fox sparrow; our finches in that of the purple finch, etc.

The same thing may be observed in other fields. The idea of the flying fish, the fish that leaves the water and takes for a moment to the air, does not seem to have exhausted itself till we reach the walking fish of tropical America, or the tree-climbing fish of India. From the protective coloring of certain insects, animals, and birds, the step is not far to actual mimicry of certain special forms and colors. The naturalists find in Java a spider that exactly copies upon a leaf the form and colors of bird droppings. How many studies of honey-gathering bees did Nature make before she achieved her masterpiece in this line in the honey-bee of our hives ? The skunk's peculiar weapon of defense is suggested by the mink and the weasel. Is not the beaver the head

of the series of gnawers, the loon of divers, the condor of soarers ? Always one species that goes beyond
any other. Look over a collection of African animals
and see how high shouldered they are, how many
hints or prophecies of the giraffe there are before
the giraffe is reached. After Nature had made the
common turtle, of course she would not stop till
she had made the box tortoise. In him the idea is
fully realized. On the body of the porcupine the
quills are detached and stuck into the flesh of its
enemy on being touched; but Nature has not stopped
here. With the tail, the animal strikes its quills
into its assailant. Now if some animal. could be
found that actually threw its quills, at a distance of
several feet, the idea would be still further carried
out.

The rattlesnake is not the only rattler. I have
seen the black snake and the harmless little garter
snake vibrate their tails when disturbed in precisely
the same manner. The black snake's tail was in
contact with a dry leaf, and it gave forth a loud
humming sound which at once put me on the alert.

I met a little mouse in my travels the other day
that interested me. He was on his travels also, and
we met in the middle of a mountain lake. I was
casting my fly there when I saw just sketched or
etched upon the glassy surface a delicate V-shaped
figure, the point of which reached about the middle
of the lake, while the two sides as they diverged

337

faded out toward the shore. I saw the point of this V was being slowly pushed toward the opposite shore. I drew near in my boat, and beheld a little mouse swimming vigorously for the opposite shore. His little legs appeared like swiftly revolving wheels beneath him. As I came near, he dived under the water to escape me, but came up again like a cork and just as quickly. It was laughable to see him repeatedly duck beneath the surface and pop back again in a twinkling. He could not keep under water more than a second or two. Presently I reached him my oar, when he ran up it and into the palm of my hand, where he sat for some time and arranged his fur and warmed himself. He did not show the slightest fear. It was probably the first time he had ever shaken hands with a human being. He was what we call a meadow mouse, but he had doubtless lived all his life in the woods, and was strangely unsophisticated. How his little round eyes did shine, and how he sniffed me to find out if I was more dangerous than I appeared to his sight.

After a while I put him down in the bottom of the boat and resumed my fishing. But it was not long before he became very restless and evidently wanted to go about his business. He would climb up to the edge of the boat and peer down into the water. Finally he could brook the delay no longer and plunged boldly overboard, but he had either changed his mind or lost his reckoning, for he started back in the direction he had come, and the last I saw of him he was a mere speck vanishing in the shadows near the other shore.

Later on I saw another mouse while we were at work in the fields that interested me also. This one was our native white-footed mouse. We disturbed the mother with her young in her nest, and she rushed out with her little ones clinging to her teats. A curious spectacle she presented as she rushed along, as if slit and torn into rags. Her pace was so precipitate that two of the young could not keep their hold and were left in the weeds. We remained quiet, and presently the mother came back looking for them. When she had found one, she seized it as a cat seizes her kitten and made off with it. In a moment or two she came back and found the other one and carried it away. I was curious to see if the young would take hold of her teats again as at first and be dragged away in that manner, but they did not. It would be interesting to know if they seize hold of their mother by instinct when danger threatens, or if they simply retain the hold which they already have. I believe the flight of the family always takes place in this manner, with this species of mouse.

VII

The other day I was walking in the silent, naked April woods when I said to myself, "There is nothing in the woods."

I sat down upon a rock. Then I lifted up my eyes and beheld a newly constructed crow's nest in a hemlock-tree near by. The nest was but little above the level of the top of a ledge of rocks only a few yards away that crowned the rim of the valley. But it was placed behind the stem of the tree from the rocks, so as to be secure from observation on that side. The crow evidently knew what she was about. Presently I heard what appeared to be the voice of a young crow in the treetops not far off. This I knew to be the voice of the female, and that she was being fed by the male. She was probably laying, or about beginning to lay, eggs in the nest. Crows, as well as most of our smaller birds, always go through the rehearsal of this act of the parent feeding the young many times while the young are yet a long way in the future. The mother bird seems timid and babyish, and both in voice and manner assumes the character of a young fledgeling. The male brings the food and seems more than usually solicitous about her welfare. Is it to conserve her strength or to make an impression on the developing eggs? The same thing may be observed among the domestic pigeons, and is always a sign that a new brood is not far off.

When the young do come, the female is usually more active in feeding them than the male. Among the birds of prey, like hawks and eagles, the female is the larger and more powerful, and therefore better

able to defend and to care for her young. Among
all animals, the affection of the mother for her off-
spring seems to be greater than that of her mate,
though among the birds the male sometimes shows
a superabundance of paternal regard that takes in
the young of other species. Thus a correspondent
sends me this curious incident of a male bluebird
and some young vireos. A pair of bluebirds were
rearing their second brood in a box on the porch of
my correspondent, and a pair of vireos had a nest
with young in some lilac bushes but a few feet away.
The writer had observed the male bluebird perch in
the lilacs near the young vireos, and, he feared, with
murderous intent. On such occasions the mother
vireo would move among the upper branches much
agitated. If she grew demonstrative, the bluebird
would drive her away. One afternoon the observer
pulled away the leaves so as to have a full view
of the vireo's nest from the seat where he sat not
ten feet away. Presently he saw the male bluebird
come to the nest with a worm in his beak, and, as
the young vireos stretched up their gaping mouths,
he dropped the worm into one of them. Then he
reached over and waited upon one of the young
birds as its own mother would have done. A few
moments after, he came to his own brood with a
worm or insect, and then the next trip he visited the
nest of the neighbor again, greatly to the displeasure
of the vireo, who scolded him sharply as she watched

his movements from a near branch. My corre-spondent says: "I watched them for several days; sometimes the bluebird would visit his own nest several times before lending a hand to the vireos. Sometimes he resented the vireos' plaintive fault-finding and drove them away. I never saw the fe-male bluebird near the vireos' nest."

That the male bird should be broader in his sym-pathies and affections will not, to most men at least, seem strange.

Another correspondent relates an equally curious incident about a wren and some young robins. "One day last summer," he says, "while watching a robin feeding her young, I was surprised to see a wren alight on the edge of the nest in the absence of the robin, and deposit a little worm in the throat of one of the young robins. It then flew off about ten feet, and it seemed as if it would almost burst with exces-sive volubility. It then disappeared, and the robin came and went, just as the wren returned with an-other worm for the young robins. This was kept up for an hour. Once they arrived simultaneously, when the wren was apparently much agitated, but waited impatiently on its previous perch, some ten feet off, until the robin had left, when it visited the nest as before. I climbed the tree for a closer inspection, and found only a well-regulated robin household, but nowhere a wren's nest. After coming down I walked around the tree and discovered a hole, and upon looking in saw a nest of sleeping, featherless wrens. At no time while I was in the vicinity had the wren visited these little ones."

Of all our birds, the wren seems the most over-flowing with life and activity. Probably in this in-stance it had stuffed its own young to repletion, when its own activity bubbled over into the nest of its neighbor. It is well known that the male wren frequently builds what are called "cock-nests." It is simply so full of life and joy and of the propa-gating instinct, that after the real nest is completed, and while the eggs are being laid, it gives vent to itself in constructing these sham, or cock-nests. I have found the nest of the long-billed marsh wren surrounded by half a dozen or more of these make-believers. The gushing, ecstatic nature of the bird expresses itself in this way.

I have myself known but one instance of a bird lending a hand in feeding young not its own. This instance is to be set down to the credit of a female English sparrow. A little "chippie" had on her hands the task of supplying the wants of that horse-leech, young cow-bunting. The sparrow looked on from its perch a few yards away, and when the "chippie" was off looking up food, it would now and then bring something and place it in the beak of the clamorous bunting. I think the "chippie" ap-preciated its good offices. Certainly its dusky foster-child did. This bird, when young, seems the most greedy of all fledgelings. It cries "More," "More,' incessantly. When its foster parent is a small bird like "chippie" or one of the warblers, one would think it would swallow its parent when food is brought it. I suppose a similar spectacle is witnessed in England when the cuckoo is brought up by a smaller bird, as is always the case. Sings the fool in "Lear:" —

"The hedge-sparrow fed the cuckoo so long,
That it had it head bit off by it young."

Last season I saw a cow-bunting fully grown following a "chippie" sparrow about, clamoring for food, and really looking large enough to bite off and swallow the head of its parent, and apparently hungry enough to do it. The "chippie" was evidently trying to shake it off and let it shift for itself, for it avoided it and flew from point to point to escape it. Its life was probably made wretched by the greedy monster it had unwittingly reared.

INDEX

INDEX

347

INDEX

Blue-weed. *See* Bugloss, viper's.
Bobolink (*Dolichonyx oryzivorus*), 203, 258; song of, 258, 259; nest of, 203.
Bob-white. *See* Quail.
Boneset, climbing, 35.
Boswell, James, 273.
Botany, the study of, 31, 32; a needed aid in, 35, 36.
Boulders, refusing to stay down, 109, 110.
Brooks. *See* Trout streams.
Bugloss, viper's, *or* blue-weed, 33.
Bullfrog, 277.
Bumblebee, 17; visiting the closed gentian, 30 and note; drones, 293.
Bunting, black-throated, *or* dick-cissel (*Spiza americana*), 258; song of, 258.
Bunting, indigo. *See* Indigo-bird.
Bunting, snow, *or* snowflake (*Passerina nivalis*), 217.

Calf, fear in the young, 211, 212.
Calypso, the orchid, 3, 4.
Cambium layer, the, 170, 171.
Camp, repairing, 52, 58; rain in, 53; a cold night in, 57–59.
Camping, in the southern Catskills, 37–66.
Campion, bladder, 33.
Canary, 105, 206, 207, 332.
Cardinal (*Cardinalis cardinalis*), 258.
Cardinal-flower, 13, 14, 33.
Carlyle, Thomas, a woman's opinion of, 117, 118; quotation from, 324.
Catbird (*Galeoscoptes carolinensis*), 153; song of, 336.
Cats, chipmunks and, 158–160; red squirrels and, 211.
Catskills, mountaineering in the southern, 37–66; the rocks of, 38, 52; the water of, 44, 45.
Cattle, backwoods, 64.
Cedar-bird, *or* cedar waxwing (*Ampelis cedrorum*), 79, 217; nest and eggs of, 77, 79.

Charming, the power of, 278–280.
Chat, yellow-breasted (*Icteria virens*), 258.
Chelone, *or* turtle-head, 33.
Cherry pits, 162.
Chewink, *or* towhee (*Pipilo erythrophthalmus*), 17.
Chickadee (*Parus atricapillus*), 130; young leaving the nest, 319, 320; family life continued after the nest is left, 320, 321; a fatal malady, 321; a male feeding his mate, 325; notes of, 319, 320; nest of, 77, 280, 319, 320, 325, 326.
Chipmunk, 150; spring awakening of, 155, 175; breeding habits of, 156; manners and conversation of, 156; enemies of, 156–158; nervous, impetuous ways of, 157, 158; a hermit, 158, 162, 163; adventures with cats, 158–160; the digging and furnishing of the den, 161; food for the winter, 161, 162, 210; sociability, 162; pursued by a weasel, 163–165.
Chippie, *or* social sparrow (*Spizella socialis*), 79; a curious mishap, 133, 134; and young cowbird, 343, 344; nest and eggs of, 70.
Claytonia, *or* spring beauty, 47.
Clintonia, 47.
Clover, red, 47.
Clover, sweet, *or* melilotus, 33.
Columbine, 16.
Condor, 337.
Cone-flower, *or* rudbeckia, 107.
Contentment, 95–98.
Coon. *See* Raccoon.
Corydalis, 16.
Cowbird, *or* cow-bunting (*Molothrus ater*), desecrating a vireo's nest, 316, 317; the young bird and its foster-parent, 343, 344.
Crane, sandhill (*Grus mexicana*), 114–116; nest and eggs of, 114, 115.
Crickets, field, hibernating of, 277.
Crow, American (*Corvus brachy-*

348

INDEX

349

INDEX

INDEX

INDEX

Neversink, the, 38.

Newt, water, 174.

Night, Jefferies on, 229; Whitman on, 230; in Senancour's *Obermann*, 231, 232.

Nightingale, song of, 336.

Oaks, English, 228.

Obermann, by Étienne Pivert de Senancour, quotation from, 231, 232.

Observation, the gift of, 98; alertness of mind necessary in, 126, 312; a translation of nature's language into human speech necessary in, 127; on the part of wild creatures, 127; selective and detective, 224, 227; an unbiased mind necessary in, 274; specialized, 274, 275; all possible sources of error to be taken into account in, 275, 276; a steady and patient as well as sharp eye necessary in, 285–292, 312; love of nature the first step in, 309; the critical habit of mind necessary in, 318.

Oriole, Baltimore (*Icterus galbula*), 256, 257, 312; nest and eggs of, 71, 72, 133, 256, 257.

Osmunda fern, royal, 19.

Osprey, American, *or* fish hawk (*Pandion haliaëtus carolinensis*), regular habits of an osprey, 187, 279.

Ostrich, 92, 93.

Otter, American, tracks of, 330, 331; habits of, 331, 332.

Oven-bird. *See* Thrush, golden-crowned.

Owl, great horned (*Bubo virginianus*), 214; nest of, 67.

Owl, screech (*Megascops asio*), a brood of young, 320, 321; notes of, 237; nest of, 67.

Owl, snowy (*Nyctea nyctea*), 214.

Owls, the eggs of, 68; 214.

Oxen, 108, 109.

Panther, Mountain, 49, 62, 63.

Partridge. *See* Grouse, ruffed.

Peak-o'-Moose, 49.

Peeper. *See* Hyla.

Perch, 19, 229.

Phœbe - bird (*Sayornis phœbe*), 313, 320; nest and eggs of, 68, 69, 77, 270, 282, 324, 325.

Pickerel, 19.

Pigeon, passenger (*Ectopistes migratorius*), 110; nest of, 68.

Pike, barrèd, 229.

Pink, prairie, 107.

Pitcher plant, 9.

Polygala, fringed, 23, 24.

Pond-lily, 16–22.

Porcupine, Canada, 40, 41, 53, 59, 64, 337.

Prairie, the, notes from, 95–118; like the ocean, 96; life in the fifties on, 106–116; game on, 110–113; a *dead* level, 242.

Prairie hen. *See* Grouse, pinnated.

Primrose. *See* Evening primrose.

Proctor, Professor, 242.

Pussy-willows, 237.

Quail, *or* bob-white (*Colinus virginianus*), 110; setting, 146, 147; young of, 147; answering a call, 190; hatching of the young, 318, 319; notes of, 190; nest and eggs of, 82, 145–147, 318, 319.

Rabbit, 53.

Rabbit, gray, 191; a captive, 197, 198; timidity and witlessness of, 213, 214.

Raccoon, 175; a captive, 192, 193; courage of, 213.

Rain, in camp, 53.

Rat, pet squirrel and, 104, 105; 113.

Redbird, summer, *or* summer tanager (*Piranga rubra*), 256; song of, 256.

Rhexia. *See* Meadow-beauty.

Roads, in Kentucky, 251.

Robin, American (*Merula migratoria*), 79; courtship of, 84, 85; duels of, 84, 85; 153, 206; singing a brown thrasher's song, 290,

352

INDEX

INDEX

INDEX

The Riverside Press
CAMBRIDGE . MASSACHUSETTS
U . S . A